D1408877

Demons and Angels

A Life of
JACOB EPSTEIN

By the same author

Modigliani: The Pure Bohemian
For the Sake of the Children: A History of Barnardos
Elizabeth Fry
A Perfect Gentleman: A History of Doctor James Barry
Marie Stopes and the Sexual Revolution
Suzanne Valadon: Mistress of Montmartre

Demons and Angels

A Life of
JACOB EPSTEIN

JUNE ROSE

CARROLL & GRAF PUBLISHERS
New York

Carroll & Graf Publishers
An imprint of Avalon Publishing Group, Inc.
161 William Street
New York
NY 10038-2607
www.carrollandgraf.com

First Carroll & Graf edition 2002

First published in the UK by Constable,
an imprint of Constable & Robinson Ltd 2002

Copyright © June Rose 2002

ISBN 0-7867-1000-4

Printed and bound in the EU

For Renate

Acknowledgements

M Y THANKS FIRST of all must go to Epstein's three surviving children, Peggie Jean Lewis, the Hon. Kitty Godley and Jackie Epstein. When I began to research this biography I wrote to them of my intention and purpose. The response in each case was encouraging and helpful. Peggy Jean Lewis offered me warm hospitality over a weekend in North Carolina. She unearthed letters from her father to show me during my visit, which subsequently went to the Tate Archives. I have visited Kitty Godley at her home in Suffolk and in upstate New York and we have kept closely in touch during the years that I have been working on her father's life. I am grateful to Kitty and her husband Wynne for their interest and support. Jackie Epstein and his wife Isabel have been kind and generous at our meetings. I am indebted to Epstein's family for their help; their enthusiasm for the project spurred me on.

I owe a particular debt of gratitude to Dr Evelyn Silber, formerly Director of Leeds City Art Galleries and Museums, for her encouragement and illuminating advice. As well as generously sharing her expert knowledge, she offered me hospitality and guided my steps from the beginning. In the final stages, she scrutinised the typescript and made invaluable suggestions. Any errors that remain are all my own.

My special thanks go to Jo Digger, Keeper of Fine Art at the New Art Gallery, Walsall. When I first visited Walsall, the Gallery had not yet moved to its splendid new home and the archives were in cramped quarters. In spite of the difficulties, Jo offered unstinting help and hospitality and I greatly enjoyed our conversations. I am grateful to Peter Jenkinson, Director of the NGAW, and to Sheila McGregor, the author of the Catalogue of the collection at Walsall, for their help.

Agi Katz of the Boundary Gallery is a friend who encouraged me throughout the writing of this book and kindly showed me her Epstein treasures and lent me books from her own Epstein collection.

The nucleus of valuable contacts led me closer to Epstein's life. Through Peggy Jean Lewis I was introduced to Teresa Henry and Sandra Kovylak, great nieces of 'Meum', Dorothy Lindsell-Stewart. With their help I was able to speak to Maria Hollingsworth, Meum's niece, and to gain permission to use extracts from her diaries as well as a previously unpublished letter from Epstein to Meum.

The conversations with the descendants of Epstein's vast circle of friends and acquaintances were most rewarding. Alice Kadel (Keene) gave me permission to quote from Matthew Smith's unpublished notes about Epstein as well as from her own book, *The Two Mr Smiths*. I must also thank my friend Renate Koenigsberger, whose connections in India located Siraj Ayesha Sayani, the great niece of Epstein's most famous model, Sunita. We had a delightful electronic correspondence and Siraj Sayani was most helpful and informative. Again, through a network of friends I was enabled to meet Noreen Smith, widow of Jan Smith, Epstein's plaster moulder in the 1950s. She and her husband worked closely in the studio with Epstein in his last years. Noreen has a remarkable memory as well as a tape and notes made by Jan about Epstein. She shared her information most graciously. My thanks too to Michael Gillespie for his insights; he worked for a shorter time as Epstein's plaster moulder.

Geoffrey Ireland was Epstein's photographer during his later years and he too contributed valuable observations about the artist.

Josef Herman and Epstein became friends during the Second World War and Josef spoke with affection and discernment about Epstein and his wife. He and his wife Ninni welcomed me warmly into their home.

I would also like to acknowledge with appreciation the work of Janice Rossen of Austin, Texas, who researched in the Harry Ransom Center on my behalf, and of Francis McMeen of New York who scanned through press cuttings for me.

Finally, in my own family, my cousin Esther Mishkin combed the archives of YIVO, the Institute for Jewish Research in New York, where she works as a volunteer; my grateful thanks go to her and to YIVO. In Nottingham, Judge David Lipman, another cousin, kindly offered advice on marriage and divorce in the early years of the last century.

Personal friends gave generously of their advice and professional judgement: in particular I would like to thank Linden Stafford, Pat Chetwyn and Christine Casley, who supported me in the writing of this book. Suzy Donat of Camden Libraries helped me to find the books I needed. Alison Smith of the Tate Gallery provided introductions and information as well as encouragement.

I am grateful to Terry Friedman, Richard Cork and Victor Arwas for their expert advice. Thanks too to Cressida Connolly for sharing information about the Garman family; to John and Susan Lade, friends of Kathleen and Epstein; to Marcella Barzetti, friend and model of the artist, and to Astrid Zydower and Ralph Brown, who met Epstein when they were students at the Royal College of Art.

I am indebted to the institutions who made my work possible: to the staff of the British Library; to the Archive Department of the Tate Gallery, and in particular to Caroline Cuthbert; to the archivist and library staff of the Henry Moore Institute for the Study of Sculpture in Leeds City Art Galleries; to the exceptionally helpful staff of the New Art Gallery, Walsall, to the Artists' Archivist of the Imperial War Museum and to Vivien Knight, Curator of the Guildhall Art Gallery and to the librarian at Hansard, I would like to express my thanks. In New York I gratefully acknowledge the help of the Department of Rare Books and Manuscripts at the New York Public Library and in Philadelphia I am indebted to Felice Fishcher of the Philadelphia Museum of Art and to their Archive Department.

I am deeply grateful to the Society of Authors who gave me a grant which helped me in the research for this book.

I wish to express my thanks to the authors and publishers of all the quoted texts; I have endeavoured to trace them all.

Finally I should like to thank my publisher and editor, Ben Glazebrook, for his belief in this project.

Contents

GENEALOGY

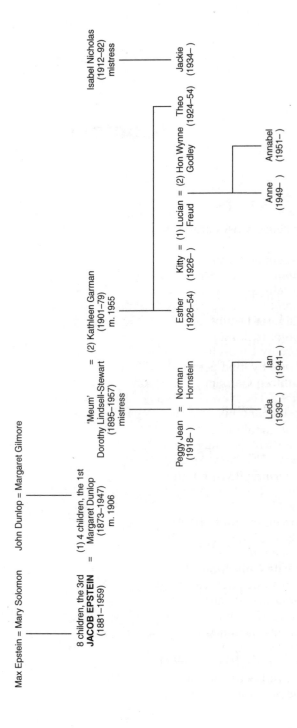

Max Epstein = Mary Solomon

John Dunlop = Margaret Gilmore

8 children, the 3rd
JACOB EPSTEIN
(1881–1959)

= (1) 4 children, the 1st
Margaret Dunlop
(1873–1947)
m. 1906

'Meum'
Dorothy Lindsell-Stewart
(1895–1957)
mistress

= (2) Kathleen Garman
(1901–79)
m. 1955

Isabel Nicholas
(1912–92)
mistress

Peggy Jean
(1918–)

= Norman
Hornstein

Esther
(1926–54)

Kitty = (1) Lucian = (2) Hon Wynne
(1926–)   Freud   Godley

Theo
(1924–54)

Jackie
(1934–)

Leda
(1939–)

Ian
(1941–)

Anne
(1949–)

Annabel
(1951–)

Illustrations

San Stefano Stone, 58.5 x 26.0 x 24.0 cm, Felton Bequest, 1983,
  National Gallery of Victoria, Melbourne, Australia
Isobel
Private collection. *Photo:* Leeds Museums & Galleries (Henry Moore
  Institute Archive)
Fifth Portrait of Mrs Jacob Epstein
Photo: Leeds Museums & Galleries (Henry Moore Institute Archive)
Bust of Albert Einstein
Fitzwilliam Museum, University of Cambridge. *Photo:* Bridgeman Art
  Library, London & New York

Between pages 204 and 205

Rock Drill
Birmingham Museums & Art Gallery
The Visitation
© Tate, London 2002
The Risen Christ
Private Collection. *Photo*: Leeds Museums & Galleries (Henry Moore
  Institute Archive)
Adam
Reproduced by kind permission of the Earl and Countess of Harewood
  and the Trustees of the Harewood House Trust
Jacob and the Angel
© Tate, London 2002
Blackpool Exhibition (exterior)
Photo: Hulton Archive/Getty Images
War Memorial, TUC building
Photo: Geoffrey Ireland
The seventh and final portrait of Kathleen Garman
Photo: Hulton Archive/Getty Images
Epstein's studio in Hyde Park Gate
Photo: Hulton Archive/Getty Images

The works of Epstein are reproduced by permission of the Estate of
Jacob Epstein/Tate, London.

Preface

Throughout his life Jacob Epstein carved monuments that express uniquely the power and pain of human existence and aspirations. He began to create his life-sized statues of naked figures before the First World War, when sculpture was regarded as a decorative and illustrative art. In Edwardian London, the art establishment favoured a flattering and sentimental realism and foreign influences were deeply distrusted. Epstein was a young American and his statues, with their explicit sexuality and their humanity, flouted contemporary conventions and roused fanatical antagonism.

He was the first 'sensation', the first sculptor to stir the public to passion about works of art, even if it was to a frenzy of disapproval. From the early years of the twentieth century when Epstein began to create his nude statues, public interest in sculpture has never waned.

In his virile early work with Eric Gill, Epstein began to carve directly into the stone block, a practice abandoned in this country since the Middle Ages. He was a young man, barely thirty, with a vaulting ambition and a passion that was wholly un-English:

'I feel that I can do the best, most profound things and life is short. How I wish I was living in an age when Man wanted to raise temples and cathedrals to Man or God or the devil,' he wrote to his dealer in 1910.[1]

Epstein looked to the continents of Africa and Asia for inspiration to contain his radical ideas. His example inspired a younger colleague, the French artist, Gaudier-Brzeska; later direct carving was taken up enthusiastically by Henry Moore, Barbara Hepworth and others. Until his old age Epstein's carvings were regarded as barbaric, each new work savagely attacked, although early on his work as a portrait sculptor was celebrated. The hostility and venom extended to the artist as well as his art grew partly out of his complex, and very un-English, personality. He was not only an American, but also a Jew with radical political views, handsome, combative and as virile as his own sculptures. Totally unschooled in the social graces needed to negotiate even the fringes of bohemian English life, Epstein was unapologetic about his origins and delighted in baiting authority. He was no more of a womanizer than some of his colleagues, but he was far less discreet about his conquests. His brash and poetic personality was puzzling and the English marvelled that it never occurred to him to be 'grateful' for the opportunity to work.

Fortunately a nucleus of discriminating artist friends championed Epstein's talent and remained admirably loyal to him throughout his tempestuous career. He was, said his son-in-law Wynne Godley, 'a life force'.[2]

Before the First World War Epstein was irrepressible. 'I want to carve mountains,' he told his American dealer, John Quinn, and he dreamt of creating sculpture on the grand scale. In 1920 he conceived, with Eric Gill, a plan of creating colossal figures of stone in the English countryside: 'a sort of twentieth-century Stonehenge' is how Gill described it. Two years later, in Paris, he met Modigliani and the two artists felt an instant sympathy. Together they decided to create a 'Temple of Beauty' and they tramped all over the Butte of Montmartre searching for a plot where they could set up a studio.

Both schemes failed, but in 1913 Epstein was inspired to create the most original sculpture yet seen in this country, *Rock Drill*, a creature that would not look alien in *Star Wars*, but with roots reaching back to primitive art. To construct his mysterious figure Epstein bought a second-hand pneumatic drill to use as the base of his work. Then he created a robot and mounted it on his drill 'visored, menacing and carrying within itself its progeny, protectively ensconced'. He was the first artist in Britain to dare to introduce a mass-produced object into the art gallery. Epstein realized that his creature was too outlandish to sell but, despite his poverty at the time, felt compelled to make *Rock Drill*. 'It is one of those things that one is tempted to do occasionally, and which, for the artist, is an indulgence,' he wrote to his dealer excited by his creation. 'I've rendered the subject in a manner that gives the utmost driving force, of hard, relentless, steel-like power.'[3]

In this experimental work, Epstein's passion for the machine collides with the sculptor's sense of awe at the might of mechanized superman. His vision of man merged into machine and rendered impotent without it is uncannily prophetic. Although Epstein was to renounce abstraction, and concentrate on the human form after the First World War, with *Rock Drill*, he had began to free British sculpture from the oppression of 'museum art' and signalled the beginning of the Modern Movement. Unsurprisingly, his most imaginative and revolutionary work provoked an even more ferocious storm of criticism than usual.

Between the wars, it was not only the art establishment and prudish members of the public who disliked Epstein. In an anti-Semitic climate, Fascists and hooligans made sporadic raids on his works of art and daubed them with swastikas and graffiti. As orchestrated opposition to his work grew, it was made impossible for him to gain public commissions to carve monumental works.

From his student days Epstein had been deeply interested in portraiture; whenever his larger works suffered a reverse, he turned to modelling, making busts and figures with increasing success. He had a marvellous gift for breathing life into his portraits and he created a gallery of characters, from Joseph Conrad and Albert Einstein, to Ralph Vaughan Williams and Churchill, as well as dozens of beautiful women. Both the critics and the public admired the vitality of his naturalistic heads. At a time when he was supporting two families, the constant flow of commissioned work provided him with an indispensable source of income.

Yet he never gave up his dream of 'carving mountains'. Between the thirties and the fifties, Epstein continued to carve huge Christ figures and supercharged Biblical characters without a hope of selling them. His carvings were regularly savaged as obscene, irreligious and barbaric. The press were always ready to pounce on an Epstein scandal, and when there was a large Epstein carving on display, the tabloids often sent a general reporter rather than an art critic to a preview. The artist possessed, half knowingly, the dangerous gift of attracting publicity and his colourful private life contributed greatly to the interest in him. In the studios of Chelsea and in West End restaurants, surrounded by beautiful women, he cut a dashing figure even when he was in his fifties and sixties and putting on weight. With his unruly greying hair, blue eyes and a body that seemed about to escape from his clothes, Epstein retained a strong personal magnetism. For cartoonists and versifiers he was an easy target:

> I don't like the family Stein
> There is Gert, there is Ep there is Ein
> Gert's writings are punk
> Ep's statues are junk
> Nor can anyone understand Ein.[4]

For most of Epstein's life his sculpture was held up to ridicule. In the forties, the shrewd showman Louis Tussaud of Blackpool offered holiday crowds the thrill of gawping at *Jacob and the Angel* in a fun fair. It is a comment on changing tastes that Epstein's magnificent alabaster carving of *Jacob*, once disdained by The Tate Gallery, has recently been cleaned and is now a prime possession of Tate Collections.

During Epstein's lifetime, the scandals, the sensational headlines and the politicization of his work made reasoned criticism difficult. His reputation at the time rested largely on his portrait bronzes, regarded as the finest of the century and represented in art galleries all over the country. Today critical appreciation focuses mainly on his early carvings, particularly *Rock Drill*, and sees in them his major and lasting achievement. Because of the range of his work, he has always been an artist who is difficult to categorize.

What I am certain of is that Epstein's contribution to the artistic

and cultural life of this country, his rousing of public awareness to
wider, more dynamic possibilities in sculpture has been shame-
fully neglected. My biography is an attempt to see the man and his
work as a whole.

1

The Ghetto

JACOB EPSTEIN'S CHILDHOOD in the Jewish ghetto of New York was a lonely and suffocating existence, yet the ghetto haunted his dreams. He was born into a family of Jewish traders from Augustow in Russian Poland on 10 November 1880. By the time Jacob was born, his parents had lived in the USA for fifteen years and were adjusting well to their new life. Max Epstein, his father, was a relatively well-to-do and devout member of the Jewish community; an important local figure, he had contributed most of the money to build a neighbourhood synagogue.

He had married well: Mary Solomon Epstein, from the same home-town, came from a family of mill-owners who had emigrated to America in 1865. Max ran a bakery and bagel business and had begun to buy up tenements in the poor, depressed neighbourhood where they lived. They were not the poverty-stricken immigrants of Hollywood legend. Jacob remembered the two Polish Christian servant girls who worked for them, who wore kerchiefs and went about the house barefoot.

Max Epstein owned the tenement building at 102 Hester Street and let out rooms to immigrants who arrived at the nearby docks. He was the first person to install a bathroom in their street, and the kind-hearted Mary allowed their lodgers to take a weekly bath, much to her husband's annoyance. Mary bore twelve children, but only eight survived, five boys and three girls; Jacob was the third eldest. Family life was punctuated by prayers morning and evening, and by Bible readings in Yiddish at home and, for the boys, daily lessons in Hebrew from a visiting rabbi.

Even as a small boy of five, Jacob went to synagogue with his father and his elder brother Louis. He came to dread Saturdays, when he had to attend the services for practically the whole day. Both sets of grandparents lived near by, and in the evening hordes of relatives and their children, dressed in their Sabbath best, came to visit. Max wanted to move uptown to a better district, to educate his sons to become solid businessmen or members of the respectable professions, the law or medicine, and his daughters to marry well. He succeeded for the most part: one of his sons became a doctor; another ran a grocery store. Only Jacob remained outside the orbit of the 'old tyrant'.

Perhaps it was his illness at the age of six which set him apart. He suffered from pleurisy, and for almost two years he remembered being carried about a great deal and no doubt spoiled. The family called him 'the sick one'. He began to shrink from family gatherings, to live in the world of the imagination, drawing whenever he could and reading voraciously. As a grown man he could not remember a time when he did not draw. He soon grew strong and delighted in roaming the city of New York before the skyscrapers dominated the skyline, crossing the great Brooklyn Bridge and watching the bay with its constant traffic of steamers and ferry-boats. From his home in Hester Street he looked down on a teeming crush of people in the open-air market crammed with push-carts and peddlers selling fruit, herrings, horseradish, books and cheeses. The people nicknamed Hester Street 'the pig market': pork was the one thing not to be found in the Orthodox surroundings. Shops or sweatshops made up the ground floor of most of the buildings; signs in Yiddish, Hebrew and English advertized hats, frocks and boots, while kettles, pots and pans hung in the ground-floor windows.

Russians, Poles, Italians, Greek and Chinese came hunting for bargains in Hester Street, and Jacob stared fascinated at the 'unique and crowded humanity' on his doorstep. He began to explore and play on the roofs where all the East Side boys flew kites; he was particularly drawn to the docks. To reach the Hudson river on the West Side of the docks, the boys from the Jewish quarter had to pass through the Irish quarter. That meant fighting their way through, and Epstein learned early on how to defend himself and to use his elbows. He would brave the Irish quarter regularly to get to the open-air seawater baths and remained a keen swimmer all his life.

Often his wanderings kept him out late so that he missed meals at home and risked his father's wrath. He attended a free public school in the area, PS7, but concentrated on literature and history, which he loved. According to his own account, when he should have been studying grammar or mathematics he was allowed to spend lessons drawing in his exercise books. The teachers were so proud of the young prodigy that they permitted him to follow his bent.

Young Jacob revelled in the variety and vitality of the people of the streets but at home he was forced to study the Bible and to behave like a pious youth in Poland. He felt American but his parents spoke Yiddish in the house, although they had both learned English. At night the boy would lie awake listening to his father reading a florid romance in Yiddish to his wife, but it was the Saturdays that he could not stand. In the synagogue, where the men and women sat separately, he was achingly bored with the 'wailing prayers' and longed to make some excuse to escape.

In 1886, when Jacob was six years old, a handful of idealistic young college graduates moved to the lower East Side of New York City, to live among the ghetto children, take them to the museums, the parks and the countryside, where they learned that 'apples came from trees not pushcarts'.[1] For boys like Jacob to have friendly neighbours, not teachers or preachers, inviting them into a house with pictures on the wall and secular books on the shelves, offered a tempting glimpse of a wider world. The Settlement House Movement aimed to improve the neighbourhood, offer practical help and give the newcomers an awareness of America while respecting their own culture and religion. Jacob Riis, in his book about the immigrant problem at the time, commented, 'If ever there was material for citizenship, the Jew is such material. He is the yeast of any slum. I for one am a firm believer in the Jew and his boy . . . Ignorant they may be but with a thirst for knowledge that surmounts any barrier . . . the boy takes all the prizes in school.'[2]

The Settlement House Movement and the complex educational and social reform programmes associated with it, many of them sponsored by Jewish charities, freed the immigrant children from their narrow horizons, bounded by home, synagogue and the streets in between. The children 'adored' their youth leaders. One young contemporary of Jacob saw the contact with the Christian reformers as liberating him from the sense of ethnic and religious isolation inculcated by Hebrew teachers and parents.[3] Once freed from the strictures of a closed orthodoxy, they were soon in touch with the vigorous Yiddish culture of the intelligentsia of Polish Jewry: writers, journalists and socialists, nearly all of them non-Orthodox.

Young Jacob, moody, artistic, sitting drawing by a poor light at the kitchen table when he should have been studying, had a longing to escape. His talent helped to free him when he won a prize for art from the Cooper Union School at the age of eleven. With the encouragement of his art teacher Epstein began to dream of a future as an artist. In writing about his early life, Epstein skims over the painful period when he was living at home, struggling to find his way: he loathed the feeling of dependence all his life. The important role the leaders of the Settlement House Movement played in the artist's development, by supporting him both morally and, to a significant extent, financially in his student years, has come to light only recently, from his letters and other documents.

He probably attended classes and talks at the nearby Neighborhood Guild (later renamed the University Settlement) while he was still at school. He was certainly befriended by at least two of the Guild's workers. They were mostly male graduates in their late twenties and thirties from professional families with left-wing tendencies. Miss Helen Moore from Iowa was an exception: she had studied literature and, more significantly, painting under Thomas Eakins; on her own initiative she opened the first library for children (five cents a loan) in the USA.

The other Neighborhood Guild worker who encouraged Jacob

was James Kirk Paulding, a literary man in his late twenties and a graduate of Harvard, Leipzig and Berlin. Paulding read aloud to a small group of immigrant boys on Sunday mornings. The selection of readings, which included works by Emerson, Spinoza and Mazzini, reflected the youth leaders' sympathies: Jacob remembered hearing Conrad's *Typhoon* and *The Nigger of the Narcissus* as well as most of Turgenev. The readings were sometimes held at the Education Alliance (formerly the Hebrew Guild), a Jewish-sponsored community centre with English classes for immigrants, drama and literary societies, a People's Synagogue and an impressive free (adult) lending library which was a part of the New York public library system.

Epstein mentions James Kirk Paulding in his autobiography, although the personal letters that survive from him are mainly to Helen Moore. One such, dated 12 July but without a year, was written while he was on holiday with a dozen other boys celebrating America's Independence Day at the Settlement summer camp at Lake Greenwood, New Jersey. Miss Moore had presented the boys with an American flag for the occasion, and a wealthy philanthropist, Mrs Stuyvesant Fish, one of the New York hostesses who patronised the Settlement House Movement, sent a cheque to Jacob, the leader, to buy cream for their 4 July dinner. Jacob dutifully wrote to thank Mrs Fish, but apparently his letter had gone astray. 'I directed my letter to Tuxedo, NY, and if you will write to Mrs Fish and tell her . . . I will be very glad,' he wrote. 'Tell Mrs Fish that although we were too late for cream yet we had many other good things. The boys are all thankful to her . . . Bernard [almost certainly Bernard Gussow, who was a particular friend of Jacob's] and I and all the boys send our love to you and to Mrs Moore.' He ended with a hint of the charm which later endeared him to women. 'Miss Moore, this I believe, is the first time I've written to you. Do you know out here I am rather glad of this opportunity of writing and feel happy when I send this off? Jake Epstein.'[4]

To Mrs Fish, after thanking her for the money for cream, he wrote a graphic account of the new Americans at camp:

We celebrated yesterday the 4th. Going into the forest we cut down a tall and slim ash, after taking of [*sic*] the bark had a beautiful flag-staff. This we raised on a mound facing the lake in front of the tents and at about ten o'clock read the declaration and raised a beautiful new American flag which Miss Moore had presented us. We then sang the 'Star-Spangled Banner'. We had truly a glorious fourth and considerable [sic] with which to enjoy ourselves. Bathing, swimming is best. I wish you could have been here this splendid Independence Day and seen the flag-raising ceremonies and the fun . . . Out here I paint and try to represent the many things that I see. All is different from the city. All is colour and cloud and atmosphere, green and blue. Yet it is the life here also, the country-life that I see, I would also get into my painting. I go out for long rambles.[5]

Mrs Stuyvesant Fish was obviously very taken with the talented and good-looking Jacob Epstein, regularly sending an open carriage with a footman to fetch him and his drawings from his tenement in the slums to her fashionable uptown house. At tea parties she introduced the boy to her smart friends and persuaded them to buy his sketches, as she did herself. According to a family story she had lost a son and wanted to adopt Jacob. She even sent a letter to Max Epstein with the proposition that she should adopt Jacob, since she could offer him so many more advantages and help to further his career. Max, who was a proud man and, by his own standards, not poor, was furious. He blamed Jacob, although the boy knew nothing of the idea. In time, Jacob grew tired of Mrs Fish's patronage, but Miss Moore's friendship was to remain important to him.

In another undated letter from the summer camp Jacob told Miss Moore that he had been home to Hester Street for a week and was 'glad to see my dear mother and brothers and my dear sisters once again'.[6] The absence of any mention of his father in the letter speaks volumes.

The first time that Jacob's activities can be dated for certain is, curiously enough, the year of his bar mitzvah, which was held in the synagogue his father had helped to build. He must have learned enough Scripture and Hebrew to read a passage from the Bible aloud to the congregation. He was just thirteen at the time, in November 1893. 'How I ever got through this trying ordeal I cannot now imagine,' he wrote.

Up until that age Jacob had to conform, outwardly at least, to the demands of a strict regime. But he was a youth who could not tolerate authority and he was growing up, growing away from his family. 'The New York ghetto was a city at that time transplanted from Poland,' Epstein recalled, and he was fast absorbing American culture. The clash in the family was always between Jacob and his father. He disliked his paternal grandmother, 'a cantankerous old creature' who swore that her grandchildren were losing their Jewish heritage in America and becoming irreligious; she spent her old age travelling between New York and Poland. She did not want to die in a pagan country. But he was fond of his mother and loved her parents. He wrote with feeling of Friday evenings when the old couple would take the children's heads in their hands, give them their blessing in front of the Sabbath candles and reward them with fruits and sweets. He remembered their kindness and patriarchal simplicity with great affection. Although he dropped all ceremonial forms of religion as soon as he could, the Old Testament stories drummed into him at Hebrew classes and in synagogue haunted his imagination all his life.

Soon after his thirteenth birthday, Jacob, encouraged no doubt by the friends who had recognized his talent, registered at the Art Students' League. The League, founded in 1875 by a group of artists, had moved the year before to a building on West 57th Street, where it still stands. To this day there is no entrance examination and students are not required to have had any previous formal training in art. The term began in February 1894 and marked Jacob's first steps in his real life.

Max Epstein did not actively discourage his son. He recognised that the boy had a gift for drawing, but to him the yearning to be an artist remained a mystery. He thought the boy was *meshugga* (mad) and could not understand why he wanted to study a subject which could not possibly earn him any money.

As an art student Jacob inevitably became more independent and increasingly estranged from his father. In his teens he began to frequent anarchist and black American circles, anathema to the inward-looking world of his parents. He knew 'Red Emma' Goldman and made a drawing of her. When she came to visit Jacob at home during the Passover holidays to invite him to a meeting, Max Epstein, furious at the invasion of his home by a woman who mixed with non-Jews and dangerous politicos, shouted at her in Yiddish, 'Get out of my house, you tramp!'[7]

Jacob could not be contained. He loved to wander down the Bowery, a street made up of a long line of saloons, crowded by night with visitors to New York, sailors and prostitutes. One saloon filled with photographs of famous boxers, its floor inlaid with silver dollars, particularly intrigued him. The Bowery led to Chinatown, and Epstein peered into Chinese shop windows and even wandered into a Chinese temple, but he could never persuade the inmates to allow him to sketch them; they would slip away into their houses as soon as they were aware of being watched. His visual senses were constantly stimulated by the city. But he also loved to escape the press of people.

As he grew older he would go off on his own to the woods, or to a secluded spot in Central Park with a book. He read the Russian novelists, absorbed the New Testament, which would have horrified his parents, and became enamoured of Walt Whitman's poems embracing the new America. 'I am large: I contain multitudes,' Whitman wrote, and that would certainly have chimed with Epstein's growing aspirations. Freed from his father's narrow orthodoxy, Jacob was able to explore the parallel world of the Polish Jewish intellectuals who brought Yiddish newspapers, Yiddish theatres, clubs and classes and a rich cultural mix to the lower East Side. He met students and scholars, poets and playwrights, freethinkers and even 'free lovers'. Max Epstein found such Jewish types utterly shocking. Jacob's daughter Peggy Jean remembers her grandfather as a kindly man but 'very narrow and

uncultured'.[8] His son, by contrast, was intensely receptive to the
new influences around him. Jacob went to symphony concerts,
even to hear Wagner's Ring Cycle performed at the Metropolitan
Opera House, sitting high up in the gallery. He attended political
meetings and heard the Russian anarchist Kropotkin speak.
Although instinctively drawn to left-wing causes, he held back
from participating and remained an observer: 'My loyalties were
all for the practice of art and I have always grudged the time that
is given to anything but that.'

As an art student he had the opportunity to develop his visual
sense. He often dropped in to Durand-Ruel's Fifth Avenue gallery
to see fine paintings by Manet, Renoir and Pissarro, who were just
beginning to become known. Durand-Ruel, the French dealer who
had done so much to support the Impressionists, noted the interest
of the young student and allowed him to look closely at the paintings before they were shipped back to Europe. Jacob also learned
to appreciate the works of the 'old masters' of America; he
admired Winslow Homer and Thomas Eakins among others. He
made friends with James Beckwith, an American painter who
taught drawing at the Art Students' League, but Epstein stood
somewhat aloof from student life. He was too earnest and too
driven to enjoy the rags and beer-drinking of his fellows. There
was a tinge of the puritan about him; he felt out of place and found
their horseplay and 'bad jokes' distasteful. Although he was very
short of money, he refused to finance his studies by the hateful
work of touching up, enlarging and colouring photographs as other
students did. But all his life Epstein found that there were people
ready to help him.

In the students' register of 1896, he lists his address as 26
Delancey Street. He did not mention, understandably, that from
1893 to 1898 the house was the home of the University Settlement.
In 1896 his friend Helen Moore was one of the workers at the
Settlement. During term-time Jacob, now in his sixteenth year,
lived at the Settlement house, which was far more congenial for
him, although his home address was still 102 Hester Street.

He spent most of the summer at home. Now that he lived away

and had gained some sense of distance, he found the moving mass in Hester Street more absorbing to watch. There were the crowds, bartering and buying and gossiping, the day workers, carpenters and washerwomen who stood by waiting to be hired, and the odd, elusive characters who excited his imagination. He noticed

> a tall, lean and bearded young man with the ascetic face of a religious fanatic, who wandered through the streets lost in a profound melancholy. His hair grew to his shoulders and upon this was perched an old bowler hat. He carried a box in one hand and as he passed the push-carts, the vendors would put food into his box, here an apple, there a herring. He was a holy man and I followed him into synagogues where he brooded and spent his days and nights.

Now Jacob entered the synagogue not as a bored and reluctant worshipper but as a clandestine artist. His activities would have been considered shockingly sacrilegious.

He was a loner by temperament, and the men he sought as his friends were older people he could look up to, men like James Kirk Paulding and James Beckwith. Around this time, Jacob did have a girlfriend, Adèle Rabinowitz, a young teacher whom he mentioned affectionately in his letters to Miss Moore. Jacob wanted to live with Adèle in the style of the 'free lovers' of the ghetto, rather than marry and settle down. But both sets of parents were so shocked that the notion was dropped.

Yet he did make one close friend in the ghetto. Bernard Gussow, a Russian Jew, was a fellow student at the League, and Epstein knew him from their camping holiday at Lake Greenwood. The son of a rabbi, Gussow was a year younger than Epstein and had studied at the National Academy of Design before registering with the League. The two young men from the same background wanted to dignify and record the life of the East Side. They dreamed of founding a distinctive ghetto art that was truthful, not sentimental or distorting.

Jacob did not study at the League in 1898. He was beginning to sell his drawings; also the University Settlement in Delancey Street, which had been his term-time home for two years, moved to a four-storey building with room for expanded facilities in Elridge Street. That year he helped to organise an exhibition called 'The East Side in Oil and Crayon' and held in Madison House, Madison Street. Jacob breathed imagination and life into the characters of the ghetto in his numerous rough charcoal sketches. He also exhibited a few paintings, rather crudely coloured. Henry Moskowitz, head worker of the Madison Street Settlement, stated that the show helped to demonstrate that the American of the future should be 'an amalgam of Old World and New World qualities'.

Importantly it brought Jacob's talent to the notice of local people and to one very perceptive outsider: Hutchins Hapgood, of the *New York Commercial Advertiser*. A well-educated and adventurous young man, Hapgood was one of the few non-Jewish journalists who had come to live in the Jewish quarter of New York, considered by most New Yorkers as a squalid and crime-ridden district. Hapgood was fascinated by the strange and vibrant life he found, the theatre, the press, the religion and the extraordinary mélange of people. Hapgood's work served to introduce New Yorkers to ghetto life. When he needed an illustrator for his articles, he went to find 'the youth with the melancholy, wistful face'.[9] Commissions for illustrations from journals and newspapers began to come in and Epstein felt a surge of confidence. Perhaps that spurred him to give up his studies at the League in 1898–9 and brave a winter in the countryside.

In summer he had always felt the need to leave town; he escaped from the city by exploring the suburbs, Harlem, Yonkers, Long Island and Coney Island. He bathed in the surf off Rockaway, explored Staten Island, which was then not built up, and scrambled down the rocks to the Hudson river. 'I was not altogether a city boy,' he wrote years later, 'and my excursions to the country bred in me a delight in outdoors.' The outdoor life he chose that winter was stark and harsh. He persuaded Bernard Gussow to share with him a small cabin on the shore of Lake Greenwood, an area they both knew well from the Settlement's summer camp. The two youths foraged in snowbound forests for firewood, cooking simple meals; in the evenings they sketched and read by oil lamp. For a fortnight, when their funds ran low, they cut ice on the deep frozen lake. Early each morning they clambered on to sledges drawn by a team of horses, travelling across the deep frozen lake to hack off slabs of ice. In the evenings as they returned home the snow-covered mountainside blazed with sunset colours. Jacob was eighteen, highly sexed and passionate, Bernard a year younger: both boys came from families where sexual licence was abhorred. Since a strict morality emanated from both his father and his mother, and the youth leaders they admired, Jacob was deeply conscious of the need for restraint. In the seclusion of a freezing winter, however, the temptation for the boys to huddle together for warmth and comfort must have been overwhelming. Jacob, who already admired Walt Whitman's poems, was later to make drawings illustrating Whitman's 'Calamus' poems, specifically the poem 'We two boys together clinging', depicting two naked boys in an embrace.

The return to New York City in 1899, although not a chronological milestone, marked Jacob's coming of age. That year his parents achieved an ambition to move out of the grimy, crowded ghetto to a more respectable and, as Jacob saw it, duller address in Madison Avenue. To Max's bafflement his son hired a small room in Hester Street, in a ramshackle, wooden building overlooking the market, and drew daily, although a room was kept for him in the family home. The stream of new immigrants and the ceaseless activity of the 'pig market' interested him far more than seeing well-dressed and suited citizens hurrying into offices. His instinct was sound. Hutchins Hapgood began to employ him to illustrate his articles. Hapgood described visiting Jacob at the top of a rickety building:

> The stairs that ascend to the garret are pestiferous and dingy ... There is one window which commands a good view of the push-cart market in Hester Street. Near the window is a

diminutive oil stove on which the artist prepares his tea and eggs. On a peg on the door hang an old mackintosh and an extra coat – his only additional wardrobe . . . he lives alone on his beloved Hester Street . . . For his modest room he pays $4 a month and as he cooks his own meals, $12 a month is quite sufficient to satisfy all his needs. This amount he can usually manage through the sale of his sketches but when he does not he 'goes to bed' as he puts it and lies low until one of his various little art enterprises brings him in a small cheque.[10]

Jacob was not quite as passive as Hapgood Hutchins implies. He was a strong youth and he had enjoyed the struggle of hard physical work. After the ice-cutting vacation on Greenwood Lake, which he described as 'hard but congenial', he began to feel that he could express himself more profoundly in sculpture, although it took him some time to find the means of fulfilling his ambition.

In 1899 he took on the job of physical instructor on a nearby children's playground. After two weeks in the park he gave up the job and insisted that Bernard Gussow should replace him. He told his mother that Bernard had no money to live on and needed the job more desperately than he did.[11] Mary Epstein believed in Jacob's talent; she told her children that he would be a great man one day. She surreptitiously slipped him money, although he was always loath to take it. Then Jacob found a job as inspector of dwellings in the Tenement House Department, where his responsibilities included inspecting the tenement property his father owned. One can only imagine the satisfaction he must have felt in telling his father and uncle, who was in the business, that they had violated the regulations governing fire risk by allowing people to sleep on the fire escapes with all their bedding! That job did not last long either, but by now Jacob was getting commissions to illustrate journals and beginning to make his way. Through Hutchins Hapgood he came to know the outstanding personalities in the ghetto, the poets and actors. The great Yiddish actor Jacob Adler made a huge impression. He lived in a house full of dependants in an atmosphere of confusion and excitement. 'Finding a clean collar out of bags that contained hundreds of collars took up most of the time,' Jacob recalled almost forty years later. The actor 'had a head like one of those you see in Japanese prints, long and white and with chameleon-like eyelids'. Adler always had a court of admirers, and when he walked in the streets he was preceded and followed by fans. He also drew Jacob Gordon, who had written a version of *King Lear* in Yiddish. Jacob went to the homes and dressing rooms of the actors and of course to the play, and conceived a lifelong love of theatre which was to influence his later work.

In March 1900 one of Hutchins Hapgood's early articles, 'Four Poets of the Ghetto', appeared in the *Critic* with illustrations 'each sketched from the life by Jacob Epstein'. Some months later Hapgood's article 'The Foreign Stage in New York', with drawings by Epstein, was published by the *Bookman*. This exposure brought Epstein to the notice of a wider public and kept him busily employed chronicling the people of the ghetto. Hapgood found him 'very happy altho' serious, like his race in general and full of idealism and ambition'.[12] Epstein talked to the sympathetic Hapgood about his love of the natural world but admitted that it held no inspiration for him. 'There is no nature in the sweat-shop,' he said, 'and yet it is there and in crowded streets that my love and my imagination call me. It is only the minds and souls of my people that fill me with a desire to work.' For a year, until he was twenty, Epstein made sketches of ghetto life for Hapgood.

Disaster faced him one day when he came back to his room in Hester Street. 'I found it burnt to the ground, and my charred drawings (hundreds of them) floating about in water with dead cats.' That is all he says about a disaster which cost him months, perhaps years of work and left him homeless. There is something almost chilling in Epstein's terse dismissal of the fire, even though it was written forty years after the event. He remained determinedly distant, refusing to lay blame or to pity himself; he had just turned twenty when it happened: his stock of drawings and material was destroyed; funds were desperately low and he had nowhere to live. Having walked out of his father's house he could not bring himself to go back. Instead he went to stay at the University Settlement, now at 184 Eldridge Street, where Helen Moore was working, and asked her for help. She immediately tried to find a way for Jacob to continue studying and working as an artist. First she wrote to her old art teacher, Thomas Eakins, in Philadelphia, sending two of Jacob's published drawings. 'I feel I cannot give him any information with regard to supporting himself while studying art,' Eakins replied on 4 December 1900. 'Perhaps with his drawings he might get on the newspapers or periodicals [he had been published, but sporadically]. Perhaps', continued Eakins,

by manual labor of some kind he could earn leisure enough to study. I never advise anyone to study art who has not a means of support while studying. I have seen so many noble fellows go down overwhelmed. Nevertheless, if he does study, I shall be glad to give him advice and instruction without compensation. The East Side is the picturesque side of New York and Rembrandt could have painted all his life without exhausting a single block of it. I like Epstein's drawings very well. I see that he has the sentiment of action. If he was under my care I should have him model the naked figure a good deal and sketch in wax and then paint.

Have you seen his painting? Has he the sentiment of color? . . . I think if I come to New York I will call upon him. He should understand perspective which is generally very foolishly taught in composition.

Does he know my work at all that he would have faith in what I should say?

Yours truly

Thomas Eakins[13]

This was valuable advice but not of much practical help. That Eakins, who was an established artist, obviously recognized Jacob's talent boosted his morale. Epstein remembered all his life what Eakins had said about the inspiration that Rembrandt would have drawn from the East Side of New York, and he later gave it as his own opinion. More importantly he took on the suggestion of trying to find labouring work to fund his studies. Once again it was Helen Moore who showed him the way. She wrote to a lawyer friend in Boston, Henry Rogers, setting out the problem and asking him whether he knew of a farm in Massachusetts that would employ Epstein, as he wanted to build up his strength, save money to go to art school and get away from New York. Rogers replied promptly and asked Miss Moore for a frank assessment of Epstein's character and suitability to work as a farmhand. The answer must have been satisfactory. By 17 December 1900 Jacob was working as a farmhand on a large estate in Southboro, Massachusetts, owned by one of the richest men in Boston. On trial for a month, he had a room to himself and a kindly manager who was instructed to keep an eye on him and allow him the privilege of visiting art exhibitions in Boston occasionally. He boarded at a farmhouse with seven older men, breakfasted at 6 a.m. by the bell and worked until 5 p.m. sawing and stacking wood and crushing stones in the deep winter. Most nights he went to bed by eight, completely 'tuckered out'. The farm was huge with about fifty hands in all, with cows, horses, sheep and pigs, a large chicken house, a carpenter, a blacksmith, shepherds and engineers.

Epstein had a gift for writing and described his life in a series of letters to Helen Moore which give a portrait of the artist on the brink of his career. He buckled down to the work, banking $20 a month in Boston at Helen Moore's suggestion, enjoying the excellent food and accepting the routine. 'Of course,' he explained to her, 'all is different from New York here. No social questions, no arguments very little lintelectual [sic]. Nothing else can be expected.'[14]

At first he left his sketching things behind and took no books because he was suffering badly from eyestrain. He observed his work-fellows closely. 'They are all goodnatured hearty men . . . they seem always in good spirit. Perhaps this is because their natures are so elementary,' he commented. 'Their pleasures are the sensual ones, eating, drinking & a good deal of lewd talk.' Epstein admired the good spirit among them and they accepted the earnest youth readily. But he was, as he said, 'more than half a dreamer . . . Last night the sky was thick sprinkled with stars & I thought of Adele and you. I think I love the sky & the earth more than ever before.'[15]

Jacob was not yet twenty-one, with both a poetical and a puritanical side to his complex nature. On 19 January 1901 he went with his workmates to a dance, a surprise party for a newly married couple. 'I am not sorry I went because I now know what they are & will never go to one again,' he told Miss Moore.

> The promiscuous hugging & kissing only disgusted me. If I had known the road home I would have left early . . . I consider it the first dissipation since my coming here. The next time I will find some good excuses for staying at home. Indeed what more can I want than what I came for, fresh air & plenty of sleep & Nature, always beautiful, wherever or however.
> Yours always Jacob.[16]

The farm work was taxing – his arms ached from crushing stones and his fingers felt painful from milking – but, in the grind of tending the herd of Jersey cows and cleaning out the barn, he kept his senses alive. 'There is something about [milking in the early morning] picturesque and strange. The moving of heads and clinking of chains, the restless mooing of animals in the dark with an occasional hoarse bellow, the growing light of the sunrise make it interesting.'[17] In February he used his pay cheque of $20 to repay Mr Ordway, a left-wing philanthropist connected with the Settlement who had loaned him money. In March he went, by special arrangement, to an exhibition of 'Fair Children' held at Copley Hall in Boston and admired a portrait of a young girl by Sargent.

Helen Moore obviously kept a motherly eye on him:

I am making my best effort to do as you would like to have me do. I have bought whatever clothes I need, overalls and working shirts, and change my underclothes often. I have to as I get quite sweaty while at work. I try to keep my room clean and neat, and as there is a bathroom I take baths all over, often. I think I will become a man if I train properly for it. I have been but a boy and an exceedingly foolish one . . . There is much in the past that I am ashamed of and very much that I wonder at . . . if I told you half the things I have done you would be astonished.[18]

Jacob was half boasting, half penitent when he wrote to Helen Moore about his exploits. There is no doubt that he had matured and faced up to the work well. He longed to study, yet realized that his health was benefiting, and now he was at least solvent. He gained two and a half stone in weight; his body had toughened up and by the spring he was helping to build a road. Best of all his eyes had improved and the Boston doctor he consulted prescribed new glasses for him. Helen Moore continued to encourage and support him. He wrote to thank her for a parcel on 18 May 1901:

The clothes are sc[r]umptious, tip-top! The dark trousers fit to a tee but the light ones will have to be sheared off at the bottom but are none too wide. I am going to ask you now for something: that is for a place to put the clothes for I have no room to put them away properly in my room. I mean of course a trunk if you can get me one. I would buy one anyhow for future use if I thought I could spare the money, but in truth I cannot. Let the trunk be old, battered, travel worn, the more so the better – but big.

I am going into Boston next week to see the doctor . . . I wish you could be there so I could see you also.

Many thanks for the things,
Yours truly
Jacob Epstein[19]

There are no more letters to Miss Moore, since Jacob returned to New York in June 1901 to resume work as an artist. Earlier that year he had told her how much her faith in him had meant: 'as you know I had lost faith in myself and I was surprised that . . . you should believe in me. I owe a great deal to you.' He signed that letter 'Yours with *great love*, Jacob'.[20] But in his autobiography, written half a century later, Epstein shabbily omitted the whole episode, ashamed perhaps to admit how much he had been helped by the University Settlement. Helen Moore does not rate a mention.

Back in New York he was burning with his ambition to study and become a sculptor. The lack of eyestrain caused by drawing and his relish for physical work made the handling of clay a pleasure and a relief. By September, Jacob had found a job at a bronze foundry, working hard and gaining valuable experience. After work he attended a modelling class at the Art Students' League taught by George Gray Barnard, an American sculptor with a passion for his subject, greatly influenced by the heroic works of Michelangelo. Epstein's fellow students, mainly sculptors' assistants, were men with an equally ardent desire to learn who came to study after a day's work. Barnard, who had been trained at the Ecole des Beaux-Arts in Paris, was the only American sculptor whom Epstein respected. One evening a week Barnard came in to look at the students' work and offer criticism. He rarely managed to get through the entire class and he finished off the evening with a general talk. A man of great earnestness, he impressed Epstein, who remained in touch with him for years. Barnard helped to forge in his pupil a desire to see the masterpieces of European sculpture, originals of Michelangelo and Donatello and, of course, Rodin, as well as of the ancients. 'Europe meant the Louvre and Florence', and Epstein was burning to get there – to study in Paris, at that time the most exciting city in the world for artists.

The sculpture class at the Art Students' League continued until May 1902. That summer, Hutchins Hapgood approached Epstein to illustrate a book of his collected essays, *The Spirit of the Ghetto*. He needed over fifty drawings of the types that Epstein knew so well:

pious men praying in the synagogue with complete concentration, bony workers in the sweatshop snatching a lunch-break, women students reading. That Epstein poured youthful idealism and dreams into these drawings is clear from his subsequent remarks. He regretted their loss and looked for them later. 'I took this East Side drawing work very serious and my drawings were not just sketches.'

He had taken another room in Hester Street, for the summer of 1902, this time in a tenement with clothing workers. 'I never remember giving up this second room,' Epstein wrote as a man of sixty, 'and it has returned to me in dreams with a strange persistence, even in Paris and London.' But he was impatient at the time to get to Paris, impatient to start on his new life. The sculpture class at the League ended in May 1902. Determined to be on his way, Epstein did not stop to finish all the illustrations to Hapgood's work but, to the author's disappointment, passed on the last few charcoal drawings to Bernard Gussow to finish. For his work he received the largest sum of money he had ever earned, $400, enabling him at last to make the trip to Europe. On 10 September 1902, aged twenty-one, he obtained a passport – in which he was described as 'five foot ten with blue eyes and a wide forehead'. His excitement at the prospect of Paris is reflected in the notes he made on the back of his new passport: 'Musée Guimet, Trocadero and the Cernucci Museum'. By the end of the month he had bought his ticket to Paris. There he was to study at the Ecole des Beaux-Arts.

2

Expanding

EPSTEIN BOUNDED UP the gangway of the ship that was to take him to France – with the 'heedlessness of youth', he recalled forty years later. His mother ran after him and embraced him for the last time. Despite his close bond with her, he was so focused on the future that he felt elated to be on his way and free of family ties. His elder brother Louis was to help him with money from time to time. He also had the backing of a prominent left-wing lawyer, Edward Warren Ordway, whom he had met through the Settlement House Movement. Ordway had loaned young Epstein money when he was struggling in New York. Epstein repaid the debt. The lawyer was a prominent figure in left-wing politics, the secretary of the New York branch of the Anti-Imperialist League, an organisation led by Mark Twain which championed the rights of immigrant workers as well as opposing American expansionism. For at least five years Ordway supported Epstein, encouraging him and sending him money orders of $50 (equivalent to about $1,000 today) every month or two. Fortunately Ordway kept several of Epstein's letters, which, combined with his own autobiography, build up a portrait of his student years.

When he arrived in Paris in October 1902 Epstein, at almost twenty-two, was aware that he was older than most first-year students. He could think of nothing but the excitement of studying and working in Paris. He was desperately keen to acquire the skills he needed to become independent as quickly as possible. His sculpture teacher in New York, George Grey Barnard, had warned his students about the dangers of drink and dissipation and of the lure of bohemian life. So Jacob, who in any case could not afford to indulge, decided that cafés and women were not for him.

Nevertheless he found Paris a delightful city to explore, even for a penniless student, and his love of the city lasted all his life. On his first visit he allowed himself barely three days to get acquainted with the realities of a place he knew so well in his imagination. He went straight to Notre-Dame and looked at the treasures of the cathedral, then strolled across the bridges of the Seine. He loved the water. In crossing one bridge he noticed a small building in the centre, a morgue. Curiosity drew him in but he came out again quickly. The grim presence of dead bodies made him regret his idle curiosity. On his second day in Paris, Epstein was plunged into a political maelstrom: he was on his way up to Montmartre when he was caught up in a funeral procession. Emile Zola, the polemical author, was to be buried in Montmartre Cemetery that day. Zola's championship of Alfred Dreyfus, the Jewish army captain wrongfully accused of treason, had made him highly unpopular in certain quarters; at that date the Dreyfus case was still unresolved. Even at his burial the writer was allowed no rest. Anti-Semites shouted insults and disturbed the mourners while the gendarmes tried to keep order. By a bizarre coincidence Epstein witnessed the incident, which was almost a curtain-raiser to his life.

Epstein never forgot the thrill he felt on his third day in Paris when he crossed the Pont des Arts to enter the Louvre. He wandered through the sculpture and painting rooms for hours and was to visit the great museum again and again. But he had come to study, and the next day he enrolled, in halting French, at the leading art school in Paris, the Ecole des Beaux-Arts. To test his ability he was placed with other candidates in an amphitheatre and told to construct a figure from a live model. 'I hurled myself at the clay,' he said. He was confident and passed the test with ease, but the unofficial initiation proved more daunting. All new students were ragged and roughed up by the senior ones, but the few foreigners among them were particularly unpopular, and Epstein's poor command of French and his strong American accent cannot have helped. He was put up to fight a boxing match with a deaf and dumb student, a stocky powerful man, who hurled himself at Epstein grunting. When Epstein struck first and knocked out his opponent, the French students howled in protest. He was no sports-man, they shouted; he took it all too seriously. Epstein's assured attitude, coupled with his obvious poverty, made him disliked by many students from well-to-do families. For his part, Epstein could not conceal his distaste for their coarse behaviour; he was told, for his pains, to go back to his own country.

He soon discovered academic disadvantages in being a new boy. New students had to take their modelling stands to the back of the large studio; in order to get a close look at the model they had to 'scamper backwards and forwards'. Epstein took to darting round the model with a measuring tape. A new model was chosen each week. On Monday mornings, the *massier*, or monitor, a real 'apache' type, according to Epstein, who recalled those early student days vividly, introduced a model to the studio. The girl stripped and the class voted noisily on whether to accept her or not. During the morning she was 'generally traded' among them. That took up far too much time, in Epstein's opinion; but he discovered that by Wednesdays most of the students had dropped out of class and he could move closer to the model and see her better. He worked 'aflame with ardour . . . in a frenzied almost mad manner', building up a study at the beginning of the week only to smash it to pieces at the end and start again the next Monday. For relaxation he went to the Luxembourg gardens and listened to the band playing on Sunday afternoons.

His absolute dedication to his art estranged him from most of his classmates, although he said that he learned more from the capable ones than from the masters, who seemed to him to do as little work as possible. He spent his mornings modelling from life, and after a hurried lunch, which he had brought with him, went into the carving class, where there was practically no instruction. He spotted two or three professional marble carvers who came in to take advantage of a free studio and materials, making small copies of Italian Renaissance heads and smuggling them out under their overcoats. The room was full of casts of Michelangelo's work, and Epstein often drew from them when he was not engaged in a carving.

When he had first come to Paris, Epstein had hoped to find that the Ecole des Beaux-Arts had modernized, reflecting the influence of Rodin's powerful expressionism. But neither the work of Rodin, nor of other realist sculptors in Paris, such as the Belgian Constantin Meunier, who carved figures of labouring men in heroic poses, or the Italian Medardo Rosso, who modelled small coloured wax figures in motion, were reflected in the curriculum of the Ecole des Beaux-Arts.

In the Salon and art schools of Paris, and in academies of art all over the Western world, plaster limbs from famous sculptures of the past and forests of smooth, second-rate marble Venuses and sham Apollos were held up to students as ideals. Archaeological discoveries in the eighteenth century had led to a revival of interest in Graeco-Roman works of classical grandeur. As a result, neoclassicism, a style easily reduced to a banal formula, had evolved.

Since he knew that Michelangelo and other great Renaissance artists had made careful studies of corpses, he forced himself, although naturally squeamish, to attend the anatomy lecture one morning when a corpse was used as a model. A green arm was handed round for the students to inspect, but that was too much for Jacob. He nearly fainted, and hurried out of the class never to return. He felt embarrassed about the episode, but the shame went deeper. Although Jacob liked to present himself as strong and manly, he possessed a deeply 'feminine' sensibility and intuition.

After six months at the school, Epstein was chafing to get on; he greatly resented the two years of 'fagging' imposed on new students. Matters came to a head in the spring of 1903 when the seniors were beginning the competition for the prestigious Prix de Rome, the prize that could lead to state honours and commissions and an assured future. By tradition new students were expected to fetch and carry the clay and modelling stands for the examinees and generally wait on the seniors. To the amazement of the French, the truculent American refused point blank to waste his morning in that way, especially as there were uniformed attendants standing by. He went off to his studio and began as usual to work on a study. The next morning, when he turned up ready to start work, he found the study he had begun smashed, a ruined heap on the ground. He ignored the incident and built up another study, but found the next day that that too had been destroyed. A group of French students stood around watching, hoping to see Epstein provoked into a furious rage. Instead he said nothing, but picked up his modelling stand and went over to the Académie Julian to enrol there.

He had been at the Ecole des Beaux-Arts for six months when the break came, lonely, hard-working months, but exciting too as he prowled through the museums discovering his own favourite works: the Egyptian, the early Greek, Cycladic goddesses and Iberian art in the Louvre, the Trocadéro with its ill-assembled mass of primitive art, and the Chinese collection in the Cernucci Museum.

In later years Epstein insisted that he had concentrated with 'fanatic zeal' on his studies in Paris and the descriptions of his work, together with the photographs, sketches and casts he sent to his patron, Edward Ordway, bear this out. But all through his life Epstein contrived to work in a frenzy of intensity while leading a hectic private life. During his first year in Paris, in April 1903, he was invited to a dinner party in Passy, a fashionable suburb, by a Belgian publisher and anarchist, Victor Dave. The political connection suggests that the invitation was arranged by Edward Ordway. Epstein notes that his host had been imprisoned for years for publishing anarchist propaganda. At the dinner he met a striking redhead, a married Scottish woman who had just turned thirty; Margaret Williams was to play an important part in his future.

Soon after the encounter with Margaret, Epstein's close friend Bernard Gussow arrived from New York to share a studio with him. The two had been close for years, taking camping holidays together; more than once Epstein, whose parents were better off than Gussow's, had put work his friend's way. 'I was very pleased that Gussow was there as by nature I am timid and Gussow was a very solid, firmly fixed, level headed person who we, the small American colony of artists, looked upon as a sort of Daddy. He was a man we could trust and for me a real boon . . . he was a painter and there was no feeling of emulation.'[1]

This revealing passage in the notes for Epstein's autobiography, written years later, was not included in the published work. Although outwardly forceful and quick to defend himself, Epstein obviously thought of himself as vulnerable; fearful perhaps of his own aggression, he recognised the value of a steady, well-balanced companion.

The two young men, intimate friends, possibly lovers, lived at no. 7 rue Belloni, a rambling, draughty building behind the Gare Montparnasse inhabited by art students. Epstein had just begun to study sculpture at the Académie Julian, while Bernard was studying painting, but the two spent their leisure time together. Epstein was working on his fine pen-and-ink drawing, *We Two Boys Together*, depicting two naked youths embracing, inspired by Walt Whitman's poem from the 1860 edition of *Leaves of Grass*:

> We two boys together clinging,
> One the other never leaving,
> Up and down the roads going, North and South excursions
>   making,
> Power enjoying, elbows stretching, fingers clutching,
> Arm'd and fearless, eating, drinking, sleeping, loving,
> No law less than ourselves owning, sailing, soldiering,
>   thieving, threatening,
> Misers, menials, priests alarming, air breathing, water
>   drinking, on the turf or the sea-beach dancing,
> Cities wrenching, ease scorning, statutes mocking, feebleness
>   chasing,
> Fulfilling our foray.[2]

The bravado and bond of the boys in the poem, their self-reliance and energy, their disdain for the values and vanities of the world, and the movement and breadth of Whitman's writing, called to Epstein as a young man in his twenties. He planned to make a bronze based on the 'Calamus' poems, a testimony of friendship, perhaps to Gussow, but the work was never realised. Whitman's inspiration remained important to Epstein: when he was in his seventies he carved a quotation from the poet on his group *Social Consciousness*, which now stands at the entrance to the Philadelphia Fine Art Museum.

Epstein felt happier at the Académie Julian, where he started work in April 1903. The Julian was a private school, less academic, less encumbered by tradition than the Ecole des Beaux-Arts, and with a group of students from all over the world. Women were admitted to attend the art school too, although they had to pay double the fees. The light was good; the studio where he worked was spacious, and, although some of the students were less attentive than Epstein would have liked, and he had to contend with the 'usual distractions of noise and singing', he was able to make better progress. He wrote to his patron Edward Ordway frankly, in an account which has resonance in the light of his later work.

> My chief faults lie in over-accentuating and exaggerating. My object to start with was to get life into my figures, to have them look living. I think that I have got that life in all the figures I have made at the school, but I have neglected proportion and got lots of exaggeration in the figures, so now I will have to give my attention to that.[3]

He still attended the carving class at the Ecole des Beaux-Arts in the afternoons, but spent his mornings at the Julian, where once again his sense of his own capabilities soon had him branded an outsider. Jean-Paul Laurens, a well-known artist at the time, was in charge of drawing at the life class. His routine was to process from drawing to drawing, while the students followed respectfully and listened to his criticism. When he came to Epstein, he sat down on his pupil's stool, gazed at the drawing, then at the model, looked up at Epstein and walked on without a word. Epstein termed it scornfully 'a silent criticism'.

He was no more impressed when a visiting luminary, William Bougereau, the most eminent French academic painter of his day, took the class. The 'great Bougereau' figured prominently at the Salon each year and his work sold for thousands of dollars in America. The students were reverential to the old man, then almost eighty, and listened carefully to his every word. Epstein remained sceptical about the visiting master and his work, and time has vindicated his judgement. After one or two disparaging remarks about his work, Epstein refused to accept criticism from any quarter and covered his work impatiently when the master entered the room. Laurens noticed Epstein's dismissive gesture and condemned '*ce sauvage Américain*' ('this American barbarian'), in audible tones.

Impatient and censorious of his educators, Epstein made his own programme, learning tirelessly from the art around him. Even when he was a student at the Art Students' League in New York, he had seen photographs of Rodin's work and read articles about him. Every day he visited the work of the artist who had thrown off the yoke of classical sculpture and pointed the way to heroic modern work. Auguste Rodin was a vitalizing force for many young artists; as a contemporary critic wrote, his sculpture had 'learnt to suggest more than it says, to embody dreams in his flesh, to become at once a living thing and symbol'.[4] In the Luxembourg gardens Epstein admired the subtle modelling of *The Age of Bronze* and the masterly technique used by the artist in *St John the Baptist*. In his first year as a student, Epstein contrived to gain an entrée to Rodin's studio. An elderly English painter, a Mr Cayley-Robinson, who was studying modelling at the Julian, knew Rodin slightly and offered to take Epstein with him on a Saturday afternoon, when guests were shown round the studio. 'You'll be interested to know', he wrote to Ordway with a hint of a swagger, 'that Gussow and I went to visit [Rodin] in his studio.' At the rue de l'Université, Rodin had several adjoining studios given to him by the state. His unfinished marble statue, *Monument to Victor Hugo*, made a great impression:

Hugo is seated nude, with one arm outstretched in a powerful movement, while in his ear, a genius pours his voice. The other figure was still more unfinished than the Hugo with a tremendous sweeping movement like a great bird . . . Rodin himself gives you an impression of great strength of personality. His manner was quiet and he did not speak much, only showing something in one or two of his works, a beauty here and there.[5]

'I did not speak to Rodin as I had only just arrived in Paris and knew no French,' he wrote in a later account. 'I was quite content to look at things and watch Rodin himself.' Epstein described Rodin as 'short, bearded, with a sort of round flat cap on his head. [He] looked calm and watchful at the same time. His neck was of enormous thickness and gave his head a tapering shape upwards. Rodin went about amongst his guests and he would roll tissue paper around a small bronze head and show it that way . . . I never saw him again, although he was several times in England.' A note of seasonal greetings from Rodin to Epstein and 'Madame', sent in December 1904 when Epstein was still a student in Paris, indicates that there was in fact a further meeting.[6]

Now that Gussow was with him and as the spring weather improved, Epstein began to enjoy Paris more. He had already roamed all over the city and loved every quarter, except the fashionable district around the Arc de Triomphe, the Elysées. Characteristically he avoided the 'desert of boring streets' with their glittering shops and exorbitant prices. There were memorable days: Epstein heard Paderewsky play the piano and watched Richard Strauss conduct symphony concerts. He was among the frenzied crowd at the Trocadéro who witnessed Isadora Duncan dance across the stage to the accompaniment of Beethoven's Seventh Symphony. Occasionally, on a mild evening, the two young men would board a little steamer going upriver and delight in the illuminations at dusk: 'then it was like fairyland'. They bought their food in a Russian students' canteen near the Jardin des Plantes. Here they could get a meal for 1 franc 50, mostly kasha (cracked wheat), but they could fill up on bread, which was free, washed down by Russian tea, familiar to Epstein and Gussow from their East European backgrounds. Refugees from tsarist Russia were welcomed in the canteen, where students ate by candlelight when the lights failed in the dingy little room. But as Americans Epstein and Gussow were looked upon with suspicion, and once denounced as spies. In his writing Epstein manages to convey a useful sense of superiority to those who taunted him. In the studios where he lived on the rue Belloni, 'only the Frenchmen had mistresses, and they naturally laughed at us Americans and English who seemed able to do without. For one thing, the mistress was also the model, and we "foreigners" had to pose for each other and mark up the hours on the walls.'

Epstein was working hard at his studies 'in a sustained explosion of energy', so driven that a fellow student at the Julian, a Czech, warned him that he was too zealous and would wear himself out before his time. His letters to Ordway that April and May suggest that he was feeling more confident and optimistic, even to the point of returning money loaned by his benefactor. 'I am returning the fifty dollars you sent me as I find I have money enough and will not need this. I should have written to you not to send it. I have no trouble in getting on.'[7] He had paid for three months' tuition at the Julian but wrote that he was considering staying on in the summer, as it would be cheaper to take a six-month course. Even if his brother had sent him money at that time it was a brave and generous gesture for an impoverished student to make.

His friendship with Margaret Williams had grown and deepened since their first meeting at the dinner party. Despite having told Ordway that he would stay in Paris through the summer, Epstein took a night train to London in July and wrote to him from Margaret's address, 49 Clovelly Mansions, Gray's Inn Road. He gave no explanation for his change of mind, but assured Ordway that he had toured the galleries, seen the Parthenon sculptures in the British Museum, visited the National Gallery, the Wallace Collection, the South Kensington Museum (the Victoria and Albert

Museum) as well as private galleries and studios. London was 'pretty dirty and horribly busy', but the National Gallery in particular impressed him: 'in some of their Old Masters they eclipse the Louvre'. He told Ordway that he was staying with two friends, Mr Duncan Williams and his wife Margaret. (In fact, Margaret's husband's name, according to their marriage certificate, was Thomas Charles.) His hosts, wrote Epstein, had taken him around and 'been very kind . . . They want me to go with them up the Thames and camping out on the banks of the river . . . I think this will be a splendid vacation.'[8]

Margaret Williams, Epstein's hostess on his first vacation in England, was a remarkably independent and determined woman. Born in January 1873 on a small croft in Fife in Scotland, she was a bright and ambitious child who managed to acquire a good enough education to pass the Civil Service examination as a woman clerk in the GPO when she was nineteen. Candidates were examined in two of three languages, Latin, French and German, as well as in handwriting and spelling, maths and English history. The knowledge of foreign languages was demanded as a guarantee that the women who succeeded were of the 'proper' social standing, as distinct from the menial outside staff. Margaret and her civil servant husband had a fifth-floor flat in Gray's Inn Road where they were 'at home' once a week. One of their other visitors in 1904, the year when Epstein came to London, was Arthur Ransome, the author of *Swallows and Amazons* and then a freelance writer and reviewer, who arrived with the poet Edward Thomas. Describing the Williamses, Ransome wrote, 'He was a compact little Welshman with a fine voice, she a large handsome peasant lass who had educated herself and made her way in the Post Office . . . Peggy wore long green dresses with big beads about her columnar throat.'[9] Ransome, who was a little bit in love with her, used to bicycle from Balham, where he lived, to the Gray's Inn Road and then run up five storeys carrying his bicycle shoulder high to visit Margaret – or Peggy, as she was known.

By an awkward coincidence Ordway had planned a surprise visit to Europe with his wife that summer and had thought that he

would visit Epstein in Paris. When he discovered that Jacob was in
London, he proposed a meeting there. Epstein put him off in a
letter of 18 August 1904, saying that he was off to Wales the next
day and planning to climb in Snowdonia. When Epstein was back
in Paris and Ordway safely back in New York, Epstein wrote an
unusually apologetic letter to his patron: 'I am so sorry that the
gods were unwilling we should meet . . . I cannot say I did
Snowdonia – I was quite unprepared as to shoe and my shoes naturally gave out after one day's climbing.' He did manage to climb
'quite a picturesque peak opposite Snowdonia . . . the top looked
as if jagged rocks had been thrown there in some mighty upheaval
ages ago . . . I like the bareness [of the mountains] and as it was
the first really high mountain I had ever seen it was something new
for me.'[10] Epstein told Ordway that he was attending the Académie
Colarossi during September, since the Julian, which he thought
was better, was not open until 1 October, and that he intended to
take an afternoon course in modelling from the antique.

Ordway remained remarkably constant and sent Epstein a
money order for $50 that autumn. He did suggest that Epstein
might consider returning to America to work. It is quite clear from
the tone of Epstein's letters to Ordway that he regarded his patron
as a discerning friend who recognized his need for support but
could in no way exert an influence on his artistic future. He told
Ordway firmly that he planned to stay at the Académie Julian until
the end of the school year and would use the money Ordway had
sent him to pay the fees. Then he intended to find a studio of his
own, large enough to house the group of figures he had been
sketching. He wanted to be able to return to America with something to show. His argument seems sensible: 'I do not think it wise
to return . . . with nothing but my technique in my fingers. If I have
something to exhibit I will gain much.' Also, if he obtained some
recognition of his artistic ability in France, it would increase his
reputation. 'If I were to exhibit at the Salon here and receive a
mention or a medal . . . it would go a long way to introducing me
to America.' Not that he thought much of the Salon, but he thought
even less of the Metropolitan Museum's Hall of Sculpture, which

Ordway had mentioned. 'I have been told that it is filled with horrors made by our early American sculptors . . . like some of those imitation Greek and Roman works.'[11] In October he entered the sculpture competition at the Ecole des Beaux-Arts, working for a week from eight in the morning until four in the afternoon at his figures, but without success.

With as much tact and patience as he could muster, Ordway was trying to persuade Epstein to return to America. He warned his protégé that he might become too academic if he remained too long in art school. That was a charge Epstein could easily refute. Throughout his student days in Paris he educated himself by looking at art, ancient and modern. He kept in touch with contemporary art by visiting his friend Durand-Ruel's gallery in the narrow rue Lafitte, the heart of the modern art market. Next door at Ambrose Vollard's, the untidiest shop in Paris, hung Gauguin and Van Gogh and a large stack of Cézannes, and he knew the work of Picasso, Matisse and Rouault, whom he particularly admired. In 1903 he had visited the first, and in his view the finest, Salon d'Automne, which opened with an exhibition of Gauguin's work; and like any alert art student looking for an outlet he also visited the official Salon as well as the Salon des Indépendants and the Salon de la Nationale. He also saw a fine collection of Japanese prints owned by Leopold Stein, Gertrude's brother.

By 1904 Epstein was totally immersed in the world of art. In an earlier letter he had expressed a polite interest in Ordway's philanthropic work for the children of the East Side; after all, it was partly thanks to that interest that he was able to study in Paris. But now he no longer troubled to conceal his distance from American politics: 'Just at present I have left theories of most kinds and do not read the papers at all so that I have lost touch of events . . . in a way my life has become very limited.'[12]

He had moved on, left the Julian, and after searching for some time found a studio by himself without Gussow, at no. 5 rue de la Campagne-Première in Montparnasse, large enough for him to work on a group of figures he was planning. Ideas flooded his imagination, poetry and music inspired him, as did the strange and stirring figures in the primitive art collections of the museums of Paris. Outwardly confident and buoyed up by grand plans, he struggled to give form to his concepts. He held high hopes for two groups. The theme of primitive man greeting the sun enthralled him for years. In the streets of Paris he came across a model who seemed ideal, a Sikh youth from the Punjab. 'He is quite slender and tall and finely formed and his brown colour gives him a very sculptural appearance. He has a good head and altogether I am greatly pleased that I have got him. I daresay there is not another model like him,' he wrote to Ordway.[13] In another, undated letter to Ordway he enthused over 'a lad with a splendid figure, long and slender, a negro model'.[14] The youth, from Martinique, sat for Epstein only on Sunday morning when he could not get other work.

From boyhood Epstein's artistic instinct and his rebellion against his own narrow circle in New York had drawn him to delight in diverse racial types, but, by breaking away from the idealized Greek hero, fair skinned and delicate, to create brown-skinned idols, Epstein was out of step with current taste and storing up trouble for the future. He knew that Ordway, with his anti-imperialist beliefs, would be in sympathy. Nevertheless he desperately needed money. Now that he was on his own, he was discovering how expensive it was to start up as a sculptor. Apart from the rent, even a small piece of marble cost 250 francs, and Epstein, 'high and dry', had grand plans. Nothing could be allowed to hold them up. 'I am asking you to let me have fifty dollars if you can spare it,' he wrote to Ordway, in the same letter in which he had announced his lack of interest in American politics.

I hope that you can and that you will trust me to use the money to the best advantage. A model costs a good deal of money, models' wages in Paris are 8 francs a day, this is less than either New York or London where models get from 40–50 cents an hour. I live on as little as I can . . . I would not ask it for anything but the work and I feel that I am not asking it for myself, that is why I am free to ask.

Ordway obliged.

The group of figures based on Whitman's 'Calamus' poems were the inspiration for Epstein's second great theme. Because of the scale of the bronze he was planning, he had made only part of the figures: arms, head and shoulders. For Ordway's benefit he had plaster casts made of the fragmented statues, photographed them with a borrowed camera and sent the results to his patron in New York. He wrote enthusiastically of the two models he had used, both from London, a young man and a young woman. 'He is not a regular model but has got a fine figure. The woman is a model and has the best arms of any model I saw . . . I am making drawings of the young man now and I think that I will have the chance to exhibit them in London.'[15]

Epstein had intended to go to London in September 1904 to see whether he could arrange an exhibition and look around for a suitable studio. Ordway, it seems clear, had hoped that Epstein would return to America and express through his sculptures the struggle of the immigrant. 'I know you will think that I ought to return to America as soon as I can,' Epstein wrote to him, but added that he wanted to stay in Paris at least until the summer Salon and then perhaps return to America. But the lure of London creeps into his letter again and again. He didn't think his expenses there would be any larger than in Paris. Food, he had heard, was cheaper; as for models, 'I have two friends who have promised to pose for me for nothing.' Epstein's restlessness, his vaulting ambition, his urge to find an ideal solution in art and in life, animate his letters. He wrote to Ordway of plans to visit Florence to see the work of Michelangelo, Donatello and the other Renaissance sculptors in the original, and to go to London to visit the British Museum. Whether he went either to Italy or to England during that year remains unknown. But London was never far from his thoughts. 'An English artist I know advised me to exhibit [the drawings] in London . . . I may do this.'[16] These pen-and-ink drawings were to give him his introduction to the English art scene.

A few months after leaving art school, Epstein became unsure of himself, unclear how to work out his plans for sculpture and dissatisfied with his attempts. In Paris, at the end of 1904, he smashed up his two heroic-sized groups, the sun-worshippers and the 'Calamus' figures, with a youthful disregard of their worth. In retrospect he regretted having destroyed the men hailing the sunrise, telling a friend, 'I have since seen early Egyptian figures which bear a remarkable resemblance to mine.' He felt at the time, however, that he needed a fresh start in new surroundings.

Although later there were rumours of casual girlfriends in Paris, and Epstein had begun to realise his potent attraction for women, Margaret Williams was the only woman of importance in his life at the time. She was, in her quiet way, as passionate and determined as he was. By the end of 1904 she had fallen so deeply in love with Jacob that she even considered the brave and scandalous step of asking her husband to divorce her. She was cosmopolitan, intellectual, with splendid contacts in the art world, a deeply spiritual woman but with her feet solidly on the ground. Even in his twenties Epstein was a connoisseur of human beings and he recognised Peggy's rare strength and magnetism.

Through her he evidently met Rodin again in a more personal capacity. On Christmas Eve 1904, the great sculptor wrote the couple a note from 182 rue de l'Université:

> *Chère Madame,*
> *Cher Monsieur,*
>   *Je vous envoie mes souvenirs et amitiés pour Noël. Mes souhaits pour qu'on aime le grand poète et sa valeur et pour votre bonheur chère Madame*
> *A. Rodin*[17]

At the beginning of 1905 Jacob Epstein left Paris to start a new life.

3

Taking Off

'BY THE WAY, there is a young American sculptor named Jacob Epstein of 219 Stanhope Street, N.W. (therefore poor) who has come to London with amazing drawings of human creatures like withered trees embracing. He wants to exhibit them at Carfax, which is to him the real centre of art in London,' wrote George Bernard Shaw to Robert Ross, the owner of the avant-garde Carfax Gallery in Ryder Street, St James's.

He has a commendatory letter from Rodin and when I advised him to get commissions of railway directors [the millionaires of the Edwardian era] he repudiated me with such utter scorn that I relented and promised to ask you to look at his portfolio. It is a bad case of helpless genius in the first flush of youth, and the drawings are queer and Rodinesque enough to be presentable at this particular moment. If you feel disposed to be bothered with him for ten minutes, send him a card and he'll call on you. There may be something in him.[1]

Barely two months in London and Epstein had already made his mark on the cultural elite. George Bernard Shaw was almost fifty, with several of his plays produced in West End theatres influencing a shift in Edwardian attitudes, and experience as an art as well as a music critic; Robert Ross, the devoted friend and executor of Oscar Wilde, was an important man of letters.

Early in February 1905 Epstein had written to Edward Ordway full of hope. He was working on the group inspired by Whitman's

'We two boys together clinging', a sculpture of two male figures with arms entwined. 'I have not the arms on as yet, as I take the figures away from one another to work on,' he wrote. He intended to have the group cast in bronze and finished in time to submit to the Royal Academy for the summer exhibition. But he added realistically, 'Whether I can find any public to come for anything I do, that is to be seen.'[2] The other group he was working on – 'representing primitive men greeting the sun' – was even more ambitious. He planned to make the figures life-sized in marble and he had, in imagination, visualised the symbolic effect of the play of light, as Elizabeth Barker points out, 'If I were to translate the group into marble I would make the hands transparent, so that the light would glow through them when placed facing the light.'[3] This early preoccupation with the effects of light, distance and position on his work endured throughout his career.

Soon after he arrived in London, Epstein met the Young Turks of modern art. John Fothergill, an eccentric dandy who had founded the Carfax Gallery while still a student at the Slade, was immediately generous. He commissioned a portrait in crayon of himself and 'bought and made his friends buy' some of Epstein's paintings.

The Carfax came to be the site where progressive and unknown young artists could find a sympathetic viewing. Dominant among the circle was Augustus John, a man as famous for his flamboyant appearance and bohemian lifestyle as for his draughtsmanship. An admirer of the Romanies, he sported large gold earrings, a silk scarf with a brooch and a broad gypsy hat on his thick brown hair. He refused to shave or polish his shoes and pursued beautiful women with brazen success, as well as living in a ménage à trois. In Chelsea, where he was co-principal of the Chelsea Art School, he strode through the streets like a king; when he made an entrance at the Café Royal, so it was said, young girls had to be led away fainting. Epstein, from puritan America, had never met such a vital exhibitionist before, and in his early years in London he was greatly influenced by John; later he was to compete with him. Augustus John, for his part, was amused and interested in the raw and talented young American; and he offered Epstein his studio floor to sleep on one night in February. When Epstein was very short of cash in his first years in England he could occasionally earn a few shillings by modelling at John's Chelsea Art School in the Rossetti studios in Flood Street.

Most of the artists Epstein met at the Carfax Gallery had been influenced by the French Impressionists and in some cases had trained in France. They found the English art establishment stolidly opposed to any work that reflected foreign influence; the insular and reactionary Royal Academy refused to exhibit the work of any 'unconventional' artist. Twenty years earlier the rebel painters had founded the New English Art Club, an alternative exhibiting society open to new trends in art. In the year that Epstein came to London, Durand-Ruel, the dealer who supported the Impressionists, brought paintings by Degas, Monet and Manet, among many others, to exhibit them for the first time in London. The show was ridiculed by the press and shunned by the public. Naturally Epstein shared whole-heartedly the anti-academic stance of the younger, progressive artists. He made friends with the rebels, among them three members of the New English Art Club, Ambrose McEvoy, Muirhead Bone and Francis Dodd. He made portraits of their wives and the trio were to remain staunch allies and supporters throughout his life. Epstein could not fail to be aware of official taste in sculpture as well as painting, as reflected in the statues in public places. After a day's work in his studio he liked to explore London, and on fine evenings he enjoyed listening to the tub-thumpers at Speakers' Corner in Hyde Park, thundering to the public from their soapboxes. There is unfortunately no record of his comments on the Albert Memorial with its fussy, over-elaborate profusion of bronze and marble statues, gilding and coloured stones and mosaics. The 1901 Victoria Memorial outside Buckingham Palace was so popular that 'replicas of large, identical ladies in night-gowns holding up symbols of Empire or Commerce or Righteousness'[4] were to be found prominently displayed in public settings all over the country. Ezra Pound, who made this caustic comment about the Queen's image, also remarked that most sculptors of the day were 'engaged in making gas-fittings and ornaments for electric-light globes'; in other words, sculpture was seen at best as the icing on the cake. Epstein's plans to create heroic sculpture for the capital were hopelessly out of touch with both popular and official taste.

He did submit his bronze group of two male figures to the Royal Academy in April; predictably, however, it was rejected. About this time he went to visit William Rothenstein, one of the painters responsible for selecting work exhibited at the Carfax Gallery: 'a stranger came to see me bringing a letter from Bernard Shaw,' Rothenstein wrote in his memoirs.

> Epstein was a young sculptor with a powerful head and frame, determined looking, enthusiastic. His people were Russians who lived in New York, he told me. He wanted to work in Europe but he had no means. Shaw couldn't help him; he thought his drawings mad, like burnt furze-bushes, he wrote, but Epstein deemed I would think otherwise, so Shaw sent him to me. He showed me his drawings, illustrations to Walt Whitman, which were intense in feeling if somewhat thin and tenuous. Judging from the style of the drawings I believed he would find more sympathy in Paris or Berlin than in London. But Epstein replied that he had reasons for wishing to work in London. For the moment he must go back to New York but must somehow get back to England.
>
> A friend of Epstein told me that his parents wouldn't hear of his being an artist; if he remained in New York they would ruin his career. Perhaps if I wrote to them [as a fellow Jew] they might be persuaded. There was a brother too who might help. [5]

That Epstein, at the age of twenty-four, felt so vulnerable and so threatened by his father's authority reveals just how painful the struggle for him to break free had been. The family, particularly his mother, was anxious to see Jacob again after an absence of almost three years. His eldest brother Louis sent him the money for a ticket, and on impulse Jacob booked a passage to New York, travelling steerage. After the Royal Academy had rejected his figures, he was feeling discouraged about his work. Epstein enjoyed the voyage and recalled that, although the food was atrocious, fellow passengers who had laid in a stock of sausages and other tasty snacks shared them with him. He was an avid observer of the passing scene and spent most of the journey on his bunk bed, watching four Chinese men play a game of chance with chips, day and night, until they reached New York.

His family met the boat, and his sister Sylvia vividly recalled the shock of seeing Jacob disembark wearing only sandals and an open shirt, his trousers wretched and his hair long. As they were newly middle class, they perceived good clothes, well-polished shoes and a covered head as being immensely important to their status. The Epsteins had no knowledge of the artist's world; to them Jacob looked and behaved like a lunatic. During his stay at home, the gulf between Jacob and his father widened. Sylvia believed that their father had made Jacob so miserable that he felt obliged to leave after two weeks. The parting with his mother was painful and he was never to see her again.

Back in London, Epstein found new lodgings off the Fulham Road at 412 Wanham Street. The dilapidated Stamford Bridge studios were nicknamed by the young artists and students who lodged there 'The Railway Accident' because they were built on a gap between the London North-Western and South-Western lines. For two years Epstein lived there, existing precariously on a grant William Rothenstein had managed to get for him from the Jewish Educational Aid Society, together with a modest monthly cheque from Rothenstein's own pocket.

Even in the shabby lodgings where he lived, Epstein's neglect of his appearance almost resulted in his being thrown out. One day he learned that the landlady, who lived on the premises, had been asked by some of the artists to have him removed because his clothes, in Epstein's words, were 'somewhat bohemian for the place, not in fact respectable enough'. The 'ludicrous snobbishness' came principally from a young Australian sculptor with

social ambitions who was making a portrait of the Australian
Prime Minister at the time. Fortunately the women artists living in
the Railway Accident rallied to his defence and wouldn't hear of
his being evicted.

Epstein haunted the British Museum in those years. His passion
for Greek sculpture – in particular for the Elgin Marbles – and the
influence of Rodin hampered him in his search to forge his own
style. When William Rothenstein came to visit him in his small
shed of a studio, he found Epstein modelling 'Rodinesque figures,
wanting in form, I thought, but with a strange and uncouth power'.
'What you say about my work is true,' replied Epstein, '*but* do not
think that I am satisfied with what I have done myself; I know its
faults & if a regard for perfect form makes an artist a classicist, I
am a classicist of classicists.' Rothenstein believed that Epstein
had not yet had the time or peace of mind to work out his ideas.[6]

In those early days Epstein was sleeping on a mattress, covering
himself with newspaper to keep warm. He had become a
bohemian, out of necessity as well as temperament. He found a
community of interests with Augustus John; they were both impatient with convention, and had free and easy manners and an
intense love of women. But John, who came from a middle-class
solicitor's family, was at home in an English drawing room as well
as in a Chelsea studio, able to sip tea and make small talk at a time
when the arts were regarded as 'an occupation akin to crochet or
knitting'.[7] And although he liked to rampage in the Café Royal, or
consort with gypsies, John could always go home to the comfort of
a salary, an increasing reputation as a portrait painter and one
woman or another who would provide him with a cooked supper
and a warm fire. There was some rivalry between the two men,
who both exuded magnetism, yet, while Epstein envied John his
dazzling artistic success, John was well aware of Epstein's great
talent. He also found his American colleague a rich source of anec-
dotes. 'I don't believe in the modern ideal of living in a cowshed
and puddling clay with somebody else's wife concealed in a soap-
box, like our friend Epstein,' wrote John to Alick Schepeler in the
summer of 1906. The notion of Augustus John as moralist seems

bizarre, since he was writing to a lover and former model and was at the time heavily involved with his wife and a third woman. A few days later, perhaps in answer to an enquiry from Schepeler, he changed the story: 'The soap-box or packing-can is well known in Bohemia as a substitute for a bed – and if turned over might very well be used to conceal somebody else's wife, provided she were not too fat – I was wrong however to provide Epstein with this piece of furniture. I forgot that he used to keep somebody else's wife in his dustbin. I hear recently that he has married her – so it's all right.'[8]

John had the date wrong. Epstein was not married to Margaret until November 1906, but in September they did announce their engagement. This prompted another of John's light-hearted, malicious gibes. 'I hope Epstein will find his wife a powerful reinforcement in his studio,' he wrote to William Rothenstein, who supported both men financially. 'Perhaps she will coax him out of some of his unduly democratic habits.'[9] Margaret was living at Epstein's studio at the time, although he never made it clear when this arrangement first began, probably because he wanted to protect her. When her decree absolute came through on 5 November 1906 they lost no time in regularizing their union. The couple were married eight days later on 13 November at Chelsea Register Office. Three days earlier Jacob had celebrated his twenty-sixth birthday. Margaret, who would be thirty-four the following January, almost eight years older than her husband, was troubled by the age difference and throughout her married life she ignored her birthday. Both the lovers had to brave public opprobrium, even from artists like Augustus John, as well as hardship and disapproval from both families. A contemporary account, however, does suggest that the wedding itself was an unalloyed joy.

Arthur Ransome, who had been a frequent visitor at Margaret's home when she was married to Thomas Williams, was asked to write a book about bohemian London in the autumn of 1906. The book was published in 1907 and one chapter is devoted to 'The Sculptor's Wedding'. Ransome's tale concerns a sculptor and a

painter (he would have wanted to protect the identity of Margaret,
a divorced woman) who decide to get married. Ten of their friends
join together to give them a wedding party. They book a small
French restaurant in Bloomsbury, buy roses cheaply from Covent
Garden, a modelling tool and a huge paint-brush as wedding
presents, and deck them with ribbons.

The sculptor shaves his beard for the marriage, and bride and
groom and ten guests set off from Chelsea, processing gaily
through the streets. An art student playing the accordion leads the
company and Arthur Ransome brings up the rear, blowing on his
penny whistle. When they arrive at the restaurant in a back street,
the proprietor, red cheeked, with a blue-checked blouse and white
apron, stands beaming in the street to greet them. She ushers them
upstairs to a private room, where a paper crown lies on the bride's
plate and a huge cigar on the sculptor's, gifts from the proprietor
and her husband. Bouillon is served with cheap claret, and the
party drink toasts and make speeches. 'Suddenly the sculptor's
self-possession left him. He put down his spoon and fairly loosed
himself in laughter . . . the food disappeared and the beer and wine
but by 10.30 in the evening they were still thirsty.' Two of the party
volunteer to buy drink and come back carrying twelve bottles of
claret and one of crème de menthe. To get back into the building
they have to break a window. 'Hail', cries the sculptor, 'to the two
brave fellows who gave their all to buy us this liquor. Gentlemen,
brother artists, your very good health.'

At 12.30 at night the proprietor appears, most apologetic. She
explains that, alas, they must leave. 'We have broken a window,'
confesses the sculptor, and insists that he must at least pay for that.
But the proprietor does not agree: 'What it is to be young,' she
says. 'One does not get married every day. The window shall be
my wedding present to Monsieur and Madame.' With many fond
goodbyes, the party bowls into the street leaving the proprietor at
the window, waving goodbye energetically. This time the party
walks twelve deep through the empty streets to the sound of the
'Soldiers' Chorus' played on the accordion. They finally arrive at
a flat in the Gray's Inn Road (where Margaret had lived when

Ransome first met her). 'As long as the wine and the jollity kept us awake we made speeches and sang and prophesied the success of the sculptor.' Then the twelve camp on chairs or crouch on the floor and fall asleep. The party awakes just in time to 'take the bride and groom to the station where their luggage, such as it was, was waiting and to see them off, dishevelled, dirty and weary as ourselves'. The sculptor and his wife catch the morning boat train for Paris, where they are spending their honeymoon in the Latin Quarter.[10]

By its subject, 'The Sculptor's Wedding', its author and the coincidence of time and place, this account seems almost certainly to have been based on the marriage of Jacob and Margaret Epstein, although there is no conclusive evidence.

After the brief excitement of the wedding, Epstein was as usual struggling. 'He never complained of having to live on a very small sum but worked ceaselessly,' remarked William Rothenstein.[11] Soon after his marriage, Epstein did achieve a small measure of recognition. The Whitechapel Art Gallery held a large exhibition of Jewish art and antiquities, and among the entries discovered by Evelyn Silber in the catalogue was a sketch model in black wax by Epstein, No. 11, entitled *Kishineff*. He had made the study in 1903 in Paris when he was still a student, in response to the pogrom in the then Russian city of Kishinev (now in Moldova). In April that year, 47 Jews were murdered, 592 injured and hundreds of homes pillaged and destroyed in a pogrom that outraged the civilized world. Although Epstein went on to create important sculptures with Christian themes, this previously unknown model reveals his deep feeling for his Jewish heritage.

In the New English Art Club's December 1906 show, Epstein exhibited an oil painting: *Konhong Sara*, presumably a portrait. Two members on the jury for the NEAC's exhibition that year, Francis Dodd and his brother-in-law, Muirhead Bone, both accomplished artists, were good friends of Epstein and keen admirers of his work; through an almost incestuous network of friends and family they exerted a strong influence on his progress. In 1907 Charles Holden, also Muirhead Bone's brother-in-law, won a competition for the design of a new British Medical Association building to be placed in the Strand in the heart of London. Holden wanted his imposing building to look both solid and dignified and yet convey a feeling of excitement. The lower half of the building was to be constructed in grey Cornish granite; the upper half in white Portland stone. He planned a frieze of eighteen stone figures placed in narrow recesses, flanking the second-floor windows, to blend the two levels. Charles Holden was an architect who believed that the artist was a vital ally, and he was gripped by a desire to find a sculptor with imagination who could infuse human meaning into his buildings. Francis Dodd suggested Epstein. The choice of a struggling young sculptor, a foreigner at the beginning of his career with no experience of collaborating with an architect, would have been more remarkable without the network of friends.

'One day in the spring of 1907 Mr Francis Dodd asked me if I could accept a commission from an architect he knew and decorate a building,' Epstein wrote. The project was on the grand scale that Epstein had long dreamed of – eighteen statues, seven feet high, to adorn a prominent London building. Paradoxically it was Epstein's untamed quality which was his greatest attraction. 'My appearance at the time was of the traditional anarchist,' he wrote. Perhaps Epstein, with his uncompromising idealism, reminded Charles Holden of his own youth. A Quaker from an impoverished background, Holden, like Epstein, was a man in love with the arts and a passionate admirer of Walt Whitman. He himself wrote poetry, but since he had recently become a partner in a flourishing architectural practice he published his poetry anonymously in the *Architectural Review* and kept his ardent inner life to himself.

When he visited Epstein's chaotic shed at the Railway Accident, Holden knew at once that he had found the sculptor he wanted. Epstein had been working on a *Mother and Child* and on two very tender images of babies, vulnerable yet sturdy,[12] but it was the life-sized figure of a naked girl holding a dove which won Holden's commitment. The two men seem to have understood each other at once. Epstein was shaking with excitement and accepted the terms, £100 for each of the eighteen figures, far less than an experienced sculptor would have asked. He was overjoyed at the prospect: 'It was a tremendous change for me to move away from the Railway Accident to a fine studio and to receive an advance payment on the commission. I thought I was wealthy and the future looked bright.' At last he felt he could fulfil his ambitions: 'I had been like a hound on a leash and I was suddenly set free and I never reckoned the cost.' Epstein was housed congenially in a terrace of artisan dwellings on the Chelsea Embankment, all individually designed by the architect C. R. Ashbee, a colleague of Holden's. In his spacious, pleasant riverside studio, No. 72 Cheyne Walk, Whistler's old home, Epstein set to work. Holden's original idea had been to have a series of figures representing the Seven Ages of Man adorning the building. Epstein took it farther: 'I tried to represent man and woman in their various stages from birth to old age . . . a primitive but in no way bizarre programme.' He rapidly produced sketches and maquettes to show to the British Medical Association representatives. When a BMA official suggested that a frieze of famous medical men in history would be more appropriate, Epstein would not hear of it: 'Surgeons in side-whiskers, no matter how eminent, could hardly have suited my purpose,' he wrote. Epstein took a wide and Whitmanesque view of his brief and Holden thoroughly approved. 'Apart from my desire to decorate a beautiful building,' wrote Epstein, 'I wished to create noble and heroic forms to embody in sculpture the great primal facts of man and woman.'

The BMA insisted upon having figures that would symbolise medicine, health and chemical research, but Epstein managed to impose his enduring interest in the life-cycle, sexual arousal, birth and infancy, and humanity in general into his series of naked men and women. In one of the figures, *Form Emerging from Chaos*, for example, a solemn bearded old man carefully cradles a block of a stone with a foetus engraved on the outside: life emerging from stone, Epstein's metaphor for the sculptor's magic which would recur in important work.

Epstein hired models in his new studio and worked furiously for months. He was buoyed up with the excitement of creation, despite working in all weathers. 'Epstein called yesterday and I went back with him to see his figure which is nearly done,' Augustus John wrote to Dorelia McNeill in 1907. 'It is a monstrous thing – but of course it has its merits – he now has a baby to do. The scotch girl [Margaret Epstein] was there – she is the one who poses for the mother – he might at least have got a real mother for his "Maternity". He is going about borrowing babies.'[13] The 'monstrous thing' was a beautiful study of a nursing mother for the BMA. It sounds as though John was boasting about his own virility as a prolific father, since Epstein had not yet produced a child.

Despite his derisory remarks to Dorelia, John obviously had a great deal of respect for Epstein's work. He asked the sculptor to make a head of his two-year-old son Romilly; Epstein created one of his most enchanting portraits during that busy year. His imaginative study captures the vulnerability and the courage of childhood by turning the chubby little boy into a warrior, his smoothed hair a glinting helmet when the work was cast in bronze. Epstein valued the head. He carved a life-size copy and kept it all his life. John was obviously pleased with the result and even sent the sculptor 'a fiver on account of Rom's portrait'. (The full financial arrangement between them is unknown.) Augustus John did mention the couple enthusiastically, at the opening of his exhibition of drawings at the Carfax Gallery in December 1907. 'The show opened most successfully,' he wrote to Dorelia. ''Twas a scene of great brilliance. Epstein and his wife looked grand.'[14]

That sounds as if both Margaret and Jacob Epstein had sported new clothes for the occasion, but the advance on the BMA work did not last long. In his inexperience he had not reckoned with the heavy cost of models, material and technical assistance. On one occasion when Epstein was short of money for the rent he found a novel solution. He 'paid it in kind with a naked male torso, member erect' dumped in a garden close to where Mrs Ashbee, the architect's mother, lived. She was horrified by the vision![15]

As soon as the plaster casts were completed and photographed, Epstein had them transported to the building in the Strand. A team of experts in architectural carving performed the complex task of reproducing Epstein's plaster casts in stone on site. For the first half of 1908 Epstein spent most of his days forty feet up from the pavement in the Strand, supervising and touching up. His working base was a cage on the scaffolding protected from the weather by a tarpaulin roof.

By June 1908 the plaster cast of *Maternity*, the tender and modest statue of a young woman holding her baby close to her bare breast, with a long skirt covering the rest of her body, arrived at the Agar Street façade of the new building. Unfortunately, the cast of the baby came on later and although the figures were far above street level they were, by a quirk of fate, placed directly opposite the offices of the National Vigilance Association. Officials of that august body craned their heads out of the window in their indignation and excitement at the figure of a full-breasted, pregnant mother in their view. After the scaffolding was removed from the first four figures in the Strand, a storm of protest broke out.

The *Evening Standard and St James's Gazette* took up the cudgels on behalf of public morality with a front-page headline: BOLD SCULPTURE, AMAZING FIGURES ON A STRAND BUILDING. IS IT ART? 'With regard to their appearance, it is unnecessary to say more than they are a form of art which no careful father would wish his daughter or no discriminating young man his fiancée to see,' the journalist remarked. 'The degree of nudity which has been chosen for the figures . . . is not calculated to enhance the artistic effect.' In an art gallery, where nude figures were viewed by those 'who knew how to appreciate the art they represent', the *Standard* pontificated, the statues were acceptable. It was laying bare the naked figures to the 'gaze of all classes, young and old' which was damaging.[16] Public morality decreed that a knowledge of art, like a knowledge of sex, should be restricted to members of the upper classes and the male gender. To the architect's implicit question 'Are we ashamed of our nakedness?' the newspaper gave the resounding answer 'Yes'. And it had many supporters.

As well as the Secretary of the National Vigilance Association, who attempted to bully the BMA into removing the statues, Father

Vaughan, a Roman Catholic cleric, wrote in inflamed indignation to the *Strand*,

> As a Christian citizen in a Christian city, I claim the right to say that I object most emphatically to such indecent and inartistic statuary being thrust upon my view in a public thoroughfare . . . [The figures could only be seen at eye level from the top of a double-decker bus.] Let us teach self-reverence and self-respect and not convert London into a Fiji island where there may be some excuse for want of drapery. In the name of public decency I beg the British Medical Association not to sanction the uncovering of these statues before the eyes of the public, many of whom, I regretfully say, will not look upon them with the temperament of our artist, but will feast upon them with the hunger of sensuality.[17]

The farce and the fuss continued. A policeman arrived on the site and demanded to see the figures more closely. The officer was taking notes, and Epstein spotted the word 'rude' in the policeman's notebook. The Bishop of Stepney, Dr Cosmo Gordon Lang, asked Epstein to show him the statues and climbed the ladder to the scaffolding, only to pronounce that he saw nothing indecent or shocking about them. Epstein's work had succeeded in polarizing public opinion; while passengers on the top deck of the buses stood up to gawp as they passed the building, a surprising number of fellow artists and dignitaries from the art world defended him. C. J. Holmes, Slade Professor of Fine Art at Oxford, wrote,

> I believe [Epstein] is a young man, and as with most sculptors of keen perception there are some traces of the influence of Rodin here and there in his work, but its main impulse is derived entirely from nature, as its technical treatment is derived from pre-Pheidian Greece, and of all the work done in England of recent years I know none that is more truly living, scholarly and monumental.[18]

Professor Holmes's view that the statues on the Strand were grave and heroic in mood was echoed by the artists Ricketts and Shannon, who made the point that the *Evening Standard* was ignorant of the degree of nudity allowed in public buildings in England and abroad, in the Sistine Chapel for example. Artist friends like Ambrose McEvoy and Muirhead Bone wrote to the press. Augustus John exerted himself by writing to the poet Arthur Symons,

> These decorations seem to me to be the only decent attempts at monumental sculpture of which the streets of London can boast. A few of the nude male figures, however . . . have been provided with the indispensable apparatus of generation . . . This flagrant indelicacy has naturally infuriated our susceptible citizens . . . Being a foreigner, Epstein is quite innocent of the parochial sentiment which is the breath of our metropolis, he has merely contrived to inform his figures with a World-Passion to which we are strangers over here.[19]

Even *The Times* came out with a leader in favour of Epstein's sculpture, commenting that it was surprised to find any section of the London press 'assuming the moral attitude of the Pope, who ordered the Vatican Venus and some of her marble sisters to wear petticoats'.[20]

By the time the BMA held its Council Meeting on the fate of the sculptures in July, the flood of letters in the artist's favour, from sculptors, scholars and museum directors, was large enough to stiffen the organization's resolve and save the threatened figures. 'My dear friend Rothenstein,' Epstein wrote after the ordeal was over, 'I am overjoyed at the splendid result of the meeting on Wed. & I will go on now quietly to the end. Your letter made me very happy & this grave wave of sympathy from everyone has filled me with happiness.'[21]

When the relief and euphoria had worn off, Epstein found himself battered physically and emotionally. The experience had been shattering; and he was left in debt, unable to pay the workmen. The affair of the Strand statues was a harsh lesson and rankled with Epstein for years. On the positive side he had woken up one morning to find himself famous – and notorious. Cartoonists and music-hall artists found rich material in the Strand statues. Public sculpture in England would never again be ignored, but the scandal of the statues never left him and was to surface years later.

4

The Liberty of Art

URIOUSLY ENOUGH IT was Augustus John who helped to
rescue Epstein from his debts and depression after the
Strand statues scandal. The onslaught of publicity about
them left him feeling 'like a criminal in the dock'. All his life he
wanted publicity – needed publicity – to bring his work to the
attention of the public. But he never became reconciled to the
dangers inherent in being in the spotlight. When he received the
commission, he thought he was wealthy; after it was done he was
struggling again, and since he had little choice he decided to scale
down his work and his expenses. He began a series of studies made
from a close scrutiny of the model. 'I worked with great care and
followed the forms of the model in quarter inches, I should say, not
letting up on any detail of construction of plane, but always
keeping the finished construction in view.'

Epstein wrote years later of taking himself in hand as a sculptor
after the fiasco of the Strand building. Yet two months after the
public outcry, in September 1908, Augustus John told his generous
new lover, Ottoline Morrell, that 'Epstein is slowly being killed in
London. It seems to be a general superstition that artists live on air
– whereas the truth is that their appetites, like their other capaci-
ties, are extremely good.'[1] He was trying to persuade Ottoline to
extend her patronage to his friend. At the end of September, John
reminded Ottoline that Epstein was desperately short of cash. 'It
would be good if Portland [the Duke of Portland, Ottoline's half-
brother] or anyone else gave him a commission.'[2]

Ottoline had already persuaded her brother to buy some of
John's drawings. This time she responded swiftly and generously

to Epstein's need. She ordered a figure for the fountain in her country house at Garsington Manor, near Oxford. Epstein wrote to her on 22 October 1908 from his Chelsea studio,

> Dear Lady Ottoline Morrell
> I shall be in on Saturday afternoon and will be pleased to see your husband. A garden statue sounds delightful; sculpture outdoors are amongst trees and shrubs, it is reminiscent of Italy and Greece.
> Yours sincerely
> Jacob Epstein[3]

That Epstein, with his dreams of carving temples, would write with such polite enthusiasm about a garden piece seems highly unlikely; the letter bears Margaret's tone and it seems clear that, while Ottoline initiated the project, Margaret Epstein agreed terms: Epstein was to receive £25 for a statue in marble. The men were, ostensibly, left to settle the business.

The model Epstein used for his fountain was a long-limbed blonde with a pale oval face, Euphemia Lamb. She was the wife of Henry Lamb, another of Augustus John's protégés. Epstein captured the sensual grace of his model in the statue of a tall young woman in loose yet clinging 'Greek' robes, one hand fluttering expressively. Euphemia was a popular model who had posed for Orpen, John and Rothenstein among others. She had been trained at the Slade and was therefore an intelligent and adaptable sitter. Her husband called her Euphemia because of her likeness to Mantegna's *St Euphemia*. As in all his best portraits, Epstein draws us close to the essence of his subject by capturing a characteristic expression. Euphemia seems to be gazing suggestively, her head on one side, her sensual lips parted. Epstein made many drawings and at least three busts of the accommodating Euphemia.

Ottoline Morrell sold the fountain figure later, but she proved a valuable patron to Epstein. She spread the word about his work and brought influential friends to his studio to see it. Yeats visited with Lady Gregory, the Irish playwright and nationalist. At the time Lady Gregory's nephew, Hugh Lane, a London picture dealer, was forming a collection of art for a National Gallery of Art in Dublin, and he commissioned a portrait of 'Aunt Augusta'. She was a formidable woman: 'intellectual and somewhat school-marmish' is how Epstein saw her, 'quite a dignified lady'. That was not, however, how Lady Gregory saw herself. Epstein modelled her carefully for days and was almost satisfied when Lady Gregory turned up for a last sitting. To his horror she arrived with 'the most astonishing head of curls' and asked Epstein to alter the head. 'You should come to the theatre tonight,' she told him, 'then you would see how much finer I look with bare shoulders.' 'It is amazing how English women of no uncertain age fancy themselves dressed as Venus,' he noted wryly. Lady Gregory said later that Epstein had 'cut through the clay throat, tilting head and chin in an eternal eagerness'. But when Hugh Lane first saw the head he exclaimed, 'Poor Aunt Augusta. She looks as if she could eat her own children.'[4] The finished portrait reveals a severe and implacable woman, and Epstein specifically states that he told Lady Gregory he could not alter it. 'In my headstrong way I kept to my guns: this practically terminated the sittings.'

As he began to earn some money to pay his debts late in 1908, Epstein learned that it was almost impossible to please both the sitter and himself. 'The successful portrait sculptor . . . needs a front of brass, the hide of a rhinoceros and all the guile of a courtier,' he said. He learned to his cost that it was often the model he chose himself, the model he paid for himself, who produced his best work. Even when funds were low, he often visited the Café Royal with Augustus John after a day in the studio. Models and artists regularly dropped in to the café at 68 Regent Street with its gilt mirrors, glass chandeliers and glamorous past. Oscar Wilde used to lunch there with Bosie and aspiring writers and students still crowded in. It was almost certainly there that he met Nan Condron, a gypsy girl who became the prototype of the Epstein woman. Nan was a professional who had sat for John, Rothenstein, Orpen and many others; she must have been something of a relief after the demands of titled ladies. She was a splendid model:

strong, angular, dark skinned and sensual with an innate dignity. Taciturn and undemanding, she had a supple body and was able to hold difficult, almost acrobatic poses for him. Nan's one treat was to visit the music hall, and once a week Epstein and Margaret took her out. They all enjoyed the knockabout entertainment, and Epstein wrote nostalgically of the disappearance of the old music hall in his autobiography. For over forty years Nan remained close to the family, and many years later, at a time of crisis, she came to clean and help them out.

Until December Epstein worked quietly at portraits. He made a dignified, even demure portrait of Mary McEvoy, the wife of the painter Ambrose McEvoy, one of his staunchest supporters; the later marble version was bought by the Johannesburg Art Gallery in 1910. His first brush with the British art establishment occurred when he was proposed by Havard Thomas for membership of the Royal Society of British Sculptors but rejected. This was even before his work showed any influence of the 'primitive' art so distressing to the academic sculptors. Despite the setback, he was beginning to make a name and to attract interest and admiration beyond the now less radical New English Art Club when another major intervention from outside completely changed the course of his career.

Six months after Epstein's work on the Strand statues had been denounced as a 'gross offence', he was named as the sculptor designated to create a tomb for Oscar Wilde, without his knowledge or consent. The announcement was made at a grand dinner at the Ritz to celebrate the publication of Wilde's *Collected Works* and reinstate his reputation. In 1900 the Irish writer had died bankrupt and in disgrace, and Robert Ross, the guest of honour at the dinner, announced that he had received an anonymous gift of £2,000, to be used for honouring the writer with a fitting monument. Wilde's remains were to be transferred from the simple grave in Bagneux, where he lay buried, to the famous Père Lachaise cemetery in Paris. The anonymous donor stipulated that the sculptor appointed should be Jacob Epstein.[5]

The morning after the dinner, friends rang to congratulate

Epstein, who responded gruffly, thinking it was a hoax. Later, when the commission was confirmed, he was excited but annoyed, understandably, at being excluded from the conspiracy. Epstein was convinced that the trustee for the monument, Robert Ross, was afraid that, if news leaked out that he had been appointed, other sculptors who knew of the plan would be envious and obstructive. The artist Charles Ricketts, who had been a friend of Wilde's, had gone so far as to make a model of a design for the tomb. But once Epstein was named publicly little could be done.

He was in the news again, placed firmly among the rebels as the creator of a monument for the celebrated and reviled Oscar Wilde. Epstein was naturally excited and inspired by the project, but this time he refused to be hurried. He studied Wilde's works, made preliminary drawings and, under pressure from Wilde's followers who dreamed of 'a Greek youth standing by a broken column', at first made sketches of 'slender, naked young men standing beside the tomb with bowed heads'. He eventually settled on an over-life-sized, elongated figure of Narcissus, and after many months of work invited Charles Holden, the architect with whom he had worked on the Strand statues, to design the plinth for the tomb. Then Epstein mysteriously changed his mind. He himself says only, 'I was dissatisfied and scrapped quite completed work.' He had decided to take the leap of carving directly in stone. As a boy cutting ice on Greenwood Lake in New Jersey, Epstein had been stirred by the challenge and the adventure of physical work. On the scaffolding high above the Strand, supervising the work of transferring his plaster models to stone, he had been sharply reminded of the exhilaration of carving in the open air. The more he saw of early sculpture, the Greek and the Egyptian and the 'vast and wonderful collections from Polynesia and Africa', the more attractive the idea of working on the stone became.

He was going against the grain. All the successful sculptors of the day relied on firms of architectural carvers to translate their clay models into stone, with the use of pointing machines to adapt the work to scale, precision stone-cutting machines and sanders to render the works so polished and bland that all trace of the artist's chisel and original inspiration was lost. Epstein had a love for the qualities of stone, which grew as he experimented with different forms. And from 1909 onwards he began a lifelong love affair with massive stone blocks. 'I went to Derbyshire to the Hopton Wood stone quarries where I saw an immense block which had just been quarried . . . I bought this monolith weighing twenty tons on the spot, and had it transported to my London studio.'

Epstein says that he began work on the monument immediately and completed it in nine months, but his memory and calculations often seem to disagree with the record of his work obtained from catalogues and press cuttings. In this case he may have wanted to camouflage his relationship with Eric Gill, which began so promisingly.

William Rothenstein claimed the credit for Epstein's fervour for carving. He sent Eric Gill – then a stone-carver who specialised in carving inscriptions on monuments and tombstones, and who was beginning to experiment with sculpture – to see Epstein. It was Gill, Rothenstein alleged, 'who turned Epstein's attention to stone-carving'. Gill had met Epstein in 1908 when the sculptor was working on the Strand statues. When the statues were attacked as indecent, Gill rallied to Epstein's defence, arguing that Epstein was 'trying to rescue sculpture from the grave to which ignorance and indifference had consigned it'.[6]

Unlike Epstein, Gill was a methodical man who kept terse notes in his diaries of his daily activities. Unfortunately the diaries for 1909 are missing, so that the question of whether Epstein or Gill was the innovator in the return to direct carving in British sculpture cannot be answered. It seems that Rothenstein's idea to put the two men together, Epstein with his monumental inspiration and feeling for sensual human form and Gill with his knowledge of the technique and possibilities of the medium, made them valuable allies in 1910.

There was another quality they shared, which perhaps Rothenstein had spotted. In an age of prudery and prurience, both Epstein and Gill delighted in sex. In each other's company they were free to discuss it, and to plan life-enhancing work with erotic subjects. Epstein's interest had always been not only in copulation but in the cycle of generation. Gill and his wife had three daughters, while the Epsteins had no children. Margaret was perhaps unable to conceive; certainly Jacob fathered children by other women, and both were inordinately fond of children. In 1910 he carved *Maternity* in Hopton Wood stone: a woman with taut nipples and thrusting breasts reminiscent of Hindu temple sculpture of voluptuous goddesses. Epstein's pregnant figure cradles her swollen belly; she is deeply sensuous and overblown, smiling to herself and imbued with compassion and inner peace. The unfinished sculpture, exhibited at the Allied Artists' Association of 1912, was one of his great early works.

During 1910 the block of Hopton Wood stone brought from Derbyshire proved an inspiration. Epstein carved a marvellous elemental *Sun God* with arms outstretched towards his halo of hair, while Gill carved a much smaller figure, a cheerful naked boy he called *Cocky Kid*. The two men were still young – Epstein was twenty-nine and Gill twenty-seven – with a longing to burst the bonds of English hypocrisy and create a new order. Their sculpture of the period, Epstein's massive *Maternity* and Gill's *Ecstasy*, a standing couple making love, seem to be a part of a grandiose, utopian plan. 'The fact of the matter is that Epstein & I have got a great scheme of doing some colossal figures together (as a contribution to the world), a sort of twentieth-century Stonehenge, and we have been looking out for a piece of the land for the purpose,' Gill wrote to Rothenstein on 25 September.[7] They had discovered the ideal place, Asheham House (later to become the home of Virginia and Leonard Woolf), an empty farm with six acres of land hidden away in a valley on the Sussex Downs. The buildings were empty and in need of repair, but Gill was enchanted with the dream of creating an artists' colony there. He had applied to the owner and could get the place on a fourteen-year lease. 'But oh! If only we could buy the place outright,' he pleaded to the benevolent Rothenstein.

Then we should be free to do all we wanted without the fear

of hurting anyone's feelings or the risk of . . . our figures
[being] smashed up by some damned fools who didn't choose
to like them. [He was referring, of course, to the threats to
Epstein's statues.] I wish you could come down and see the
place . . . Is that quite impossible? Surely some millionaire
could be persuaded to buy the place for us.[8]

About to embark on a voyage to India to explore the art of the
subcontinent, Rothenstein replied euphorically,

You shall get a 14-years' lease and when you have turned the
potter's field into Valhalla, the nation shall reluctantly buy the
freehold . . . you shall save a little corner for me and you shall
carve neatly on it 'here lies one who loved more than he was
loved' and Epstein shall carve Shaw nude and you shall make
Wells glitter in the light of the sun.[9]

Both Gill and Epstein were enamoured of the idea of founding an
artistic community where they could work freely and without
disturbance. Since his student days Epstein had dreamed of sculpting monumental works of art to be placed in a temple where they
would be worshipped. Gill's reasons were more complex: he had
grave yearnings for the religious life and gross appetites for the life
of the flesh, and he longed to fuse them in a new order. Epstein,
liberated from his strict background, seems to have accepted his
sexual drive as a normal, joyous fact of life.

The friendship of the two men was intense during 1910 and took
on a domestic character. In June the Gills invited the Epsteins to
Sussex for the weekend. Eric Gill lived in a pleasant Georgian
house in the village of Ditchling, with his wife Ethel and three
small daughters. Margaret Epstein, a countrywoman who loved
animals and gardening, enjoyed the escape from the city. The occasion was a success, and in July the Epsteins came back for a picnic
tea on the hills. Often Gill visited them when he went to London
to see a client or attend a Fabian lecture; sometimes he stayed the
night with them in Chelsea. The men went to watch Japanese

wrestling and Margaret joined them when they visited the Tivoli to see Marie Lloyd. The two young men were proud of their uninhibited attitudes and photographed each other and the small girls nude as they wrestled with the practicalities of a utopian scheme.

Gill, the prime mover in their grandiose scheme, invited Augustus John down to Ditchling to discuss the new religion that he envisaged would spring from their colony: 'so splendid and all-embracing that the hierarchy to which it will give birth, uniting within itself the artist and the priest, will supplant and utterly destroy our present commercial age'.[10] Gill also proposed to provide a house in which artists could sell without charge, subverting the commercial age by bypassing the dealers. He pressed John into holding gatherings in his King's Road studio with Ambrose McEvoy in an attempt to further the plan. 'Gill's idea took the form of a Neo-Nietzschean cult of super-humanity under the sign of the Ithyphallus. Epstein's more simply would be realised by the apotheosis of himself on a colossal scale, alone, and blowing his own trumpet,' John wrote dismissively. 'I was in favour of the rehabilitation of the Earth-Mother and child whose image installed in a covered wagon would be drawn by oxen and attended by dancing corybantes.'[11]

Despite all the Chelsea chatter and high hopes, the plans were held up by the lack of hard cash. Written comment on Gill's utopia comes either from Gill himself, or from Rothenstein or Augustus John. Epstein did make a seductive pencil sketch of *One of the Pillars of the Secret Temple* at the time but otherwise did not refer to the plan: he rarely mentioned schemes that failed. Yet the dream of a huge temple where he could create massive figures recurs in many of his letters. His ideal, despite John's waspish words, would have been a temple to art, to beauty, and not to a specific god or gods.

Had the British public known of the plan to create a modern Stonehenge they would have put it down to yet another sign that the world had gone mad. The comfortable certainty of affluent Edwardians was under threat in 1910 from the rise of socialism, workers' activism and the women's suffrage movement.

In November, when the painter and art critic Roger Fry introduced an exhibition of French paintings, 'Manet and the Post-Impressionists', at the Grafton Galleries, Robert Ross detected the existence 'of a widespread plot to destroy the whole fabric of European painting';[12] the poet Wilfrid Scawen Blunt found the pictures 'nothing but the gross puerility which scrawls indecencies on the walls of a privy', and maiden ladies bold enough to peer at the exhibits were reported to have reached for their smelling salts.[13] These were paintings by Cézanne, Gauguin and Van Gogh, as well as the younger artists, Signac, Seurat, Rouault, Matisse and Picasso. The startled British public felt that the violence of the vivid colours and strange distorted shapes on the walls of the gallery echoed the menace of the world around them. What they wanted and expected from their paintings was a pleasing reflection of 'reality'. But the show of foreign art was of primary importance; the conventions of acceptable good taste imposed by the Royal Academy were swept aside for the first time and 1910 marked the beginning of the modern movement in English art. Augustus John described it as a 'bloody show'. Gill equivocated. For Epstein, who had seen many of the artists' works in Paris five years earlier and knew their reputation abroad, the show was hardly revolutionary. Yet for an artist who sought 'not to imitate form but create form, not to imitate life but to find an equivalent for life', the Post-Impressionist exhibition helped to create an audience for a new way of seeing.

The year had been a memorable one for Epstein. On 22 December he was naturalized as a British subject. George Bernard Shaw, who had wanted to put Epstein's name forward as a sculptor for the Shakespeare Memorial Theatre, had advised that he apply for naturalization, and Epstein, grumbling at the idiocy of nationality, reluctantly agreed. On Christmas Eve Jacob and Margaret travelled to Sussex to spend the holiday with the Gills. 'Jacob and Mrs E. for Xmas,' Gill noted in his diary. The two men had worked very closely that year. Epstein had made a limestone copy of his impressive head of Romilly, Augustus John's son. Mounted on a tall plinth, *Rom* takes on a more original and daring character than the bronze. The child's head and hair seem to grow out of the stone; the little head is a challenging small boy, his lower lip thrust out, and also a warrior. Gill cut the inscription ROM in large letters. He also made an almost exact stone copy of Epstein's bronze with the title, *Romily*, misspelled in the inscription. Epstein had apparently commissioned Gill's version in stone as early as June 1910.[14] His reason is not clear; perhaps he was not confident at that stage of his own ability to carve direct. When Gill exhibited his copy of *Romilly* at his first one-man show, held at the Chenil Gallery in January 1911, the piece was entitled *Head of Romilly John, carved from a model by J. Epstein, lent by J. Epstein.*

In all the heady activity of that year, Epstein does not seem to have touched on his large work, the tomb for Oscar Wilde, commissioned in December 1908. But early in 1911 Gill wrote to tell Rothenstein that Epstein had decided to carve the Oscar Wilde figure in stone himself, adding, 'that is why he is down here – getting into the way of stone carving'. Gill clearly wanted to claim some of the credit, although he did have the grace to note that Epstein 'is doing splendid things'.[15]

Epstein was always vague about dates. He said he worked hard for nine months carving the Oscar Wilde monument. After months if not years of wrestling with the intractable problem of devising a suitable tomb, he decided on an enigmatic theme for his enigmatic subject. 'I now conceived of a vast, winged figure . . . it was of course purely symbolical, the conception of poet as messenger.' The face of his magnificent flying demon-angel, sensual and dis-illusioned, has a small creature representing Fame with a trumpet perching on the forehead and two other creatures symbolising Intellectual Pride and Luxury balanced on the haloed head. In this commission, overloaded with literary expectations, the tomb reflects the mood of Wilde's poem 'The Sphinx'. Epstein described it as a 'work of combined simplicity and ornate decora-tion and no doubt influenced by antique carving'. The conception clearly indicates how closely he had studied the magnificent Assyrian sculpture in the British Museum. His proud creature with arms outstretched seems to be supporting enormous wings as it hovers in space. 'For me,' Epstein wrote tellingly, 'its merit lay in its being a direct carving and on a grand scale.' On the back of the tomb Gill designed the inscription:

> And alien tears shall fill for him
> Pity's long-broken urn
> For his mourners will be outcast men
> And outcasts always mourn.[16]

Those lines, one feels, held particular resonance for Epstein.

Though Gill was closely involved with Epstein's conception of the Oscar Wilde tomb, and one witness even claimed to have seen him working in Epstein's studio on the wings of the Sphinx,[17] their close friendship ended long before the tomb was finished. Gill's utopian scheme to create an artists' colony and a new religion had fallen through and he blamed Epstein. He called at Epstein's studio in Cheyne Walk at the end of March and wrote a bitter letter. Epstein replied,

> I can't think why Mrs Philpot [presumably the Epsteins' cleaner] didn't let you in to write a letter even though she was scrubbing. Why didn't you let me know you were coming . . . I don't understand your fury . . . about our fellowship. Certainly it came to nothing but why do you blame me or John or McEvoy for that. Why aren't you to blame? In our first talks it was wonderful and worthwhile but it seemed to resolve itself with merely schemes for exhibitions . . . This is an awful whimper about letter. Artists be damned and the world of artists. I don't want to be in it. I prefer wives and whores and fucking and working.[18]

At a stroke Epstein shrugged off not only the grandiose idea of a new religion but also the pretensions and persiflage of the Chelsea set.

Up until then Augustus John had played an important role in promoting Epstein's work. In the autumn of 1910 he invited

Epstein and Margaret to a party at the Café Royal to meet John Quinn, a wealthy Irish-American lawyer, who was establishing himself as a patron of artists and writers. The company included George Moore, the Anglo-Irish writer, and the painter J. D. Innes. It was a riotous success, and Epstein obviously made an impression. In the autumn of 1911 Quinn was back in London and visited Epstein's Chelsea studio. He greatly admired the tomb of Oscar Wilde, which dominated the space. From that visit onwards Quinn became one of Epstein's most important patrons and confidants. On 29 September he sent Quinn photographs of the monument, urging him to keep them to himself. At the same time he hoped for exposure in America. 'Is America looking out for it [the Wilde tomb],' he asked Quinn naïvely. 'Do you think the photo rights are worth anything to American publishers if they are published before the unveiling?'[19]

At the time when Quinn was stepping into the role of Epstein's patron and benefactor, Epstein had rounded on his former benefactor, William Rothenstein. 'Dear Rothenstein,' he wrote in June 1911, 'I want no more of your damned insincere invitations. This pretence of friendship has gone far enough. Yours etc. Jacob Epstein.'[20] The occasion for the bust-up is unknown; but Epstein consistently displayed what amounted to a talent for ingratitude. His needs as an artist made him dependent for most of his life on the goodwill of different patrons. But one at a time was enough. During the later stages of the Oscar Wilde tomb it was to Quinn that he turned for moral and financial support. The collector had bought a bronze statuette and ordered a stone bust, and he sent Epstein money in advance.

By the end of the year he was feeling fatigued by the enormous physical and mental effort he had expended on the tomb and was eager to start new work. 'I feel that I can do the biggest, most profound things, and life is short,' he wrote to Quinn in November 1911.

> I won't have any big commissions after the Wilde, but I
> am full of big ideas, amongst which I want to do great

> stones, representing angelic and diabolic forces . . .
> Nature in her grand design makes all the works of man
> look puny. How I wish I was living in an age when man
> wanted to raise temples and cathedrals to Man and God
> and the Devil . . . I am thinking of doing a Virgin and
> Child.[21]

Epstein told Quinn that Augustus John had exhibited a fine painting at the New English Art Club and the critics, as usual, had been
making fools of themselves. 'Creation is the only thing and critics
are not even discerning men nowadays but ignoramuses.' In his
letters to Quinn he returned again and again to his longing to carve
large works: 'I feel now in the heyday of my creative strength.' But
the cost of buying huge blocks of stone was prohibitive. He could,
he prophesied accurately, get enough portrait commissions to last
him for the rest of his life, 'but it isn't portraits I want to do or to
compromise with art lovers or aesthetes of any kind'.[22]

In March 1912, with the Oscar Wilde tomb almost finished, he
wrote to Quinn again, pouring out his longing to create monumental work: 'I don't want to rest with the Oscar Wilde but go on and
do large new things: *no work, no matter what the scope, would
appall me, the larger the better: I want to carve mountains.*'[23] It
was as if Epstein at thirty-one wanted to pit himself against the
elements.

An unexpected distraction from the Wilde tomb offered itself in
the spring of that year. Frida Strindberg, the third wife of the
Swedish playwright, wealthy and wayward, was in London,
preying on artistic and intellectual males. She was now so obsessively taken up with Augustus John that she even employed a
private detective to track down his 'infidelities'. She adored
modern art and modern artists and her latest fancy was to open a
late-night cabaret club, the Cave of the Golden Calf, deep in a
Soho basement in Heddon Street, round the corner from the Café
Royal. Madame Strindberg had extraordinary discernment, as well
as a flair for melodrama, and she persuaded the most prominent
progressive artists to give her nightclub a daring modern air. The

Camden Town artists, Harold Gilman and Spencer Gore, painted wild-coloured murals of primitive figures hunting in the jungle; the artist and writer Wyndham Lewis, one of Frida's lovers, painted a bizarre drop curtain and Eric Gill created the golden calf in the entrance to the club. Epstein covered the two iron pillars that supported the cellar with plaster heads of hawks, cats and camels painted in scarlet and white. Each night, as the Café Royal closed, wealthy old men and languorous models swarmed down the stairs of the Golden Calf to dance and carouse until the early hours. Madame Strindberg waived the annual membership fee for her favourite artists and was an accommodating hostess. Ezra Pound once heard her wave a customer away from her table, saying, 'Yes I vil sleep vit you . . . But talk to you half an hour, neffair! Vun must traw de line sommefere!!'[24] For Epstein the commission helped to bring in some money and a change of scene but, more importantly, thanks to the Golden Calf he was mixing with the most adventurous of his contemporaries, among them Wyndham Lewis, with whom he was later to collaborate.

The Golden Calf opened in June, but it is doubtful whether Epstein found much time for nightclubbing. That month he finally completed the tomb of Oscar Wilde. He had a card printed and opened his studio to the press and public:

THE TOMB OF OSCAR WILDE IS NOW ON VIEW
(1st June to 30th) at 72 Cheyne Walk . . . from 10 a.m. to 6 p.m.

After the reception of the Strand statues, he felt ready for an onslaught. To his astonishment, the *Evening Standard and St James's Gazette*, which had led the attack on the BMA figures, featured an appreciative review with the heading MR J. EPSTEIN'S DIGNIFIED SCULPTURE.

The first thing that strikes one is Mr Epstein's regard for his material and its purpose. From the earliest ages it has been the most universal instinct of humanity to set up a stone over the dead, but modern sculptors are apt to forget that every touch

of the chisel . . . is a destruction of the monumental character
of the stone . . . The conception embodied in this great block
of stone is that of a winged figure driven through space by an
irresistible fate . . . The work, in very high relief rather than
in the round, is as reserved in execution as it is monumental
in conception.[25]

The *Pall Mall Gazette* complimented him on his courage in
defying the accepted ideas of creating tombstones:

For Mr Epstein is not only a real sculptor – a carver, not a
modeller – but he is also a Sculptor in Revolt who is in deadly
conflict with the ideas of current sculpture . . . And one would
be bold in denying that he may be right . . . As the painter's
idea lies, not in literary suggestion of imitation but in the
perfection of the paint, so the carver's idea must be born in
the marble and spring directly from it . . . It is obvious that Mr
Epstein did not propose to be either a literary or a moral critic
of Oscar Wilde. This brooding winged figure . . . is a child of
the marble and is not an enlarged copy by some other hand of
a highly finished plaster model. It has been created in anguish
under the driving obsession of an idea. The hand of the sculptor has groped in the block of marble, impelled to the expression, without words or definitions of the haunting tragedy of
a great career . . . 'Go and see it at once' is my urgent advice
to all who are interested in sculpture.[26]

With advice like that from a critic and an open invitation from the
artist, both art lovers and the merely curious popped in and out of
Epstein's Chelsea studio all through the month. The French artist
Henri Gaudier-Brzeska, who was living in poverty in London and
soaking up the artistic scene, found his way to Epstein's studio one
Sunday morning. Gaudier-Brzeska was twenty-one, dressed in
tattered clothes with dark, wispy hair, a sprouting beard and eyes of
piercing intelligence. 'He was very pleasant, I thought,' Epstein
remarked to Ezra Pound in an account of this first meeting. 'I asked

him if he carved direct and, afraid to acknowledge that he hadn't, he hurried home and immediately started a carving. This was very characteristic of him.' Gaudier-Brzeska wrote of Epstein's Wilde tomb to a friend, 'I saw it in the studio last Sunday – Oscar Wilde is flying slowly into space, his eyes shut. The whole work is treated strongly – filled with insuperable movement and delicate feeling, in the expression and the medium – a piece of sculpture which will live for ever, only the total effect seems too small.'[27]

Born Henri Gaudier, the son of a joiner, Gaudier-Brzeska, a fluent and inspired draughtsman and sculptor, took makeshift jobs to allow himself to study art and work in his studio in his spare time, even making his own tools. He had a ramshackle studio under the railway arches leading to Putney Bridge and lived in a nearby tenement with his companion, Sophie Brzeska, twenty years his senior. A Polish intellectual, Sophie was utterly devoted to Henri, and his devotion was expressed in his adoption of her surname in this passionate though platonic attachment.

Epstein wrote rather patronisingly about Gaudier-Brzeska's domestic arrangements, but he would have been surprised to know that Gaudier-Brzeska found Epstein's own way of living somewhat meagre. He visited one day in the autumn of 1912:

While I was ringing the front door, his missus stuck her head out of the window to see who I was. There is an enormous difference between old Epstein's place and that of Fraser & Co [more affluent acquaintances]. Little Epstein, dirty and dusty and covered with plaster, sitting on the sill of his window cutting at marble. In the room two bunks, mean and miserable . . . one bigger than the other – a little table, very small and nothing else. No picture nor image, nothing on the large white walls, only the torso of a woman, half-broken in a corner . . . Later on he showed a little bronze, very beautiful, quite the nicest work of his I have seen – alive and sincere – a seated woman with her arms above her head. We smoked together, talked of castings and marbles as usual and I left.[28]

Before his tragic death in the trenches in France, Gaudier-Brzeska made an extraordinary contribution to art in a variety of styles. His graceful drawings and sculpture were sometimes figurative, sometimes influenced by Cubism and sometimes abstract. Epstein reckoned that he followed the fashions too readily, although he acknowledged his great gifts. Gaudier-Brzeska, who wrote occasionally for small progressive publications, placed Epstein at the head of the moderns: 'Epstein whom I consider the foremost in the small number of good sculptors in Europe.'[29]

5

Gathering Force

FTER THE ENTHUSIASTIC acceptance in England of his Oscar Wilde tomb, Epstein was anxious to see his memorial installed in the Père Lachaise cemetery in Paris by the end of July 1912. Work on a commission to carve two granite lions at the front of the government building in Pretoria was already overdue. But what should have been a triumphal reception of his work in Paris turned into more of a French farce.

The French authorities created difficulties at every step. First customs demanded that an import duty of £120 be paid on the value of the stone. This was an extortionate amount of money and a blow to Epstein and to Ross, who had commissioned the work. Two of the late writer's closest friends, Ross himself and Ada Leverson, nicknamed 'The Sphinx' by Wilde, arranged for a petition to be sent to the French government. Lytton Strachey drew up the gracefully worded letter:

> The sculptor Epstein has just completed the Tomb of Oscar Wilde . . . It is estimated that the customs duty will amount to £120 at the least . . . The monument is a serious and interesting work of art destined for a public position in Paris. It is dedicated to the memory of the English poet and author Oscar Wilde . . . Given these circumstances, it is suggested to us that we should make some approach to those concerned in the French Government in order to obtain an exemption from customs duty. The aesthetic merit of this work by Mr Epstein and the public interest it has aroused lead us to hope that the artist could be free of this onerous charge. We think that the

favour of such an exemption would be in full conformity with
the fine tradition of the French nation, which is so justly
renowned for its enlightened munificence towards the arts.[1]

The letter was signed by George Bernard Shaw, H. G. Wells, John
Lavery and Leon Bakst. The fine words, unfortunately, made no
impression.

Meanwhile, Epstein travelled to Paris in August to rally French
intellectual opinion, but was once again in debt; dependent on
friends to lend him money, he was soon back in London to work
on portrait busts. With money raised by Ross, Epstein was able to
return to Paris in September, to put the finishing touches to the
work. When he arrived in Paris he found the monument 'covered
with an enormous tarpaulin and a gendarme standing on guard
beside it. He informed me that the tomb was banned.' When the
gendarme moved away, Epstein dragged the cover off, to discover
to his horror that the angel's pendulous testicles were swaddled in
plaster and the monument looked 'horrible'. He went to see the
keeper of the cemetery, only to learn that the Préfet of the Seine
and the Keeper of the Ecole des Beaux-Arts had solemnly decided
that Epstein must either castrate his angel or disguise the offending parts with a fig-leaf. He, of course, refused, and a few days
later returned to the tomb with a group of sympathetic artists
including Brancusi and the English painter Nina Hamnett.

Every morning the group of friends arrived with Epstein to help
him drag off the tarpaulin, but almost as soon as it was removed
the police replaced it. The pantomime continued daily, with the
Parisian authorities insisting on protecting the public's eyes from
the vision. Thus the two major works Epstein had created had
brought him into conflict with police on both sides of the Channel.
'The prisoner of Reading Gaol is today the prisoner of M. le
Conservateur du Père Lachaise,' wrote Georges Bazille in a witty
and angry piece in *Commedia*.

Because of a narrow-minded official and of the obscene
remarks of some gross-minded keepers and stonemasons, a

work of art, created in a spirit of full respect and reverence, is being kept hidden like something foul and loathsome.

Does M. le Conservateur mean to say he has never seen a man in his nakedness? Let him go to the Luxembourg – the Museum as well as the Gardens – and his eyes will soon be edified. The monument was publicly exhibited in London throughout the month of June. Thousands of people, artists and otherwise, went to see it and no official objections of any kind were raised . . . it was reserved for France to be the scene of this new attack on the Liberty of Art.[2]

Letters of protest to the press organised by intellectuals on both sides of the Channel could not overturn official French prudery: the tomb which had been planned for so long remained under tarpaulin. Robert Ross asked Epstein to modify the work to appease the French authorities. The artist declined. 'I refused to do anything that would admit I had done an indecent work.' Ross eventually found a journeyman to make a bronze plaque in the shape of a butterfly to cover the genitals, and the tomb, commissioned at the end of 1908, was finally unveiled in August 1914. After all the scandal it was difficult to find anyone to perform the ceremony, which may explain Ross's somewhat unfortunate choice of Aleister Crowley, the notorious diabolist. Epstein, bitter at the treatment of his work, refused to attend the unveiling. However, that was not the end of the affair: one evening in the early autumn of 1914, Crowley, in full evening dress, walked over to Epstein's table at the Café Royal. Round his neck he was wearing a very long cord with the bronze plaque, which he had removed from the tomb. In full view of the curious onlookers he took off the cord holding the 'fig-leaf' and solemnly presented it to Epstein. Epstein had seen his work covered up, mutilated, the centre of a scandal. He had to borrow money to try in vain to combat the stupidities of the censors. On the surface, the past year had been an utterly frustrating waste of time.

But the climate in Edwardian English society was gradually changing. D. H. Lawrence was writing novels which, with their

frankness about sex and the use of four-letter words, were eventually to banish Mrs Grundy. In the art world, despite the barricades,
influences from Europe were seeping in. The 1910 Post-
Impressionist exhibition had opened the floodgates. From 1911 to
1913 the arrival of Diaghilev's spectacular Ballets Russes in
London profoundly affected art lovers in the capital with its
disturbing music by Stravinsky and Debussy, brilliantly coloured
costumes and sets by Bakst and Picasso and ecstatic dancing by
Nijinsky and Karsavina. The influence of Futurism was beginning
to be reflected in the painting of the most radical young artists.
Although Epstein was always wary of theories and groups, the
furore over his Strand statues and the farce of the Oscar Wilde
tomb, together with his fervid embrace of primal themes, allied
him with a rising generation of rebel artists and writers. The years
immediately before the First World War were to prove the most
exciting of his life.

It was the influential philosopher and poet T. E. Hulme who first
drew Epstein into the circle of iconoclastic artists and writers.
Hulme, who described himself as a 'philosophic amateur and
aesthete', went to visit Epstein when he was working on the Wilde
tomb. In revolt against Romanticism, Hulme believed that he
found in Epstein's work the re-emergence of the abstract geomet-
ric forms he had so much admired in mosaics in Ravenna. Hulme
was to write about the vitality of angular, constructive art as
opposed to 'the sloppy dregs of the Renaissance', and he was the
first critic to champion Epstein consistently. The sculptor, for his
part, always chary of making friends, said that he 'got to know
Hulme very well'. The burly, imposing intellectual had a great
personal admiration for the sculptor – almost, according to
Wyndham Lewis, who was envious, 'a dog-like devotion'.
Evidently he was not so respectful of Lewis, whom he once picked
up and held upside down.[3] Epstein flourished in the company of
discerning admirers. He went regularly to Hulme's Tuesday
evenings soirées, held at a house in Frith Street, Soho, where
writers, journalists, painters and sculptors gathered. Epstein found
Hulme a 'great conversationalist' but admitted to understanding

little of his discourse on philosophy. 'With artists,' Epstein remarked, he was 'humble and always willing to learn'. Less to Epstein's taste was Hulme's rule barring women: he was afraid that the 'sex element' would interfere with masculine intellectual talk. There was no question that Hulme was heterosexual; he once boasted that his knowledge of London's suburbs was based on his love affairs there. At the Tuesday gatherings, Epstein met a wide range of artists and intellectuals: Stanley Spencer as well as the Camden Town painters Spencer Gore and Harold Gilman, the novelist Ford Madox Ford and A. R. Orage, the editor of a revitalised left-wing journal, the *New Age*, now an important influence in the arts as well as politics.

The *New Age* had helped to create a new climate in the arts by welcoming change and experiment. As early as 1908 the journal had championed Epstein's maligned statues in the Strand, not only on aesthetic grounds but with the decidedly *New Age* viewpoint that they would provide useful tools in sex education.

The severe, massive architecture is enriched and enlightened by its gallery of shrines . . . a strong sense of nobility is the first one that awakens in you . . . We are puzzling over the problem of how best to prepare our schoolchildren for a knowledge of the facts of sex . . . Perhaps in some such series of symbolic figures . . . we shall find a way.[4]

Through his new friends Epstein was now in touch with the avant-garde of art in Britain. In March 1912 the Italian Futurists held a show at the Sackville Galleries. A talented publicist for his movement, their leader, Marinetti, turned up at the gallery and proclaimed in noisy rhetoric the glory of the modern and the need to break with the past. Modern life was a life of steel, fever, pride and headlong speed, according to the Futurist Manifesto. Marinetti brought to the gallery 'a tooth-brush and a few twigs he had found in Hyde Park and a match-box tied together with string'. Epstein described Marinetti's delivery as an imitation of the chattering of machine-guns, the booming of cannons and the whirr of aeroplane engines. 'He was a stupid-looking man and his impudence was as great as his energy.' Epstein rightly called him a 'pro-Fascist'; but there is no doubt that the energy and aggression that Marinetti and his Futurists displayed fuelled the aims of Vorticism, the embryonic English avant-garde movement born some months later.

During 1912 Epstein went to Paris four times, causing an outlay in expense and energy that was infuriating and dispiriting. But in the French capital the intense artistic life in Montparnasse and the expansive climate in the café-terraces brought Epstein new friends and new sources of inspiration that were to last all his life. Modigliani – 'Modi', as he was known in Montparnasse, a handsome and distinguished young Italian Jew – had determined to become a sculptor at the time, planning a great Temple to Humanity, with hundreds of large female figures – 'columns of tenderness', he called them. His caryatids, female figures designed to bear weight, obsessed him. In his studio, 'a miserable hole in a courtyard', stood nine or ten stone heads suggested by African masks; he talked incessantly of the inspiration of primitive art and its enriching effect upon modern artists. At night Modigliani placed candles on top of each figure, creating the effect of a primitive temple. Café gossip in Montparnasse had it that, under the influence of hashish, Modi would embrace his magnificent columns. Epstein was entranced, although when Modi gave him some hashish to try it had little effect on him.[5] However, Modi's vision of a temple peopled with imposing sculpture echoed his own long-cherished dream.

Like Epstein, Modi believed that modern sculptors were modelling too much in clay; 'too much mud', he explained. The only way to revitalise the art was to work directly in stone. With a shared vision and similar ideals, the two men took to each other immediately. Although Modigliani had not yet sold a single sculpture and scraped a living by selling or swapping his drawings for the price of a drink, Epstein recognised his quality and the two sculptors tried to find a space for a studio where they could work side by side. Both Jews with a global vision, yet acutely aware of the anti-Semitism around them, they felt easy with each other. For days they trudged all over the Butte of Montmartre looking for a suitable grass plot in the wasteland. But the sight of the two wild-eyed artists aroused the suspicions of caretakers and landlords and they were unsuccessful.

The two often ate together at Rosalie's *crémerie*, in the rue Campagne-Première. Run by a former model, the small café boasted four marble-topped tables where for a few francs artists could buy simple, hearty food. All his life Epstein treasured a beautiful Modigliani drawing of a caryatid. (It hangs today in the New Art Gallery, Walsall.[6]) Modigliani, tragically, could not continue his career as a sculptor because the stone dust from the chisel affected his lungs. After his death, Epstein wrote with great warmth of his friend.

Through Modigliani's close friend, the Chilean artist Ortiz de Zarate, Epstein visited the studio of the Romanian sculptor Constantin Brancusi, who was something of a legend in Montparnasse. Brancusi was an artist who had achieved integrity and simplicity in his art and his life. Carving in wood and stone, he pared down his forms – nudes, birds in flight, a couple kissing – to their essence. A burly, bearded man who wore a blue smock and clogs, Brancusi had created for himself a world of self-sufficiency. He built his own furniture and cooked his meals on a stone oven he had made himself, and remained firmly outside the intrigues and cliques of the Montparnasse scene. Epstein was impressed by his genial welcome, no matter how busy he was, and by his simplicity. He rarely went out and mistrusted café life, drinking only hot water because he believed that alcohol and carousing, as well as all the art talk, sapped the artist's strength. Epstein agreed, but he was more susceptible to the charm of the cafés. However, he certainly achieved a greater simplicity in his own work after his visit to Brancusi, as the art critic Richard Cork suggests.[7] It was Brancusi who specifically warned Epstein against 'imitating African art'.

A small number of avant-garde artists, notably Picasso, Matisse, Modigliani and Vlaminck, had found inspiration and interest in primitive art, but in 1912 African art was only just beginning to be recognised and valued, even by dealers. Occasionally masks and statues were to be seen on sale for a trivial sum in junk or souvenir shops. Epstein found the temptation to buy these treasures irresistible; he rapidly developed a discerning and sensitive appreciation of primitive art and an obsession to possess it which led him eventually to own the finest collection of African and Pacific art in Europe.[8] In 1912 Epstein the 'collector' was also the penniless artist, heavily in debt. 'One of [African sculpture's] greatest attractions was that it was the only sculpture I could afford,' he said. Although he and his wife Margaret were living on the narrowest of margins, she never reproached him for buying the figures that were such a source of delight and inspiration to him.

Beginning in 1912 he made a series of portraits of Margaret. 'Leaning upon her hand, she looks towards the future with supreme confidence,' he wrote in his autobiography. Of the second *Mask of Mrs Epstein*, made four years later, he said, 'it is one of my subtlest and most beautiful works. The serenity and inward calm is there . . . I can recall that I worked at this mask without effort, achieving it happily, and was pleased with the result.'[9]

The mask suggests that Margaret lived an intense inner life: her gaze and attention go beyond the sculptor and the view to a private world. Their relationship held depths of mystery. In *The Autobiography of Alice B. Toklas*, Gertrude Stein, who described Epstein as 'a large, rather stout man, not unimpressive but not beautiful', recalled, 'He had an English wife who had a very remarkable pair of brown eyes, of a shade of brown I had never seen before in eyes.'[10] Epstein, impulsive, emotional, passionate, had immense respect for the woman who had jettisoned her former life to be with him. She eased his contacts with the outside world, made very few demands and kept her absolute faith in him and her dignity in a raffish world. Epstein was taciturn about his intimate feelings, and his relationship with Margaret was complex and impenetrable. But there can be no mistaking the intensity of his feeling for her in the dignity and strength with which he imbues his modelling.

As 1912 drew to a close, the notoriety over the Oscar Wilde tomb still infuriated Epstein. He had wanted publicity in America before the scandal, but the gossipy piece in the American magazine *The World* appalled him. Headed 'Ghetto Youth Who Stirred the Paris Art World', it contrasted Jacob the artist with his brother 'Herman', who ran a grocery store and sent Jacob money, to fund his dreams. 'I have your letter with the amazingly impudent article in the *World* magazine,' he wrote to Quinn.

It was evidently concocted by a damned journalist in conjunction with a fool of a brother I have in New York. The photographs [of two life-sized figures with knees bent and arms outstretched, of a dignified old man entitled *Age* and of *The Diver*] are of things I did as a student years ago which I did not know existed or I should never allow to be published. The titles are fictitious as well as the whole of the article. I would have given anything that rubbish of that sort be prevented from publication, even were I Michelangelo, which, thank God, I have no desire to be . . . My one desire is to get to some quiet spot and do some work and leave large commissions . . . I would like to show that last Sun God, but it is impossible I know for any exhibition for the public and I won't be mad enough to think of it and yet there is a need of doing work that is significant and the desire to have others partake of a rich experience.[11]

Epstein said he had given up large commissions. He had tried, through Quinn, to build a monument to the Wright brothers, the American aviation pioneers, but that had fallen through because Wilbur Wright's brother Orville was still alive. Also the South Africans, tired of the delays, had dispensed with his services without payment, although Epstein had made a finished sketch and a model of a lion for them. 'Dirty swine, I am glad to be rid of them.'[12]

Epstein wanted peace and quiet to work, yet in a restless mood he and Margaret gave up the studio in Cheyne Walk in December

and decided to spend some time in Montparnasse. They found a
studio at 5 rue Campagne-Première, over a baker's shop, the house
where he had lived as a student in 1904, and rented it for three
months. Rosaline's artists' café was in the same little street;
Modigliani and Brancusi lived near by, and Augustus John passed
through in January 1913 in good spirits. So rapid was their move
that Epstein almost lost the chance to exhibit in the Armory Show
in New York, an important exhibition of over 1,100 modern artists
organised by the Society of American Painters and Sculptors.
Quinn wrote to London about the show and the sculptor received
Quinn's forwarded letter almost too late. His patron was a shrewd
businessman as well as an art lover and he moved quickly to buy
Epstein's model of Euphemia Lamb and have it shipped over in
time for the opening of the exhibition in February.

Epstein found the air of Paris cleaner and less oppressive than
the London fogs, but he was already dreaming of living in the
country in complete isolation. 'I am full of ideas and will yet do
something good, I think,' he wrote to Quinn. He was a man almost
unaware of material possessions but he could not resist telling
Quinn of his acquisitions in Paris.

> My African figures are wonderful . . . I possess four
> which I have got by the greatest good luck and purely by
> chance . . . they are genuine old works without a touch
> of European influence . . . The effect can't be conveyed
> in words – to feel it they must be seen. The beauty of the
> lines, of the carving, the perfect realization of forms.[13]

Two months later, on 17 March, he wrote to Quinn, who had
become infected with Epstein's enthusiasm, 'At present African
work is undervalued but soon it will be greatly valued. Gauguin
was among the first to see the great artistic value of African sculpture and he possessed a few pieces, I am told.'[14]

The Epsteins had decided to give up life in London and to live
in the country quietly and inexpensively. The Oscar Wilde débâcle
had left Jacob with large debts 'which I must endeavour to pay off

to gain peace for myself and my wife who cannot maintain a home for me without the constant threat of the bailiffs at the door'.[15] By May they were settled in seclusion in a bungalow called Bay Point, in Pett Level, a fishing hamlet near Rye. The bungalow, surrounded by fields, looked straight out to sea. In the back garden there was a shed which Epstein used for a studio. For neighbours they had only fishermen and a coastguard, so that Epstein was left absolutely undisturbed. He had three large stones to work. Here he could 'look out to sea and carve away to my heart's content without troubling a soul'. His health improved in the fresh air away from dirty London, and he revelled in the freedom of the elemental landscape.

The couple thought they had found a real home at last. Margaret was contented and worked hard in the garden. Epstein tried to persuade Quinn to lend them the money to buy their idyll. The landlord wanted £450 for the purchase and Epstein suggested that Quinn should buy the bungalow for him, holding eleven pieces of Epstein's African sculpture (a considerable sacrifice) as security while the sculptor paid back the debt at £40 a year. As Epstein was still in debt, he asked his patron to buy the property in his wife's name. Quinn was a shrewd lawyer and his interest in talented artists was not primarily philanthropic. He tried to drive down the price, but Epstein was too proud to haggle and the subject of buying the bungalow was dropped. Still, invigorated by the fresh sea air, Epstein felt a sense of release. To travel to London took him only two and a half hours, and when he needed to stay in town he could sleep on the floor of John's Chelsea studio or put up at other friends' homes. At last he felt free of the interminable discussions and self-important pronouncements about his Oscar Wilde tomb, free of committees and official bodies. Most exciting of all, at Pett Level he had 'found' 'a beautiful stone called flint which is as hard as granite and needs a lot of patience for me to make any impression on it'.[15] He coined the term 'Flenite' for the rich dark green stone know as Serpentine.

His mother, whom he had loved deeply, died in March 1913. The night before receiving the news he had dreamed about her. She had been his closest link with New York and his family there. That year he carved a moving and elegant *Mother and Child* in marble: two simplified geometrical heads, side by side, now in MOMA in New York.

At Pett Level he was at peace at last and furiously at work, able to shut out the world and carve his creations. At the time Epstein was experimenting with several different themes, inspired both by Brancusi's deceptively simple pared-down forms and by the stylised vitality of African art, to evolve his own powerful enactment of sexual energy. Wyndham Lewis captured the essence of Epstein's mysterious preoccupation: Epstein, he wrote, 'discovered in the machinery of procreation a dynamo to work the deep atavism of his spirit'.[16]

The themes of Venus, coupling doves, pregnancy, birth, and mother and child tumbled out on his drawing board, the drawings austere, geometrical, formal. The works he carved in Flenite, thought by some critics to be among his best, include *Flenite Relief*, a remarkable carving of an infant emerging from its mother's womb with only her splayed legs shown, and 'two pregnant women, one a large, mysterious figure looking down anxiously at her large and solid lap'; the other slighter figure, now in Tate Britain, shows an almost S-shaped mother engrossed in rapt contemplation of the unborn child in her belly. Epstein also modelled a black child in plaster, an African image, with the body painted red and the infant boy with upturned head wailing. *Cursed Be the Day wherein I was Born*, a quotation from the Book of Job, was the title for this outraged figure.

This was Epstein at his most original and powerful, widening the horizon of aesthetes in Britain with his raw and violent images of creation, and it was at Pett Level, inevitably, that he embarked on what he described as 'his great adventure'. The first drawings for his haunting and barbaric figure *Rock Drill* – his probe into the future; a machine-like robot, 'visored, menacing and carrying within itself' its progeny, with a pneumatic drill between its legs – were roughed out in that productive summer. 'It is one of those things that the artist is tempted to do occasionally and which for the artist is an indulgence as he has small chance of selling it,' Epstein explained in a letter to Quinn. The figure would not do for exhibition in a home, he said, but added that he thought it was very successful because 'I've rendered the subject in a manner that gives the utmost of driving force, of hard, relentless steel-like power, the work is metallic and for metal.'[17]

He was exceptionally productive that year, working on many different sculptures at the same time. The garden shed at Pett Level was too small to model *Rock Drill*, which would be over eight feet tall, so Epstein rented a small attic room above Harold Munro's Poetry Bookshop in Devonshire Street, with a garage in Devonshire Mews which served as his London studio.

Epstein went to London occasionally to work or to attend a meeting. The director of the Whitechapel Gallery invited him and the painter David Bomberg to visit Paris, to report on any talented new Jewish sculptors and painters who might be included in an exhibition the following year. A brief trip at the end of May 1913 was a welcome interlude. It gave Epstein the chance to visit old friends. Although Modigliani was at his home in Livorno recuperating from ill health and neglect he did recommend that the Italian's work be included in the exhibition of Jewish art in London. He also attended an important sale of African art.

In London in July, the Allied Artists' Association, an organisation modelled on the lines of the Parisian Salon des Indépendants, held their annual exhibition. The object of the AAA was to give subscribing artists the chance to show their work without the intervention of a jury. Epstein, on the management committee, entered the smaller of his Flenite women and the first version of his *Doves*, a sensuous and accessible representation of mating doves in translucent marble. In October the show of Post-Impressionist and Futurist work at the Doré Galleries included a second version of the *Doves*, a Flenite woman and studies for *Rock Drill*.

His work seemed extreme, even among the avant-garde, and the critics predictably excoriated him. 'Sculpture gone crazy' was a headline that represented the general tone. Epstein despised them. 'I look upon the art critics as all bought by dealers,' he told Quinn, 'and as I have not let one dealer corner me, I understand their rage.'[18] His attitude was not, of course, helpful to his standing in commercial circles, but it was a very different story among the avant-garde. Ezra Pound and T. E. Hulme praised Epstein's originality and splendour in left-wing and artistic magazines. 'Epstein is a great sculptor,' wrote Ezra Pound to his mother in November 1913. 'I wish he would wash, but I believe Michael Angelo never did so, so I suppose it is part of the tradition. Also it is nearly impossible to appear clean in London, perhaps he does remove some of the grime.'[19] Epstein lived in meagre lodgings in London and worked with steel and plaster. He was always preoccupied with his work and, even on grand social occasions, was apt to appear with daubs of plaster on his coat.

Gaudier-Brzeska was always eager to see Epstein's work. He admired the Oscar Wilde tomb, the Flenite carvings and particularly *Rock Drill*. He brought Ezra Pound to Epstein's garage studio to look at the strange figure. When the poet began to hold forth about the sculpture, Gaudier-Brzeska erupted: 'Shut up! You understand nothing.'[20]

Gaudier-Brzeska was working on an over-life-sized marble bust of Pound, and Epstein went along one afternoon to see the work in his tumbledown Putney studio with the roar of trains overhead. The sculptor had abandoned naturalism for a forceful abstraction, and his slit-eyed, totemic head of Pound had begun to look like a phallus, seen from the front or in profile. 'Pound had asked him to make it virile and this Gaudier was endeavouring to do, explaining to me the general biological significance,' Epstein said. The poet was delighted with the bold work and later named it *Hieratic Head*. That evening Gaudier-Brzeska invited Epstein to supper, and while he made a pungent stew at the kitchen stove Sophie Brzeska sat and talked to their guest. Epstein thought the young sculptor had 'any amount of talent and great energy . . . We were interested in each other's work.' He was gratified that Gaudier-Brzeska addressed him as '*Cher maître*', the French courtesy address from a younger to an older artist.

In December Epstein held his first one-man show of sculpture and drawings at Mrs Smith's Twenty-One Gallery at the Adelphi. The work on show included the newest productions from Pett Level: Flenite figures, *Doves*, the drawings of *Rock Drill* as well as earlier work, including bronzes of Nan and Romilly John. Eric Gill travelled from Ditchling to see the exhibition on 9 December. 'Epstein is mad on sex,' he wrote tersely in his diary – a rich comment, given his own intemperate sexual appetite.[21]

T. E. Hulme, writing in the *New Age*'s Christmas Day issue, felt bound to attack Epstein's critics, whom he considered exhibited 'a range and variety of fatuousness seldom equalled'. C. B., writing in the *Athenaeum*, was merely spiteful: 'The *Illustrated London News* compared [Epstein's] show unfavourably with the Exhibition of Humorous Artists.'[22] Hulme's article, entitled 'Mr Epstein and the Critics', concentrated on rebutting what he saw as the stupidities of the more serious of Epstein's critics, and the force of his feeling for his creations was vitiated. In the draft review he had prepared for the *New Age* his reaction is more direct:

Mr Epstein is certainly the most interesting and remarkable sculptor of this generation. I have seen no work in Paris or Berlin which I can so unreservedly admire. It is stronger than the mild archaisms of Malliol, and more varied than that of Modigliani or Brancusi. He possesses that peculiar energy which distinguishes the creative from the merely intelligent artist; that is he produces complete works of art, not merely work which exhibits interesting qualities. Work springing from the intellect is interesting only temporarily. Mr Epstein's carvings on the contrary have that other quality, springing ultimately perhaps from character, which bears more continued contemplation. They have a certain quality of finality, of inevitableness, which makes them seem like things discovered rather than things constructed.[23]

Hulme particularly admired the smaller 'carving in Flenite', the figure of a pregnant woman bending backwards, now in Tate Britain. After the exhibition, he bought the figure from Epstein.

For a brief period before the First World War, Epstein influenced and shared in the excitement and confusion of the birth of the modern movement in art and literature. In 1913 he had been one of the founders of the London Group, an exhibiting society for like-minded artists. Epstein called the members simply 'the best of English artists . . . There was an integrity about the London Group which is lacking today.' He also recognised the qualities of the talented and polemical Wyndham Lewis; indeed, he recommended that Ezra Pound look closely at Lewis's graphic work. 'Lewis's drawing has the qualities of sculpture,' he said. Epstein's own drawings for *Rock Drill*, with their clean, thrusting line and angularity, reflect the attraction he felt for the machine at the time. He was close to Lewis artistically, but they were both too combative to be friends, and Epstein was always on his guard against cliques and coteries.

In the summer of 1913 Roger Fry, who had promoted a second Post-Impressionist exhibition in 1912, founded the Omega Workshops, with the object of providing talented young artists with a living wage and encouraging his protégés to decorate furniture and fabrics in vibrant colours and bold modern shapes. Lewis, who had exhibited in Fry's Post-Impressionist exhibition, was invited to participate. Epstein was excluded from both ventures. Wyndham Lewis worked at the Omega briefly but left after an explosive row. He alleged that Roger Fry had appropriated an order to decorate a room for the Ideal Home Exhibition intended for the painter Spencer Gore. In a scathing round robin sent to friends and patrons of the workshops, he complained of the amateurism and snobbery bedevilling English art. 'The ideal is still Prettiness with its mid-Victorian languish of the neck and its skirt of "greenery yallery" despite the Post-What-Not fashionableness of its draperies.' Besides, he complained, painters were given no training in the applied arts: 'naturally the chairs we sold stuck to the seats of people's trousers; when they took up an Omega candlestick, they could not put it down again . . . it was glued to them and they to it'.[24]

For years splits and schisms had hampered co-operation

between progressive young artists. Wyndham Lewis believed that the 'Bloomsburies' (the 'Bloomsbuggers', as Pound called them), with their petty jealousies and ambitions, had poisoned British intellectual life at the beginning of the twentieth century. Without them, he concluded, 'the writing and painting world of London might have been less like the afternoon tea-party of a perverse spinster'.[25] When Lewis broke with the Omega Workshops, Gaudier-Brzeska, whose work was becoming increasingly abstract, left with him. The new avant-garde, outright in their rejection of naturalism and tradition, were beginning to form into a more radical force in British art. Epstein was still an outsider; he had not worked in the Omega Workshops, but as a sympathizer and friend of Lewis and Gaudier-Brzeska he was viewed with animosity by Fry and the Bloomsbury set.

Marinetti returned to England in November 1913, still trying to drum up support for his Futurist movement. The man who styled himself 'the caffeine of Europe' again recited poems at machine-gun speed, but this time was met with even less sympathy. Wyndham Lewis now saw himself as the prophet of a new art and he disliked the Italian obsession with machines and fast cars. 'You Wops', he told Marinetti, 'insist too much upon the Machine . . . We've had Machines for donkey's years.'[26]

Marinetti's attempt to woo English artists to Futurism spurred Lewis to forge his own English modern movement. In March 1914 he set up a Rebel Art Centre at 38 Great Ormond Street, financed by Kate Lechmere, a painter who was Wyndham Lewis's lover. They held Saturday tea parties and lectures for kindred spirits. Lewis invited Ezra Pound to lecture on Imagism, a contemporary Anglo-American movement of poets in revolt against Romanticism. The Imagists favoured language used with precision and clarity rather than words that carried symbolic meaning – aims that coincided with Wyndham Lewis's visual objectives. It was Ezra Pound who coined the term Vorticism, the rallying cry for a small and vital group of young English artists. The Vorticists focused their interest on a still, central object, the heart of the Vortex, a response to the Italian Futurists' love of figures and objects in movement, a movement that blurred and displaced the line. The artistic products of the Vorticist movement were to be easier to follow than their theories.

In June the short-lived Rebel Art Centre closed down over a lovers' tiff. T. E. Hulme had bedded Kate Lechmere, Wyndham Lewis's benefactor and partner, and Lechmere moved herself and her financial backing away. At the same time the painter Christopher Nevinson, Marinetti's only supporter in London, overplayed his hand. He published the 'Vital English Art Futurist Manifesto', written in collaboration with Marinetti in the *Observer* on 7 June 1914, using Rebel Art Centre notepaper and naming Bomberg, Epstein, Lewis, Roberts and Wadsworth, among others, as artists who were injecting vitality into the insipid English art scene. None of the artists named had given their permission; they were all furious. A week later, on 14 June, the rebel English artists took their revenge. Wyndham Lewis describes in his autobiography how he

> assembled in Greek Street a determined band of miscella-neous anti-futurists . . . After a hearty meal we shuffled belli-cosely round to the Doré Gallery [where Marinetti was speaking]. Marinetti had entrenched himself upon a high lecture platform, and he put down a tremendous barrage in French as we entered. Gaudier went into action at once. He was very good at the *parlez-vous*, in fact he was a Frenchman. He was sniping him without intermission . . . the remainder of our party maintained a confused uproar and the Italian intruder was worsted.[27]

The war of words was waged with renewed vigour when *Blast*, the puce-coloured magazine of the Vorticist movement, appeared at the beginning of July. The full-page advertisement that was displayed in the *Egoist* had promised 'Story by Wyndham Lewis, Poems by Ezra Pound, Reproductions of Drawings, Paintings and Sculpture by Etchells, Nevinson, Lewis, Hamilton, Brzeska, Wadsworth, Epstein, Roberts, etc. . . . NO Pornography, NO old pulp. END OF THE CHRISTIAN ERA.'

Although Epstein allowed two drawings of his most polemical work, studies of *Birth* and *Rock Drill*, to be reproduced in *Blast*, like David Bomberg he did not sign the Vorticist Manifesto. Two lines in a *Blast* poem by Ezra Pound, 'Let us be done with Jews and Jobbery,/Let us spit upon those who fawn on the Jews for their money',[28] might have influenced their decision. Although *Blast* railed against the English climate, the Royal Academy and Victorian middle-class values, ingrained and prevalent anti-Semitism was allowed to slip by.

By the summer of 1914 Epstein, at the peak of his creativity, was in confident mood. He had finished his *Rock Drill*. 'I dream of great commissions,' he wrote to Quinn. He was back in the country at Pett Level with several blocks of marble; and he had decided, he told Quinn, to 'pass by bawling theorists and cliques'.[29]

6

Surviving

IN THE FINE SUMMER before the First World War, the painter Mark Gertler was on holiday in a fisherman's cottage at Pett Level. With Epstein as a neighbour in the hamlet, Gertler hoped for inspiration. A reluctant virgin, Gertler still lived with his mother in the East End of London and was deeply shocked by the casual arrangements in the Epstein household. 'Epstein is the one fault in my holiday here, somehow he puts me off working,' he wrote in a letter to Dora Carrington, a fellow art student with whom he was passionately and unhappily in love. 'He has a filthy mind and he always has some girl living with him *including* his wife. Now he has a horrible black girl. She tells me she's sat at the Slade. She's like a Gauguin. I hate her more and more every day.'[1]

Two years earlier, when Gertler was still a student at the Slade, Epstein had taken him on a memorable tour of the British Museum. 'He revealed to me such wonders in works of art that my inspiration knew no bounds and I came to the conclusion that Egyptian art is by far, far, the greatest of all arts. We moderns are but ants in comparison.'[2] Now, however, he found that, far from inspiring him, Epstein's presence actually hampered his work.

Margaret Epstein – Peggy – by then in her early forties, had apparently decided that as an artist Epstein had needs which were different from those of other men. He could not afford to pay models, and if Jacob coupled with beautiful young women who came to pose for him and to stay in their cottage she did not make a scene. Margaret totally identified with her husband's artistic aspirations, but perhaps his sexual demands on her were excessive. 'Jacob liked women who don't have sex naturally,' she once told her sister-in-law.[3] As a modern, left-wing woman with an exceptionally broad attitude, Margaret was content to watch over the genius.

On 4 August 1914 war was declared and a fever of excitement spread through the country. In Trafalgar Square masses of people drifted past Nelson's Column to scan the headlines; when the news of Britain's mobilization came through, the murmurs of the crowd rose to a great roar. The art market was immediately affected. Dealers in the empty galleries warned their artists that no more advances would be forthcoming, and Epstein's precarious income was badly depleted. He had been relying on selling some small bronzes. 'I don't know how I will pull through the summer,' he wrote despairingly to John Quinn in New York. 'All dealers here refuse anything for sale. They are in a state of mortal funk and things have come to an absolute standstill. Everybody here is war-mad. But my life has always been a war and it is more difficult, I believe, for men to stick to their jobs than to go out . . . and fight and get patriotically drunk.'[4]

In a quiet Sussex village, Epstein was spared the jingoism and the hysteria of London, but in wartime his German-sounding name as well as the special attention he paid to pigeons – to send messages, perhaps? – made the villagers suspicious. He had a vast amount of work to finish. His most important statues, the *Sun God*, *Venus* (the second version) and *Rock Drill*, all needed attention, but none of it would bring in money immediately – if ever. Since he could not afford to have his *Rock Drill* cast in steel, he was having it made in white plaster. Quinn had commissioned him to carve another replica of the *Doves* but the work was not yet done and Epstein, of course, had not been paid.

For him, the prospect of conscription meant not only the horror and danger of war, which he had always hated, but also the worry of keeping afloat. 'I have a wife dependent upon me and with no resources in hand, to go off to war would mean leaving her to survive on a soldier's pay, which doesn't even pay the rent . . . My chances of government recognition of my work are nil. As an artist I am amongst the most hated and the most ignored.'[5] Hated Epstein might have been, but he was rarely ignored. Ezra Pound made Epstein's struggle to exist a public issue. 'Is it or is it not ludicrous that [Epstein's] *Sun God* and two other pieces which I have not seen, should be pawned, the whole lot for some £60? And that six of the other works are still on the sculptor's hands? And this is not due to the war. It was so before this war was heard of.'[6]

But Pound's tactics were as likely to deter potential buyers as to shame them. When John Quinn saw the article he was angry, taking it to be an attack on himself. Ezra Pound replied, 'I heard that you had bought an Epstein (*an* Epstein, not half a dozen). By the way if you are getting Jacob's Birds [*Doves*] for God's sake get the two that are stuck together, not the pair in which one is standing up on its legs.'[7] Quinn repeated Pound's advice in a letter to Epstein, who was furious. 'Why Pound should implore you "for God's sake" not to get the other birds passes my understanding . . . let Ezra stick to his poetry and leave the sculpture alone.'[8] That was unlikely, since Pound, together with Augustus John, was advising Quinn on his purchases of art.

Epstein's close contacts with the Vorticists had their uses, though. The Countess of Drogheda, who commissioned Wyndham Lewis to decorate her dining room in daring Vorticist style with black mirrors, asked Epstein to make a portrait of her. From January to March 1915 he worked in London. He produced an unusually conventional portrait of the countess with bare shoulders and tendrils of hair curling round her head. Lady Drogheda was evidently enchanted, although her husband could not bear the work and told her to sell the only bronze casting.[9] She put on a small, exclusive show of Epstein's work at her Knightsbridge home. The *Doves* formed a part of the little exhibition and once again caused trouble. Lord Drogheda, who seems to have had no friendly feelings towards Epstein, exploded when he saw the mating birds. 'I won't have those fucking doves in here,' he shouted. 'I'll throw them out of the window.'[10]

Perhaps Epstein's daring reputation lent a frisson to employing him as a sculptor. He was, of course, establishing a reputation as the best portrait sculptor, and he certainly built up a society connection very rapidly. His sitters came mainly from the wealthy and distinguished strata of society: those were the people who could command the work. But the beautiful models who adorned the Café Royal and occasionally a striking figure among the characters that roamed the streets produced some of his best work. His mastery of modelling technique gave him a freedom to express his intuitive understanding of the character and attitude of his sitters, and he was extraordinarily versatile, both in his range of subjects and in his approach. Some portraits he treated naturalistically; others revealed his admiration for work of the past and relied on a more decorative effect. When he was a student, his main concern was to imbue his sculptures with life; it was an intention he fulfilled in almost every work he created. Epstein's portraits seem to radiate their creator's vivid intensity. Although he was at his happiest and most fulfilled in Pett Level, portrait work meant that he was continually travelling up to London to try to make a sale or gain a commission.

At Pett Level, by the sea, 'for a long summer and almost privately', he worked 'for his own pleasure' on the second of his two ambitious figures of Venus. These austere, blank-faced goddesses personify the forces of creation and reproduction, and it was in the second, larger version that Epstein achieved the satisfaction and poise that he sought. The smooth, marble figure of Venus is perched on two mating doves, her parted legs leaning towards the cock's comb. Venus, the goddess of love, is always represented in Western art as a beautiful, idealised figure – Botticelli's maiden rising from the sea – and therefore to name his statue *Venus* was provocative. His elegantly simplified marble *Mother and Child* in the form of two adjacent heads is just as austere, with the features of the faces barely suggested but with no sexual characteristics to excite comment.

In March 1915 Epstein exhibited his most original work with the London Group at the Goupil Gallery. His exhibits included the two *Flenite Figures, Cursed Be the Day wherein I was Born,* the stylised *Mother and Child* and *Rock Drill.* The menacing *Rock Drill* was his closest encounter with the spirit of the new century and, as he said, marked a new epoch in sculpture. The creature, with its pneumatic drill, caused real disquiet in the West End gallery. At one point he had even considered attaching pneumatic power to his drill, setting it in motion and so 'completing every potentiality of form and movement in one single work'. In London the art gallery was still a world where John Singer Sargent's suave, almost photographic portraits of society ladies held sway; even in Paris, Epstein was years ahead of his time. In 1913, just as Epstein was creating *Rock Drill*, Marcel Duchamp fastened a bicycle chain to a wheel and announced that he had invented the first 'mobile' sculpture.

Besides the 'monster', Epstein defied convention in his portrayal of pregnant women, infants, motherhood, even birds. Yet the ferocity of the attack mounted by the critics surprised him. 'With the exception of the *Manchester Guardian*, the critics have exhausted their vocabulary of abuse,' he wrote to Quinn. 'I can stand a lot, but this time they have really outdone themselves and naturally sales have been affected . . . Of my three small saleable pieces none were sold. My "Rock Drill" was my great adventure and I did not expect to sell it.'[11] Yet Jacob described in the same letter his experiments with his second version of *Venus*. Quinn was impressed with Epstein's talent and his courage. He bought *Flenite Relief* and *Cursed Be the Day wherein I was Born*, and was planning to buy *Rock Drill* when Augustus John, Epstein's 'friend' as well as Quinn's adviser, put him off. '[The robot] is turning the handle for all he's worth and under his ribs is the vague shape of a rudimentary child, or is it something indigestible he's been eating? Altogether the most hideous thing I've seen.'[12] John was merely echoing the opinions of most of the critics. P. G. Konody of the *Observer* was ruthless: 'The whole effect is unutterably loathsome. Even leaving aside the nasty suggestiveness of the whole thing, there remains the irreconcilable contradiction between the crude realism of the real machinery (of American make) combined with an abstractedly treated figure.'[13]

Epstein was spending more time in London in wartime, moving from studio to studio. In the autumn of 1915 he was working at 20

Great James Street, but by December he had moved to 42 Emerald Street in Holborn, carving a *Mother and Child* in granite standing about five feet high. 'If I do nothing further and I complete this I will have the greatest satisfaction as I look upon the thing as one of my most final sculptures,' Epstein wrote.[14] He made this kind of judgement on several of his important works. Unfortunately this figure of an enormous child almost dwarfing the great granite mother who is proudly holding it up is lost. According to family legend, Epstein sent it to Quinn during the war. The collector had wanted the two elegant marble heads of *Mother and Child* and, on Epstein's instructions, had dumped the massive sculpture in the Hudson river.[15]

The war ground on and life became more difficult for everyone. Tools and sculptural material were harder to find; sending sculpture overseas required official permission and was a lengthier business as the carnage came closer. Zeppelin raids on London killed, maimed and caused destruction. One of Margaret's two brothers in a Scottish regiment was wounded. Hugh Lane, the Irishman who had commissioned Epstein's head of Lady Gregory, went down with the *Lusitania*. Even at the Café Royal the soldiers on leave were seen at the tables, bandaged and scarred. Epstein's good friend T. E. Hulme, who was preparing a book on Epstein, arrived back from the front with a shattered arm. Worst of all, on 15 June 1915, at the age of twenty-three, Henri Gaudier-Brzeska, one of the most talented and dynamic of the modern artists, was killed in battle in France. Epstein and Wyndham Lewis had been among the party who saw him off on the boat train to France when he went to enlist. 'He was a great friend of mine and his loss to sculpture was real, not only for what he had accomplished,' Epstein wrote to Quinn in the autumn from Frith Street, Soho.

Conscription for all able-bodied men was imminent; as a naturalised Briton, Epstein was liable to be called up and was anxious about the prospect. Confronted with the realities of a mechanised war, his enthusiasm for his 'great adventure', *Rock Drill*, with its real machine and futuristic operator, waned. In wartime he came to hate and mistrust the destructive power of technology. In May

1916 he reported tersely to Quinn his extraordinary decision to truncate *Rock Drill*, discarding the drill and showing only the synthetic operator in an exhibition of the London Group in 1916. He told Quinn that the black metal torso possessed the quality of the whole (which seems, from a sculptor, a very dubious statement) and added, 'I consider it one of my best things.'[16] Without the drill, however, the robot loses his dominance and aggression and looks pathetic and awkward. Later he rationalized what was almost certainly an instinctive revulsion against his creation. 'It is a thing prophetic of much in the great war and . . . within the experience of nearly all,' he said in an interview.[17] By the time the Second World War broke out Epstein had developed his analysis of *Rock Drill* in the light of an even more menacing world. 'Here is the armed sinister figure of today and tomorrow. No humanity, only the terrible Frankenstein monster we have made ourselves into.'

Rock Drill was a particularly complex work, difficult for even Epstein to describe. In contrast, the critics nearly always approved of the sculptor's bronze busts, almost as if they breathed a corporate sigh of relief at having something comprehensible to write about. His display at the National Portrait Society's exhibition included a portrait of Lilian Shelley, a singer and dancer at the Cave of the Golden Calf whom Epstein described as 'beautiful but temperamental'; a striking bust of Iris Beerbohm-Tree, daughter of the actor-manager; and a bust of Elizabeth Scott-Ellis, the daughter of Lord and Lady Howard de Walden. He had splendid reviews, which delighted him because they helped sales, but his opinion of the critics' understanding of art was caustic:

> Some of the critics have turned somersaults with great agility. When 'Rock Drill' [the complete version] was exhibited they declared it to be the end of art . . . Attempting even to put into language what lies behind a work like 'Rock Drill' or 'Cursed Be the Day that I was Born' [sic] they fail dismally. The aesthetic side of the works they entirely miss. The determination and research of planes, the opposition of lines and planes,

the spring of lines, the whole plastic side of a work exists not
at all to these gentlemen who have jobs on the newspapers.[18]

Epstein was no longer an outsider in the world of progressive art.
Augustus John, once the leader of the avant-garde, had faded from
view, while Epstein was regarded as a force for change, an innovator in a swiftly changing world. Socially too his position had
changed. Successive scandals, good looks and a pugnacious attitude had made him into a dominant character in the Café Royal
and beyond. The cult café became his club; he had his own table,
and fellow artists, models and dealers like Oliver Brown of the
Leicester Galleries began to drop in there every evening to meet
Epstein and other artists.

Epstein's name was never out of the papers for long – and not
always in the context of art criticism. Early in 1914, Epstein was
summoned before a magistrate by Lord Alfred Douglas (Oscar
Wilde's Bosie) for a letter he had sent threatening to 'spoil the
remains of your beauty double-quick . . . if you attack any monument to O.W.'.[19] Epstein had admitted to sending the letter under
great provocation and was bound over to keep the peace. But it all
made great copy and stuck in the minds of the public.

His life in the early war years had been restless – he moved studios
several times in London – and full of excitement. He had made new
friends in the world of music: Peter Warlock (Philip Heseltine), a
young composer who later committed suicide, Cecil Gray, and
Bernard Van Dieren, a Dutch composer who became a close friend
and admirer of Epstein's and later wrote a book about him. Through
his musical friends Epstein met Frederick Delius. Although the two
men visited each other, Epstein found 'this composer of sweet and
melancholy music . . . argumentative, cranky and bad-tempered and
we had many a set-to'. He thought Delius had very little sense of
humour, but his own was broad and not to everyone's taste. When
Delius laid the law down on art, he infuriated Epstein. Apparently
he considered himself an authority because his wife was a painter
and Delius himself had once bought a painting by Gauguin.

All through his life Epstein's material circumstances were

suddenly transformed by lucrative commissions. In June 1916 he received a visit at his studio in Emerald Street from Francis Dodd, his painter friend from his early days in London. Dodd asked Epstein whether he would agree to make a bust of Admiral Lord Fisher, the man who had created the Dreadnought battleship. When he agreed, Epstein was bundled into a taxi with his clay and materials and driven to the Duchess of Hamilton's flat in Piccadilly. The sculptor found the man of war arresting, with his combative stance, iron-grey hair and light eyes that could look dangerous. The men forged an immediate understanding and that morning, standing near the window in a room that was poorly lit, he started work. For the first two hours of the session Fisher stood while Epstein moulded his features, then moved obediently so that the light fell upon the aspect of his face that Epstein was modelling. If the pose allowed, Admiral Fisher liked to watch the sculptor at work through the reflection in a mirror. He posed first in civilian clothes but after four days put on his uniform, his chest covered in rows of medals. Epstein took six days, working long, regular hours to finish the bust. 'I have tried to show all the wonderful virility of the head and the grim, implacable expression of determination which is the most striking characteristic,' he wrote in a column-long article in the *Weekly Dispatch* on Christmas Eve 1916. 'Sculpturally speaking it is the most powerful head that I have ever done.'[20] A part of him had evidently admired the ruthlessness of the war leader. The work found favour and in wartime was a particularly useful commission. Epstein was exploring the possibility of exemption from call-up. Since his youth he had abhorred war, but on the other hand he detested the types who pleaded conscientious objection. He convinced himself that he was merely seeking a delay so that he could finish important carvings and set his finances in order. What really drove him was his faith in his work, a faith which convinced him that 'the future would think it important'.

Margaret Epstein was campaigning energetically to keep her husband out of the army, helped by Muirhead Bone, J. B. Manson, director of the Tate Gallery, and A. R. Orage, the editor of the *New*

Age. Margaret wrote and cabled John Quinn in New York several times, careful to sign herself Margaret Dunlop, since she was convinced that the censors were holding up correspondence in the name of Epstein. At her prompting Quinn cabled both the War Office and the Exemption Tribunal, pleading for deferment for Epstein to finish *Sun God*, *Venus* (second version), *Man and Woman*, *Maternity* and *Rock Drill* in order to stave off severe financial hardship. 'Mr Epstein is a really great sculptor,' he wrote eloquently, 'his inability to finish the works that he has in hand would be not only a great loss to art, and in particular to English art, but would be a loss to the world. His sculpture is extraordinary.'[21] Epstein, hard at work on a bust of the Duchess of Hamilton commissioned by Admiral Fisher, was unaware of all the activity on his behalf. The admiral had been so impressed by Epstein that he had written to the Director of Recruiting, offering himself, at the age of almost eighty, as a substitute for the sculptor.[22]

Margaret was unswervingly loyal and steadfast to Epstein but the age difference of almost eight years was beginning to tell. She was forty-three, Jacob a youthful thirty-five, and more and more she was taking on a protective, motherly role with him. The irony was that the sculptor so obsessed with procreation had not yet become a father.

There is no record of how Epstein met 'Meum', the slender, fair-haired young woman, both seductive and demure, who captivated him, but it seems likely that he encountered her at the Café Royal. When Epstein saw a beautiful woman, he almost devoured her with his gaze, scanning her face and body with open appreciation. The estranged wife of an army captain, Dorothy Lindsell-Stewart ('Meum' was her husband's pet name for her) was making a meagre living as a typist, although she had the grace and distinction of a dancer. Soon after he met her, Epstein began to sketch and sculpt Meum, who was flattered and elated by his attention. He even painted her in oils, an extremely unusual medium for him, and the two fell in love.

Meum was a delightful companion, playful, affectionate and sexy. Epstein left a clue to their union in a beautiful drawing of Meum in orgasm. Underneath he wrote in Latin, 'And still she is not satisfied!'[23] Like Epstein, Meum was a rebel. A convent-educated girl from a cultivated family, she could not bear to stay at home in Surrey waiting for a suitable beau and filling in time by acting as nursemaid to her little brother. Instead, in her teens she persuaded her parents to let her go dancing with Tony Lindsell-Stewart, a dark, Italian-looking man, ten years her senior, who was a professional dancer. The two partnered so well that they sometimes gave exhibitions together, and inevitably they began a passionate affair. Their liaison so shocked Meum's parents that they forced the two young people, entirely without means, to get married. This turned out to be a ghastly mistake. With the outbreak of the First World War, Tony joined the army and Meum, not yet twenty, was left to fend for herself. When Tony came home on leave they quarrelled miserably and when he pawned her engagement ring she left him.

Since to be a divorced woman was almost as scandalous as to 'live in sin', Meum went to stay with her eldest sister and her husband in Wimbledon, where she mixed with friends in the world of theatre and art. Although she was poor, she had great style and spirit. Having learned to sew and embroider expertly as a convent girl, she always cut out and designed her own crêpe-de-chine underwear and made dresses in cyclamen and blue to set off her dark blue eyes. In wartime her insouciant manner and her fresh, untroubled look were much admired. Thirty years later Epstein remembered her as the 'ever beautiful, ever youthful Meum'.[24]

The journalist Ashley Gibson, on leave from France in July 1916, was also an admirer, and his account of a wasted afternoon trailing after Meum captures something of the atmosphere of the time. He had called round at her aunt's in Wimbledon to invite Meum to lunch. She was sleeping late after a party and the wretched Gibson waited and waited.

In about an hour Miss M., her vague, fluttering, delightful

self floated down, welcoming but elusive in green velvet and
a Russian hat. Lunch would be divine, she said, but it would
be a subsequent engagement. There was Epstein, keeping
vigil even now in a Chinese restaurant. He was doing a bust
of her, a divine bust . . . 'You look so well,' she said. 'But you
were disappointed when you saw me. You tried not to show
it, but I can always tell. It's because I didn't have time to do
my face properly.' So we taxied to Glasshouse Street and
pacified Epstein, who seemed to have been waiting some
time for his lunch and was in a little mood with me.

After lunch, Meum, Epstein and Gibson took another taxi to
Epstein's studio in Great James Street.

While Mrs Epstein gravely sat and stitched, the sweet silhou-
ette of Miss M., enthroned where the light made cunning play
with the folds of her green velvet, wavered nebulously.
Epstein was quietly busy with his clay. His movements had
the stealthy quick precision of a tiger's. Miss M. slid out a
long, white snake of an arm. 'Talk to me,' she said sleepily.[25]

The domestic vigil says it all: the seductive, elegant Meum posing
centre stage, Margaret Epstein, old enough to be her mother,
keeping vigil while she sewed, and Epstein, predatory and alert,
guarding the prize from the young soldier who was longing for
consolation before he went back to the front. The newspapers
described Meum as 'Epstein's favourite model' and she was soon
a part of the Epstein household, although officially still living with
her sister in Wimbledon.

Thanks to the efforts of Margaret and his friends, Epstein was
granted three months' exemption from the army. In January 1917
he was busy preparing for his first major exhibition in London, to
be held in February at the progressive Leicester Galleries. Epstein
had met one of the directors, Oliver Brown, just before the war in
the back room of Dan Rider's bookshop in St Martin's Court,
Leicester Square, a useful meeting place for artists and writers.

The two men became friendly; Epstein sold Brown a bronze of a baby's head, which, the sculptor said, would be sure to appeal to the sentimental British public. When Brown suggested a one-man exhibition, Epstein agreed eagerly. 'My show at the Leicester Galleries . . . may be my Swan Song,' he wrote to John Quinn, then added confidently, 'These solid studies give me the right to launch out on work of a different character and establish myself as a sculptor; they give the lie to any attempt to label Epstein's vision as one of a charlatan.'[26]

Epstein exhibited a body of bronze that impressed the critics. He included portraits of the beauties and socialites of the Café Royal, a craggy study of Augustus John and a portrait of the poet W. H. Davies, as well as a bust of Mrs Epstein and two of Meum. His recently completed bust of Admiral Fisher and two fine studies of soldiers, one with a real tin hat on his head, as well as a head of his friend Hulme, on leave recovering from a war injury, and of Muirhead Bone, who was to become an official war artist, made up a section which he no doubt hoped would establish his credentials for sculpting the troops at the front.

Oliver Brown of the Leicester Galleries was a shrewd business-man as well as a discerning dealer. He made a poster of Epstein's haunting *Venus* (second version), with its evocation of primitive power, which attracted vast crowds to the galleries. The Leicester had a turnstile, and huge crowds queued to pay their shilling to view the novelty, but the gallery owners said they were gratified by the serious attention the exhibition received from the visiting public. Epstein's large granite *Mother and Child*, still unfinished, was among the twenty-six exhibits. In a preface to the catalogue he said simply, 'I rest silent in my work.'

The critics were predictably enthusiastic about the accessible bronze portraits. *The Times* called Epstein 'the master of portrai-ture', the *New Statesman* saw 'a master's hand' in his portrait work,[27] but it was a friend, Bernard Van Dieren, writing in the *New Age*, who made a connection between Epstein's portraits and his non-figurative work, and argued that both were abstract and imaginative. The fact that the bronzes 'also represent existing beings is of secondary importance'. A sitter constitutes 'sculptural conceptions expressing certain human qualities which rest clearly defined in the artist's mind until in his search for them he comes across the individual who could serve as a medium of the particular expression concerned'. Van Dieren described the dominant sculpture in the show, the *Venus*, as

> a beautiful tower of white marble which the sculptor has modelled so that a wonderful rhythm of three conspicuous planes and a base, so arranged to suggest great lightness and elegance of pose, convey a single artistic emotion . . . a suggestion of physical virginity and sterility coupled with lasciviousness constitutes what, in an exalted sense, the word Venus means to us.[28]

Epstein wrote to thank Van Dieren for his perceptive article: 'that you should point out the fact of there being no discrepancy between the portraits and the more sculptural and imaginative conceptions is what was really necessary'.[29] The question of the differing appearance and value of carving and modelling, his more imaginative work versus the representational, was constantly to recur. Despite a longing to make great monumental statements in stone, a longing that lasted all his life, as an artist Epstein defended his best portrait work. 'I think you are inclined to overrate what you call advanced work,' he wrote to Quinn, who was increasingly buying avant-garde work from Paris.

> Not all advanced work is good, some of it is damned, damned bad. I say this because there is a tendency to slight work which has any resemblance to natural objects. My own essays into abstract art have always been natural and not forced . . . I make no formula and only when I see something to be done in abstract form that better conveys my meaning than natural form then I use it. There is a solidity in natural forms though that will always attract a sculptor and great work can be done on a natural basis.[30]

The Leicester Galleries show lasted from February to March 1917, and £1,600 worth of bronzes were sold at Epstein's one-man show in the middle of the war, although of course the gallery creamed off its share. Through the exhibition Epstein attracted many new admirers, including Gladys Deacon, a wealthy and intelligent young American who had grown up in artistic circles in Venice and Paris. She had known Rodin, who died at the age of seventy-seven that year, and was delighted to find in Epstein '*un génie qui est jeune*'.[31] She commissioned her own portrait as well as a marble clock from Epstein. The clock was never made, although she paid £150 for it. Deacon, mistress of the Duke of Marlborough, who was to become the Duchess four years later, became a valuable patron and friend.

Epstein needed further exemption from the army and Gladys Deacon rallied to help Margaret Epstein and other friends to gain deferment for the artist. The local tribunal refused his application. At a second hearing he was granted three months' further deferment by the Law Society Appeal Tribunal. But this time an elaborate anti-Epstein plot, which had been hatching since March, upset his plans.

In March 1917, just as Epstein's Leicester Galleries exhibition was reaching a triumphal conclusion, a pantomime in aid of a patriotic charity, Lena Ashwell's 'Concerts at the Front', was held at the Chelsea Palace theatre. The pantomime, the *Monster Matinée,* organised by ladies of the YMCA, comprised a little history of Chelsea, with playlets and songs and dances about Rossetti and Whistler, ending up with a grand finale in praise of Augustus John, who had applied to go to France to sketch the troops. In the course of the pantomime, Epstein was caricatured on stage; he saw it as part of an elaborate conspiracy to force him into the army. He blamed John for the episode, but the more active culprit was John's friend Horace de Vere Cole, an eccentric and malicious joker. Cole, an old Etonian, was a wealthy habitué of the Café Royal, good looking and extremely vain, who delighted in practical jokes. Yeats described him as 'hardly sane'. He loathed Epstein and his friends and took every occasion to insult them. One evening he sat down at a table when Epstein was having a drink with Cecil Gray and began to abuse them both. This led to a fight and two black eyes for Cole. His hatred of Epstein verged on paranoia, and in wartime he succeeded in a damaging prank.

Cole had been closely following Epstein's attempts to gain exemption from the army. When he got wind of the latest exemption, he prompted a number of minor artists to write to the press in protest. The *Illustrated Sunday Herald* featured the correspondence in an article headed 'Art and War – Noted Sculptor's Exemption'. The paper canvassed artists and writers on their views, all of which happened to be anti-Epstein. 'That any artist's life should be considered so valuable that those in power are prepared to offer him exemption from the military duties and sacrifices which fall to the lot of other men is a new and surprising departure,' wrote Sir Philip Burne-Jones, son of the painter Sir Edward Burne-Jones.

It is surely a good omen for the civilisation of the world . . . But here a pitfall awaits . . . Who is to be the greatly favoured individual and before what tribunal shall his merits receive confirmation . . . it is essential that such high distinction should be reserved only for one or two of the nobles in the land and should not be squandered upon the popular exponent of a . . . passing fashion or the favourite of a clique.

G. K. Chesterton, who had made no secret of his anti-Semitism, commented, 'It seems to me a dangerous principle to say that because a man is a great artist he should not share the ordinary responsibilities of citizenship. The principle undoubtedly is that real national need is of annihilating superiority to any art.' Frank Brangwyn, ARA, a painter of murals, made a curious assertion: 'The point that struck me about the Epstein case is the greater the artist, the greater the patriot. I don't want to criticise Epstein but you can judge from what I say what my feelings are.' A Captain Adrian Jones, well known for his equestrian sculpture, weighed in:

'I do not think it right to those who have fought and died in the British Army that anyone should be treated in that fashion. I know something about art as well as sculpture and most of Epstein's work, in my view, is not all that it is claimed to be. There is no art or elegance or anything in it.'[32]

The newspaper that had first attacked Epstein's Strand statues, the *Evening Standard*, mounted a similar campaign, and minor artists wrote in to belittle Epstein's work with gusto and to decry the decision to exempt him from military service. Epstein was not isolated in artistic circles in seeking immunity. The Bloomsbury set were opposed to war and managed to sidestep conscription with the minimum of public attention. For example, Duncan Grant and his friend David (Bunny) Garnett worked as farm labourers on a relative's farm. Epstein, of course, did insist on his importance as an artist, which was very un-English and very unfortunate for him.

His enemies had done their work well. On 14 June, four days after the letters had appeared in the *Illustrated Sunday Herald*, a question was asked in the House. A Colonel C. Lowther asked Mr McPherson, the Under-Secretary of State, whether Mr Epstein the sculptor had been exempted from active military service on the grounds of his importance in the world of art; and, if so, who was responsible for this assertion? Mr McPherson ducked the question of Epstein's importance in the world of art. He replied that Epstein had been refused exemption by the local tribunal but that on appeal he was granted three months' exemption. But the Military Representative had claimed leave to appeal against Epstein and that appeal was now pending. In the end, Epstein's enemies and the military triumphed. Professional jealousy was, of course, one of the motives for the remarkable outpouring of spite, but one cannot overlook the anti-Semitism, xenophobia and sexual jealousy of the artists who ganged up against him. Epstein's awesome arrogance did not excuse their malice.

While the military were making up their minds whether or not Jacob Epstein could be spared from the army, he went off to his bungalow at Pett Level. 'I had to get away for a few days and am here in blessed peace with Mrs E.,' he wrote to Van Dieren on a postcard dated 18 June 1917. 'I shall get what holiday I can and be up in London before long.'[33]

Epstein's love affair with Meum was at its peak; that he could find peace with Margaret suggests how utterly devoted and strangely understanding she was. For both of them Epstein's work was of supreme importance. At the time he was occupied with a study of Van Dieren. He had admired the Dutchman's head since they first met in 1915 and saw in it 'a quality of force allied to something mystical'. He continued to work until the last moment. Despite attempts by both Margaret and finally Epstein himself to arrange for a secondment to the American Army as an artist, Epstein was called up to the British Army. 'My enemies have at last succeeded in forcing me into the army,' he told Quinn.

> I have not been averse to joining, but ever since I've seen how eager my professional brothers are to get me in I've taken a different view of the matter. To be attacked in the press is almost my daily portion. I loom too large, for our feeble small folk of the brush and chisel. I consider my life in England as a sculptor a failure.[34]

He repeated the hope he so often expressed: 'My ambition has always been to do great works.' For the small folk he derided, his ambition was overweening.

Epstein was not, however, entirely honest with Quinn or himself about his attitude to war. He had loathed it since boyhood, when he came under the influence of men like Edward Ordway of the Anti-Imperialist League. His position as a naturalized American Jew made it impossible for him to keep out of the army, but the experience of serving in it would be disastrous. By the end of September 1917, Private Epstein of the 38th Royal Fusiliers, a Jewish regiment, was stationed at Crownhill barracks, Plymouth, having given up the 'priesthood' of the artist, and loathing his daily routine of square-bashing and forming fours.

He went into the army at the worst possible time. His closest friend and ally in the art world, T. E. Hulme, had been killed in

'I already had a reputation for wildness; why I don't quite know.' Epstein on his youth in London.

Epstein and Margaret after forty years of marriage.

Margaret Dunlop in a family group, standing (*left*) behind her father. Margaret divorced her first husband to marry Epstein.

Epstein adored beautiful women. After giving birth to Epstein's first child, Dorothy Lindsell-Stewart became a professional dancer.

Kathleen Garman, the sculptor's lover for over thirty years bore him three children.

At his country cottage near Epping Forest, with his eldest daughter Peggy Jean and their dog.

The façade of the BMA building in the Strand.

Maternity, Epstein's tender study of motherhood, outraged Edwardian society and provoked a scandal that lasted for thirty years.

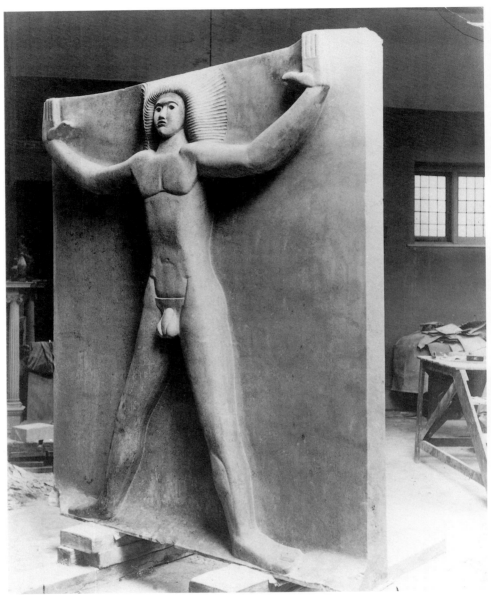

The imperious *Sun God* relief was probably designed for a large temple,
set in the Sussex Downs, 'a sort of twentieth-century Stonehenge' envisaged
by Eric Gill and Epstein.

Both of these fine carvings, *Elemental* and the voluptuous *Maternity* express Epstein's fascination with the process of generation and his reverence for life.

In *The Sick Child*, the artist captures the vulnerability of his eldest daughter. He made fifteen portraits in all of Peggy Jean.

Epstein's elegant carving, *The Sunflower*, contrasts with the exquisitely earthy bronze, *Isobel*. Isobel Nicholas, Epstein's model and studio assistant, bore him a son. Later she became an accomplished artist in her own right.

'I think of this bust as a crowning piece' Epstein wrote of the subtle bronze, the *Fifth Portrait of Mrs Jacob Epstein*.

To Epstein, *Albert Einstein* resembled the aging Rembrandt. He sculpted the famous scientist in 1933, when Einstein was taking refuge in England.

action in France that month. While he was home on sick leave, Hulme had been preparing the first critical assessment of his friend's work, and Epstein had been looking forward to it. 'I'd rather Hulme did it than anyone else, as he is sane and whatever he writes will be free from journalism and sentimentality.'[35] Hulme's critical writings had boosted the avant-garde's opinion of Epstein's carvings and influenced his work: a book would have been crucial to his development. Besides, Hulme was a close friend, a man Epstein liked and admired. His death only confirmed Epstein's horror of war.

Even when Epstein was safely in army barracks, a loyal conspiracy of friends and art lovers battled to get him out. Barely a week after he was conscripted, Cecil L. Phillips of the Leicester Galleries wrote to Sir Alfred Mond at the National War Museum, arguing that Epstein's *Tin Hat*, the head of a soldier that he had made with the intention of demonstrating his ability as a war artist, deserved to be in the museum. With its rugged strength, the slightly contemptuous look, not without a sense of humour, the head seemed to be, he wrote, typical of the English soldier in wartime. Two months later, in December 1917, Sir Martin Conway, the director of the Imperial War Museum, wrote to Sir William Robertson at the War Office proposing that Epstein should make 'a series of typical heads serving in the various contingents of the British Army . . . Jews, Turks, infidels and all the rest'.[36] Although Conway made it clear that Epstein's artistic ability was outstanding, he managed subtly to class the artist with all the riff-raff. Since the Imperial War Museum was entitled to send two artists to the front to make a record of the war, the outcome seemed certain. Epstein got wind of the proposed transfer and sent a letter to Shaw asking him to use his influence with the bigwigs at the IWM. All seemed set fair for Epstein to do some valuable work for the war effort. Suddenly and inexplicably, in January 1918 Epstein's upgrading to war artist was abruptly cancelled.

Two letters taken out of Epstein's file as confidential, and still missing from the Imperial War Museum's records, hold the secret. Sir George Frampton, ARA, a well-regarded sculptor, wrote to

Major-General Donald about Epstein. The contents were damaging enough to persuade Major-General Donald to object to the employment of Epstein and Field Marshal Sir Douglas Haig to cancel his transfer.[37]

From his wife, mistress and other friends, Epstein heard rumours and reports about the efforts made to transfer him. He was in a constant state of anxiety and tension. To become an official war artist, Epstein had to obtain a commission. After four months in Plymouth barracks he managed to get himself on a preparatory course for the OTC, firing on the range in the Cornish countryside. He detested his existence. 'It is a life of mental rot and for me of a particular kind of exasperation, knowing as I do the forces that worked against me and that have been so successful in achieving this object: my decease as an active artist,' he wrote to Van Dieren early in February. However, he found the elemental Cornish coast at Tregantle wild and beautiful, and the life was a little freer.

> We live in huts and I prefer them as there isn't a prison-like air about them as barracks have, with their gates and sentries . . . we have had wild, stormy weather and I love to see . . . nature at any rate in wild freedom, no seargant [*sic*] can bowl the wind into silence or form forces with the rain . . . I've been told that there is a very special opposition to me at the War Office, this is a compliment.[38]

It was, if not a compliment, certainly a distinction for a private soldier in the First World War to be feared and hated for his imaginative power and his refusal, or inability, to conform. But from boyhood Epstein had learned to become angry and not depressed by injustice. 'I am filled with rage when I think of the work I might have done in the last four months. I am wealth squandered and wasted.'[39] He was granted leave when he finished his training course, reunited with Margaret and with Meum, happy to be home working and seeing old friends. Private Epstein was noticed at the Café Royal one night when he was on leave drinking with two Guards officers. They were reprimanded for the breach of discipline; their name was Sitwell.

When Epstein rejoined his unit on 3 March 1918 he discovered that he was due to sail to Palestine from Southampton on the 5th. He must have telephoned Margaret, because she wrote immediately to the Imperial War Museum, thinking that the orders might have been a departmental error, since Lord Beaverbrook, Minister of Information, had asked for his release. But there was no mistake. Private Epstein 'could not be spared'. On the day the regiment left Plymouth, Epstein went missing. He was found wandering round Dartmoor and detained under medical observation, wretched and *distrait*.

The case of Private Epstein took up the time of an extraordinary number of prominent people in the first four months of 1918, and demonstrates his anomalous position in society. He was the bugbear of exhibitionists like de Vere Cole and many minor artists who did not attract either his prominence in the art world or his level of publicity; and he was hated by officialdom for his flouting of authority and lack of enthusiasm for the war effort. At the same time, sincere art lovers, friends and lovers supported him beyond the call. Lord Beaverbrook, primed by Muirhead Bone, an official war artist himself, was trying hard to get Epstein transferred to the Canadian forces, encouraged by the Duke of Marlborough. As Epstein's regiment was due to embark for Palestine in April, the flurry of letters and cables about him accelerated. C. P. Scott, the editor of the *Manchester Guardian*, was to speak to Lloyd George the moment he returned from France. Lady Randolph Churchill cabled Lady Clementine to see if Winston could help. Margaret Epstein wrote urgently to Beaverbook from Guilford Street. Perhaps the most unusual appeal came from Meum in a letter dated 25 March 1918 to Sir Martin Conway at the Imperial War Museum:

Dear Sir
As I know that you have tried to get Mr Jacob Epstein from the War Office to do work in France for the British War

Museum, I want to tell you privately that Lord Beaverbrook
has been trying for the last two months to get Mr Epstein for
the propaganda Department to do artistic work for the British
and Canadians . . . Perhaps you could encourage or help
Beaverbrook. Mr Epstein is at present in a military convalescent hospital recovering from internal inflammation [*sic*]
cystitis and he is under orders to proceed to Palestine to join
his Regiment . . . when he gets out in a few days. Let this
urgency be my excuse for my letter to you whom I do not
know personally. The loss of a great artist's time doing transport manual work in Palestine when he might be doing works
for all the world which will live for ever, will be – if it is
allowed to happen – a disaster to the art history of England
and a scandal to be spoken of in all that will be written about
Epstein and his work after the war. The English are too apt to
throw stones at the man who thinks much or in a new way
about art or science or war and will call it 'bad form'. They
caricatured Rodin as being 'not a gentleman' and they have
so far refused Epstein a commission in the Propaganda
because they say he is 'untidy' and they order him overseas.
Hoping you will be able to do something to prevent this
ludicrous decision being carried out.
I am sincerely yours
Dorothy Lindsell-Stewart[40]

Meum's letter was both courageous and cogent; it demonstrates
Epstein's ability to attract extraordinary devotion from his extraordinary women.

From an undated letter to Van Dieren, one gains a sense of
Epstein's baffled fury at his plight.

I feel of course very hopeless especially after Beaverbrook's
failure. I believe that opposition to my transfer comes from
this blessed Jewish regiment I'm in . . . I am at present imprisoned in the detention room, I hope not for long. I have passed
through a severe mental crisis as you can imagine and am

under observation of the medical office. My position . . . is horrible in the extreme. I have to submit myself to men who regard my attitude as a heinous crime. They know by this time how much I loathe the army and themselves and their ambitions, but they have me tight and look upon me only as a schoolmaster regards a recalcitrant youth. I spend bad days and worse nights. How horrible that what amounts to my incarceration for an indefinite future should be looked upon as a right, almost fit, punishment for my sins as an artist . . . It took half a dozen Holborn grocers to make me out a normal citizen, the 'exceptional creatures'.[41]

Epstein is presumably referring to the tribunal, but since his own father was a grocer who opposed his career as an artist, it seems that the rigours of army life were causing him to relive the battles of his adolescence.

When Quinn wrote to Epstein, telling him that his father had called to enquire about him and suggesting that he should write to the family, Epstein was unmoved by the appeal. In April he was transferred to Mount Tovey Military Hospital in Plymouth and remained there until he was invalided out of the army on 25 July 1918.

The nature of Epstein's illness is unclear: he told Quinn that he had suffered 'a complete breakdown' and was not allowed to see letters. He was obviously deeply depressed, disappointed and lonely. He was not a man's man; he was totally uninterested in sport, even less so in war; he had no small talk and no interests outside the arts. He was also argumentative, didactic and incapable of disguising his disdain for anyone who did not share his priorities. Ever since he had left his parental home in New York as a youth, he had pleased himself how he lived. War had deprived him of his calling, of his liberty and of his friend T. E. Hulme. Hulme's manuscript for a book on Epstein had also disappeared. Epstein was inclined to see plots and conspiracies against him everywhere and thought the manuscript had been stolen. If he was over-suspicious, it was hardly surprising.

He did make ten fine drawings of wounded men during his enforced idleness in hospital. Throughout his ten months in the army either Epstein or his wife corresponded with Quinn, sending photographs of his sculpture, negotiating prices, cabling for money and sending works of art off to the collector. Quinn had had a serious abdominal operation and Epstein, back home, had written to send his good wishes for recovery. 'Mrs Epstein', he wrote, 'has been keeping things together for me.' Back home in Guilford Street, working on 'small study heads and a portrait of my wife', he longed for some great work to stretch his powers to the full. He hoped, he told Quinn, for an opportunity to create 'some great scheme of war memorial or shrine'.[42]

7

Casting Off

THE END OF THE Great War left artists, like the rest of society, confused and unsettled. The brief burst of artistic ferment which gave rise to Wyndham Lewis's Vorticist movement spent itself; even the Bloomsbury artists and writers were geographically dispersed and spiritually demoralized. Epstein was now isolated, no longer allied to any artistic group. Fortunately, just before the war ended, a great joy entered his life: the birth of his first child, Peggy Jean. She was born to Meum in Paris on 31 October 1918. Margaret and Epstein were both there, Epstein having come to France to portray war heroes. The war was almost over and he created only one, a fine bust of Sergeant David Ferguson Hunter, VC, now in the Imperial War Museum, but his main concern was his baby daughter.

'To have a child to work from was delightful,' he wrote of the studies of his baby. 'The little Peggy Jean was a real source of inspiration. I never tired of watching her and to watch her was for me, to work from her. To make studies in clay of all her moods; and when she tired and fell asleep, there was something new to do.' He made fifteen portraits of Peggy Jean in all, the first at three months and the last when she was a young woman of seventeen, more than of any other model. He obviously adored her.

Meum seemed content to allow Margaret and Epstein to bring her child up. She was just beginning a career as a dancer – a dream she had always held – and she had no means of supporting a child. As Epstein's favourite model, Meum, who was extremely photogenic, had gained invaluable experience. 'Miss Meum Stewart', reported the *Sketch* in July 1918,

is the original of a series of marble busts and a painting by Mr
Jacob Epstein which created considerable comment when
shown at an exhibition of the International Society of
Sculptors, Painters and Engravers . . . [She] is of course well
known on the stage. We understand that she has been engaged
by Mr Charles Cochran to appear in his production,
rehearsals for which are in progress.[1]

Meum was to enjoy a successful career in musical comedy, but the
Sketch's photograph of her in a loose-fitting gown was remarkable
for more than her grace. She was five months pregnant with
Epstein's child; soon after the baby was born she went back to the
stage. During 1918 Epstein created two portraits of Meum which
reveal her air of languid distinction: a mask and an unusual three-
quarter-length figure holding a fan. 'Auntie' Meum remained a
friend of the family and continued to visit them all; Epstein's
painting of her hung in their home.[2]

A description of Epstein modelling in clay around this time was
written by Clare Sheridan, a first cousin of Winston Churchill.
Rich and well connected, she was an aspiring sculptor who had
wanted Epstein to take her on as a pupil. Towards the end of the
year, after the Armistice, she inveigled him to luncheon and
commissioned him to make a bust of her. Her lunch guests were
wealthy and eccentric, and perhaps the sculptor was a little ill at
ease with the minor aristocracy at the table. Sheridan noted the
difference in his behaviour when he came to model her:

Epstein at work was a being transformed. Not only was his
method interesting to watch, but the man himself, his movement, his stooping and bending, his leaping back, poised and
then rushing forward, his trick of passing clay from one hand
to the other over the top of his head while he scrutinised his
work from all angles, was the equivalent of a dance . . . He
wore a butcher-blue tunic and his black curly hair stood on
end; he was beautiful when he worked . . . he did not model
with his fingers but built up his planes slowly by means of

small pieces of clay, applied with a flat wooden tool . . . It is his method of building up that gives Epstein's surfaces their vibrating and pulsating quality of flesh . . . Without him ever suspecting it, I acquired from merely watching him, knowledge that revolutionised my work.[3]

Epstein's technique was no longer to model smooth faces as he had done with some of the earlier portraits: the surface was rougher and freer, allowing the sculptor more opportunity to interpret the sitter's character and respond to it. As he once explained, 'It is the rough surface that gives both character and lines to the face . . . No face is entirely round and smooth. The face is made up of numberless small planes and it is a study of where those planes begin and end, their direction, that makes the individual head.'[4]

In 1919 the Café Royal, somewhat fly-blown and seedy, was still *the* place to meet for artists, writers and models. Augustus John, a reluctant hero, had joined the Canadian Army as a war artist, and was given an honorary commission as a major. At the Café Royal, in khaki, John was a popular figure; he and Epstein were often rivals for the services of popular models. Margaret Epstein used to warn her 'girls' not to visit John.[5] As a couple they were genuinely concerned with the models' welfare. Betty May, a beautiful girl from the slums, only five foot tall, relates in her autobiography how Epstein approached her at the Café Royal, saying, 'You are very young to be here.'[6] He took her home to Guilford Street to tea and she became a great friend of the family. Epstein only agreed to model her when she was older and often advised her about her work.

During 1919 he occupied himself mainly in modelling saleable heads. It was taking him a long time to recover from the aftermath of the war, which had sapped his strength and his spirits. In the summer he suffered a severe attack of neuritis in his right arm and shoulder and was unable to work for several weeks. For years, however, he had been brooding on a large bronze.

Epstein's *The Risen Christ*, his first work of a specifically religious nature, was begun just before he was called up. He started by working on a study of his friend Bernard Van Dieren, who was ill in bed at the time, suffering from kidney stones. 'Watching the head so spiritual and worn with suffering, I thought I would like to make a mask of him. I hurried home and returned with clay and made a mask which I immediately recognized as the Christ head with its short beard, its pitying accusing eyes and the lofty and broad brow, denoting great intellectual strength.' Epstein uses the word 'recognized' as though he was in a state of trance himself. 'I drew the whole figure of Christ in the mask. With haste I began to add the torso and the arms and hands with the accusing finger. This I then cast and had, as a certainty, the beginning of my statue.' Epstein set up the bust with an armature – a structure upon which clay is supported – for the body. 'I established the whole figure down to the feet. The statue rose swathed in clothes, a pillar firmly set on two naked feet – Christ risen supernatural, a portent for all time.'

That a Jew should tackle the subject at all is astonishing. Epstein had spent a long time brooding on the subject and worked on it for over three years. He had to abandon it during his war service, and by the time he took it up again his model, Van Dieren, had returned to Holland, still ailing. The sculptor therefore recruited two friends – the Leeds-based artist Jacob Kramer and an aspiring musician, Cecil Gray – to pose for the face, hands and feet. Epstein exhibited the statue at the Leicester Galleries in February 1920. When he came to write his autobiography in 1939, he insisted that his *Christ* still represented his intention:

It stands and accuses the world for its grossness, inhumanity, cruelty and beastliness. I should like to remodel this Christ. I should like to make it hundreds of feet high and set it up on some high place where all could see it and where it would give out its warning to all lands. The Jew – the Galilean – condemns our wars and warns us that 'Shalom, Shalom' must be still the watchword between man and man.

Epstein was an innately religious man, although he subscribed to no organised religion. He read the Bible, both the Old Testament and the New, all through his life, and he grappled with the search for significance. In the 'wrath and pity of the Son of Man', he found a potent warning against the horror and slaughter of war. His interpretation of Christ emphasized 'intellect as well as sentiment; power and a rare sense of justice as well as compassion and forgiveness'. Epstein felt that Christ's weakness and passivity had been exaggerated and the 'sterner elements' repressed or passed over.

As a Jew from an Orthodox East European background, he would have been aware of the superstitious horror with which some of his co-religionists regarded all Christian images; memories of Cossack atrocities at Easter, when Jewish villages were stormed and pillaged, remained vivid. In Epstein's perception, Jesus, the Jew, assumed the guise of an imperious rabbi who led his people with stern love. But he entitled his sculpture *The Risen Christ* – which implies that he could conceive of Jesus as divine. Perhaps unconsciously Epstein had created an image in *The Risen Christ* which demonstrated his alienation from his roots, and from his father's house. In the urbane setting of the Leicester Galleries, the gaunt, accusing figure of Christ, seven feet high, dominated the room and shocked visitors accustomed to palely sentimental images of Jesus as exemplified in Holman Hunt's *The Light of the World*. The Christ Epstein revealed was as alien to the English as he was himself, and it raised a storm of abuse.

'Is Mr Epstein of British blood and is he by faith a Christian?' asked an 'artist' in the *Daily Graphic* of 3 March 1920. 'The name Epstein suggests that the sculptor is addressing an audience of British Christians without the necessary psychic equipment. He has indeed made a terrible mess of it.' A correspondent signing herself 'An American woman and an English officer's wife' deplored 'the wild deformity of the skull, the deliberate defiling of Christ's characteristics by a degenerated imagination . . . If this monstrosity were alive it would be in an asylum for mental and moral degradation.' The worst scourging of Epstein came from the Roman Catholic Church, in the person of Father Bernard Vaughan

(a crusading priest who was to do battle with Marie Stopes over
the question of birth control). Father Vaughan set himself up as
arbiter of the canons of correct taste in depicting the Christ figure.
Artists through the ages, he proclaimed, had portrayed Christ as a
beautiful, dignified figure, and any portrait that failed 'to express
tenderness, dignity, calmness and sweetness with overwhelming
majesty' must be ruthlessly cast out. Confronted with Epstein's
Christ, Father Vaughan

> felt ready to cry out with indignation that in this Christian
> England there should be exhibited the figure of Christ which
> suggested to me some degraded Chaldean or African which
> wore the appearance of an Asiatic-American or Hun-Jew,
> which reminded me of some emaciated Hindu, or a badly
> grown Egyptian swathed in the cerements of the grave. I call
> it positively wicked and insulting to perpetrate such a travesty
> of the Risen Christ.[7]

There were many detractors, among them the writer John
Galsworthy, whom Epstein noticed emerging from the room where
the *Christ* was on view, red-faced and with clenched fists. Epstein
believed that it was a matter of class, and he maintained that it was
the upper middle class who resented his work the most. An old
lady who visited the Leicester Galleries summed up the genuine
distress felt by some Christians. 'I can never forgive Mr Epstein
for his representation of Our Lord,' she told Oliver Brown of the
Leicester Galleries; 'it's so un-English.'[8] But by that time the artist
had offended conventional English sensibilities on politics, sex
and religion.

Writing in the *Nation*, the critic John Middleton Murry put
forward the most thoughtful view of Epstein's bronzes. The sculptor, he argued, had a technical mastery unequalled in the age as
well as a 'powerful and original genius',

> a genius which by its own limitations seems superbly fitted
> for the mastery of stone. Should he be sidetracked into

portraiture by the necessity of having to fill a role? Here is a man of whom it could safely be said that were he to be given a pyramid to decorate, his work would have congruity and significance. Let him then carve our monuments and leave to others the task of immortalising the houris of the hour.[9]

By that time Epstein was the most prominent sculptor in Britain; although every major work of his brought vicious attacks from the critics, to exhibit Epstein drew the crowds. The Leicester Galleries were delighted with the numbers of visitors who passed through their turnstiles to see the Epstein exhibition in 1920. Before it closed in March, Apsley Cherry-Garrard, the Antarctic explorer who had been a member of Scott's expedition to the South Pole, purchased *The Risen Christ* for £2,000. This meant that Epstein's financial difficulties were temporarily overcome.

By the spring of 1920, he was gradually recovering from the oppression of the war years; in March, restless and eager to see friends in Montparnasse again and to hunt out gems of non-European art for his collection, he returned to Paris, his second home. Margaret stayed in England to look after Peggy Jean, and he asked Cecil Gray, his musician friend, to accompany him. Modigliani had tragically died two months earlier aged thirty-six, and it is probably not coincidental that Epstein decided to visit the great stone quarries at Carrara, where the Italian made his first attempts at sculpture. Like Modigliani, Epstein tried to find a suitable studio in Carrara but was unsuccessful. With Cecil Gray he visited Florence and Rome then travelled down the coast, via Livorno (Modigliani's home town), to La Spezia, Genoa and Nice. Gladys Deacon, Epstein's patron and friend, had a villa near Nice and wanted 'to talk to Epstein about art' before she gave up her independence to marry the now divorced Duke of Marlborough. Epstein stayed in the warm south with her for a week before returning home to his wife and the 'dear little chick'.

The first book on Epstein, a critical appreciation written by his friend Van Dieren, was published in May 1921. Epstein carefully monitored both the text and illustrations, fifty photographs, before publication. Van Dieren's opaque prose lacked the authority of the late T. E. Hulme, who had prepared a monograph on Epstein before being killed in action. But his opening sentence was prophetic: 'The world does not forgive talent.'[10] Epstein wrote to Quinn from Guilford Street in September in disgust to tell him that the book had been savagely reviewed:

> London is the city of intrigue and in the world of art, the char-latan and social snob rule supreme . . . although there was a strong desire expressed both at the Tate Gallery meetings and also in the press, no work of mine was purchased by the Tate Gallery . . . the art culture of this London . . . is controlled by harlots and pederasts . . . I think of these things only occa-sionally . . . I have now a little girl Peggy Jean, of whom I've done several studies. I have my family and there are the wonderful things at the British Museum and the National Gallery which cannot be seen too often.[11]

Ever since Epstein's first visit to London as a student, the British Museum had been a source of inspiration to him. He was amazed that he never met his colleagues there. 'I discovered that sculptors would be rather ashamed to be seen in the British Museum. In fact it would be considered a lack of originality to be discovered there. Fancy a dramatist or poet willingly eschewing Shakespeare and the Elizabethans or a composer of music deliberately avoiding Beethoven.' Epstein took a personal, almost proprietorial interest in the treasures of the museum and was alarmed when he noticed that the statue of Demeter of Cnidus had been tampered with. When he saw workmen 'manhandling' the Elgin Marbles with soap and scrubbing brush he felt bound to speak out. 'Sir,' he wrote to *The Times* on 2 May 1921,

> All those who care for antique sculpture view with astonish-ment and dismay the present policy followed by the British Museum authorities in restoring the Marbles, that is working them up with new plaster noses, etc.

I have remarked with growing alarm marble after marble so treated during the last year. I felt the futility of protesting and so held my peace, but now that the incredible crime of 'restoring' the head of the Demeter of Cnidus has at last been committed, the atrocity calls for immediate protest.

No doubt the Museum authorities do not really like the Marbles in their possession, but why they should translate the masterpieces into something more nearly approaching the Albert Moore ideal of Greek [Moore was a Victorian decorative and mural painter] passes my understanding. The Demeter has not only been improved with a new plaster nose, but to bring the rest of the head into consistency with the nose, the whole face has been scraped and cleaned, thus destroying the mellow golden patina of centuries . . . How long are these vandals to have in their 'care' the golden treasury of sculpture, which at least they might leave untouched.

Epstein signed himself 'Yours respectfully'.

His boldness in challenging the authorities was met with hostility from academic quarters in an attempt to 'put him in his place'. Epstein wrote that later he was 'looked on askance' if he entered the rooms in the British Museum where antiquities were gathered. He was subsequently entirely vindicated in his concern about the effect of restoring the Marbles. His knowledge of art was profound, and experts today acknowledge that his personal collection contained 'some of the greatest, most famous and widely illustrated works of African and Pacific sculpture ever to reach Europe'.[12] To call the curators of the British Museum 'vandals' was, however, to bait the Establishment; and neither Epstein nor Margaret could resist the sport, no matter what the cost.

Epstein had an ambitious plan to create a group depicting the Deposition from the Cross that year, and he invited the artist Jacob Kramer, one of his models for *The Risen Christ*, to pose as St John. 'You could be of immense use to me and I hope you will give me an opportunity to make a study of you. I would want to do your head, torso and arms. In return I will sit to you and you can make drawings or an oil study.' Epstein did not complete the group, but the bust he made of his friend and colleague reveals the sculptor at his most perceptive. He was always keen to have his portraits 'quivering with life', but in Kramer's case he actually had to try to calm him down. Kramer 'was a model who seemed to be on fire . . . He was extraordinarily nervous. Energy seemed to leap into his hair as he sat.' Epstein's portrait of the pained and noble features of the highly strung painter, a man he described as a 'typical bohemian', conveys the intensity and thwarted idealism of both sitter and artist.

That year his life seemed becalmed: his dream of carving great monuments balked, his love affair with Meum tamed into domesticity with Peggy Jean, their daughter, now living *en famille* with the Epsteins. He was over forty, tired and still struggling. Perhaps he was ready for new inspiration.

Epstein first noticed Kathleen Garman in the Harlequin night-café in Beak Street, a small restaurant started by a former waiter at the Café Royal, 'almost gypsy in its freedom from conventional restraints'. Here the very beautiful Garman sisters were eating an evening meal. They were girls of the new 'flapper' generation, from a highly respected family in Wednesbury, south of Walsall, where their Victorian father, Walter Chancellor Garman, was a medical officer of health. The two young women had broken away from their home in Oakeswell House, a medieval manor house, to sample the excitement of London and study the arts. Mary, the elder sister, wanted to take up painting; Kathleen, a gifted pianist, wished to study music. Both were determined to get away from 'all the curates our parents wanted us to marry'.[13] Their father, a strict disciplinarian, was furious, and at first refused to give his daughters an allowance. They responded with great spirit by getting jobs driving a Lyons van delivering bread, until their father relented. Then they rented a studio at 13 Regent Square, began their lessons and drifted on the fringes of the art world.

That August evening at the Harlequin café Epstein stared across at Kathleen with such longing that she was intrigued; eventually he sent a note over with the waiter, inviting the young women to join him. They glanced at the message, laughed and strolled out. A few nights later Kathleen was eating alone at the café when Epstein came in. He invited her to join him, to sit for him; and they fell hopelessly in love with each other. They spent the night together and the next day Epstein began to sculpt his love.

Epstein, almost forty-one, found Kathleen's looks, her reckless spirit and cultivated mind utterly captivating. As a youth he had had no time for courting. Both Adele, his first love in the ghetto, and Jacob himself had been too taken up with forging a career; there had been a loving friendship with Bernard Gussow and then his relationship with Margaret, his wife, the older woman who had cared for him and given up her life to him. The other women had fallen into his lap.

Kathleen was different. She was young, just twenty, respectable and marriageable. Dark, with an olive skin, deep brown eyes and a full and graceful figure, Kathleen was physically the type of woman that Epstein loved to model. But he was spoiled, used to having his own way, and to possess Kathleen became an obsession. For the first time he had found a woman who refused to be subject to his will and his passion. Kathleen had a caring family and there was no question that she would become a part of the Epstein entourage.

The love affair was partly conducted by phone calls from the Café Royal and messages left with waiters at the Harlequin café or by post. Epstein's letters from those early days convey something of his ecstasy, suspicion and frustration. This one is headed simply 'Friday':

I wrote you yesterday hurriedly and feeling somewhat wretched. This naturally the result of hearing some gossip about you. Then I could hear nothing of what you said on that miserable Café Royal phone in the evening. Why do we meet to part and yet it is necessary. Some day it may not be. How well you know me. What you write is true and from the moment I meet you my elation is equal to yours and my happiness so genuine that you can easily discern it.

Naturally I've been annoyed at the postponement of the bronze for the Tate; I had been counting on it for a sale. In a fortnight I am to be visited by a committee from the Leicester City Art Gallery and perhaps something will happen then. I have to think of these things as the accumulation of my debts quickly rids me of any money I may make. Later I hope to do some portraits which will pay me; I pray the sitters will be interesting. I will be on the present work for at least a month more. I haven't forgotten about the Rembrandt [possibly a print or photograph Epstein had ordered for Kathleen], but it has not come yet.

Write me: your letters console me and dissipate the things I hear and often imagine to be true. What a lack of faith in myself to be thrown from the heights to which you raise me and realize what a mockery our love is. My hell is almost as intense as the heaven I've been in. When you say they are liars I believe you. I want your love and without it I would be the unhappiest man on earth.[14]

Epstein was a proud man who defended his independence ferociously, but with Kathleen he was the supplicant, tormented by her absence yet aware of the enormity of his demands. His love letters from the time he met her until the end of his life are written in white heat.

I have your note and also the news that you arrived home. I love to read what you feel and that you know my happiness was so extreme that were I to die then and there I would be an image of supreme happiness in death. I still live in the nights, the 3 nights we were together. I express myself readily enough with you but to write of it is impossible in me, our nearness, your glances and every touch of you fills me with joy & that is what makes it difficult for us to be together for long. I will try now and finish the head I am on: even unfinished I think it will be beautiful, perhaps owing to its subject [surely a head of Kathleen]. The true artist should make anything wonderful. When I look on you and am with you I see the most wonderful things and they can't be but a memory with me. No more. This I regret. Will I some day get to work on the many things that being with you inspires me to work on. It seems that the Manchester Art Gallery are trying at last to get one of my bronzes . . . but they started this 10 years ago. What can you expect though from a committee with Todds and Dodds on it. Write and tell me how you are. The Harlequin has one use anyway; otherwise the place is detestable to me.[15]

Epstein began work on his first head of Kathleen the day after he met her. He portrayed her as a visionary, her eyes rapt, a hostage to the future, and he nicknamed the bronze 'Joan of Arc'.

Margaret knew of all Epstein's diversions, but this time she sensed that the involvement was deeper. So stoical when Epstein made love to his luscious models or spent his money on collecting African sculpture, she now became wildly jealous. To Margaret, aware of every nuance of Epstein's moods, his infatuation was a torment. The suspicion that Kathleen was becoming his muse as well as his mistress was unbearable. Nearing fifty, Margaret was finding the complications of life with Epstein increasingly diffi-cult. When the twenty-year-old Roy Campbell, the future poet, fell in love with Mary Garman and came to live with the sisters, Margaret resorted to bribing waiters from the Harlequin to spy on the trio, hoping to prove that Kathleen was living in a ménage à trois. Epstein's jealousy of Kathleen was fanned by Margaret, who told or repeated stories about her keeping company with other men. Yet his love affair with Kathleen was no secret among the artists: Augustus John, Wyndham Lewis and Jacob Kramer were among the guests at Mary Garman and Roy Campbell's wedding celebration at the Harlequin.

By January 1922 Epstein was working on a second head of Kathleen; this time the portrait is frankly sensuous, with Kathleen's eyes half closed, her lips languorously parted. Margaret could have had no illusions about her husband's feelings. Furious, she enlisted Meum in her fight to detach Epstein from Kathleen. 'Dear Meum,' she wrote on 23 February 1922,

> I was amused to hear that the effect of your glances in the Café Royal made Kathleen Garman, Epstein's latest, resolve to meet him elsewhere tonight. The two were in the Café Royal with Kathleen's sister Mary of the Zulu hair, and her husband, the extremely useful Campbell, will twist your neck if they think you are a danger to the pre-eminence of their sister over all Epstein's other mistresses!
>
> If you have time at 2.45, I'm passing your door in a taxi to go to hospital. Come with me.[16]

The reason for Margaret's visit to hospital is unknown, but her note was bizarre − a message from a wife to a mistress, whose daughter she had virtually adopted, about a second mistress. By this time Margaret, respected by even the wildest of Epstein's models, was half crazed with jealousy. 'Concentrate on Epstein' was her favourite saying at home. As one mistress recorded: 'She exists solely for her husband, his interests are hers, his genius is the only god she recognizes and she deems the world well lost for his sake.'[17] Margaret had made Epstein the centre of her life and was content to live in his shadow, provided that his need of her remained constant.

Epstein was anguished: torn between his ardent love for Kathleen and his reliance on and deep feeling for his wife. After six months of the affair, Margaret could bear it no longer. She sent for Kathleen to come to Guilford Street. A brave and wayward young woman, Kathleen was, one suspects, enjoying the drama she had created. She had not anticipated the passion of Epstein's wife. Once Kathleen was inside, Margaret locked the door, took out a pistol from inside her long skirt and shot Kathleen in the left clavicle, aiming, no doubt, at her heart. The wounded girl crawled from the house bleeding. Fortunately, Kathleen's brother Douglas was passing the house, perhaps waiting for her, and he rushed her to hospital.

According to her daughter, the scar from the wound never disappeared and Kathleen was never able to wear short sleeves again. But, being young and strong, she completely recovered her health. Neither Kathleen nor her parents pressed charges against Margaret. When Mrs Garman, a wise and devout woman, came to visit her daughter in hospital she sat quietly by the bedside holding Kathleen's hand and said not a word in reproach.[18]

Once Kathleen had recovered, the shooting incident served curiously to calm the situation. Epstein and his women accepted that he now had two families, his official wife Margaret (and unofficial daughter Peggy Jean) and Kathleen. He even evolved a routine for his domestic life. Every evening after six, when he left the studio, he visited Kathleen for an hour, bringing flowers and wine. He spent Wednesday and Saturday nights with her, although he always came home early in the morning.

During 1922, Dolores, a flamboyant, dark-haired model, known later as the 'Queen of the London studios', came to live in Guilford Street with the Epsteins so that the sculptor could make a series of studies from her. Margaret was delighted. 'As soon as she understood that I represented Epstein's inspiration she took me unto herself as something very rare and precious,' wrote Dolores in highly coloured memoirs.[19] She described Margaret as 'a largely built Scotchwoman with a mop of untidy flaming red hair, turquoise stars in her ears, wearing men's golfing shoes, knitted woollen stockings and a sleeveless black dance frock over an emerald green "woollie"'.

Margaret was hoping, of course, that Dolores would replace Kathleen, but there is no evidence to suggest that the exhibitionist model, who loved to take off her clothes, ever made love to Epstein. 'I could not insult Margaret,' Dolores said. The model saw herself as 'the High Priestess of Beauty . . . In the studio she was the devoted model, never allowing anything to interfere with posing, taking it seriously; a religious rite.'[20]

At first, when she posed for Epstein, Dolores felt nervous because the sculptor stared at her with such intensity. He would get down on his knees, crawling nearer and nearer and shading his

eyes to study the naked girl. When he began to work, rolling the
little sausages of grey clay and sticking them on the face, the
model felt as if he were stealing parts of her for his work. One
morning, when Epstein was resting, Dolores was sitting sadly,
recalling her past and wondering about her future, when she began
to weep:

> tears streamed down my cheeks, in fact I quite forgot where I
> was until the strident voice of Epstein shattered my recollec-
> tions: 'My God,' he cried, 'keep that pose, it's too wonder-
> ful!' And in the face and the figure known to the world as *The
> Weeping Woman* are to be seen my train of regrets, my broken
> dreams and my soul suffering.[21]

The sculpture of a woman wringing her hands in the grip of a
violent emotion 'pushes the expression of a dramatic movement to
the verge of caricature, but is saved by its convincing truth of
gesture, which has the intensity and purpose always found in
strong natural passion unhampered by self-consciousness', wrote a
contemporary critic.

Epstein, said Dolores, spared neither himself nor his models
while he was working. When inspiration flagged, Dolores saw him
drop his tools and return to ordinary existence 'much in the same
way that a sleeper awakens from an enchanted sleep'. For Dolores,
living with the Epsteins was an enchanted existence. 'Nothing was
considered immoral or indecent,' she recalled.[22] Epstein said that
the only indecency was in the mind.

Margaret was still desperately trying to free her husband from
Kathleen's influence and decided that a place in the country
would be ideal. Early one morning she dragged Dolores out of
bed to go house-hunting with her in Epping. 'Put a cloak over
your nightdress, tie a scarf around your head and slip on your
golden sandals,' she commanded. 'We mustn't waste a moment.'
The pair found a small cottage to rent at Baldwin's Hill near
Loughton, on a ridge above the city. Set on the edge of Epping
Forest, the cottage was also within easy reach of London. That

same evening at the Café Royal, Epstein, Margaret and Dolores enjoyed a special dinner to celebrate Dolores's discovery of the 'Shrine of the Simple life'. Dolores describes the three of them wandering through Epping Forest, dressed or undressed as the fancy seized them. 'This life of sunshine and nature was an inspiration of Mrs Epstein,' she said.[23] No doubt Margaret hoped that in Epping Forest, as at Pett Level, Epstein would find new inspiration.

At the time Epstein was badly short of funds. He was no longer able to rely on selling to Quinn; his American collector had given up buying modern British work in favour of the Paris avant-garde. His output, not surprisingly, had been affected by the dramas of the year. With his new lover Kathleen as well as Margaret and Peggy Jean to support, he needed money more than ever. The love affair with Kathleen remained intense and tormenting.

'It was terribly trying to hear you on the phone tonight,' he wrote to Kathleen at her home in Wednesbury.

> You asked me if I was happy. Are you? I am working and looking forward to you. I tried to tell you that if I dreamt of you as I do, it was only a suggestion of the reality which is the best thing I know. The last letter I wrote you was on a foggy day, last Tuesday. I went out filled with the idea of you and imagined our waking up on such a day and lying all through it together. I walked the streets and thought of you. One of the things I am working on is almost completed, the others do not get on partly because [indecipherable] is busy just now. She promises to give me more sittings when her holidays commence . . . Dolores is beginning to play the fool. There was a paragraph about 'her beauty' and I am afraid this is sending her off her head. She has been interviewed by some newspaper people about her sitting to me; but I've stopped all that and she resents it. Stupidities . . . I answered you about the money if you would read my letter of Tuesday again. You are my sweetheart having my thoughts by day, my dreams, my ardent longings by night. My memory of you is

so [indecipherable] it is real torture to think of you. You only can know what I mean by this.[24]

Soon after writing this letter, Epstein was once again offered an important commission, this time to create a memorial to W. H. Hudson, the writer and naturalist whose championship of wildlife, particularly birds, had aroused ardent public sympathy. The Royal Society for the Protection of Birds wanted a sculptor to produce a panel in an enclosure which was to be called the Bird Sanctuary, and placed in Kensington Gardens, Hyde Park. Epstein's loyal friend Muirhead Bone was responsible for suggesting his name. A quiet, civilized Scot and a brilliant graphic artist himself, Bone had an eye and an enthusiasm for the talent of others, and was outstandingly generous to Epstein. He commissioned a portrait of himself during the First World War, bought some of his works and presented them to the Imperial War Museum and, as a trustee of the National Gallery and an influential figure in the art world, placed opportunities Epstein's way whenever he could.

On the face of it a portrait of a naturalist carved on a fountain in a bird sanctuary in Hyde Park did not appear to be controversial. Epstein worked quickly, made a number of sketches and early in 1923 produced for a hundred guineas a clay model of W. H. Hudson sprawled on the ground beside a tree, looking down at a bird. When he was starting the work, Margaret said optimistically, 'They will never be able to make a fuss this time.'[25]

8

A Tolerant People

IN LESS THAN twenty years in England, Epstein had received three important architectural commissions: the Strand statues, the Oscar Wilde tomb and now the Hudson memorial bird sanctuary in a royal park. Loyal friends and excellent contacts helped enormously; but they were not in themselves enough to account for his prominence. He was, at the time, the only sculptor who could inject excitement and ardent feeling into a dull project; he was also an important influence on the younger generation. Henry Moore, a student at the Royal College of Art in the autumn of 1921, acknowledged Epstein as the only sculptor whom he respected at the time, and made his way to the studio in Guilford Street. Epstein befriended the younger man and encouraged his talent. '[I] . . . have never forgotten him taking me into his bedroom to see his collection of primitive carvings – it was so overflowing with negro sculptures etc., that I wondered how he got into bed without knocking something over.'[1] Moore's own interest in primitive art was heightened by Epstein's inspired appreciation, and, as Evelyn Silber points out, Moore's *Maternity* (1924) was clearly influenced by Epstein's early *Maternity* figure.

With the commission of the monument to W. H. Hudson, however, Epstein was once again plunged into the world of committees and controversy. Many of the subscribers to the monument had known Hudson personally; since many were members of the Royal Society for the Protection of Birds (RSPB), whose cause Hudson had done so much to advance, feelings about their project ran high. Hudson had been elected the society's Chairman of Committee in 1894, and on his death in August 1922 the RSPB had received a substantial legacy from him. By January 1923 Epstein's preparatory sketches and his clay model of Hudson had been approved by the Hudson memorial committee. However, since the monument was to be sited in a royal park, the Office of Works had to sanction the design, and protocol forbade portrait sculpture in Hyde Park, although imaginary figures like Peter Pan could caper in the gardens without objection. So the design had to be abandoned.

As well as influential friends backing the memorial, Epstein had influential enemies, notably John Galsworthy, who publicly declared that Epstein was not the right man to make the monument. But Muirhead Bone acted quickly to retain his friend as sculptor with a new plan. 'I confess that I am as anxious as ever to get something really strikingly imaginative and beautiful from Epstein and I want to know what you think of the idea of the relief on the stone representing the wonderful woman spirit in *Green Mansions*,' he wrote to the committee chairman, R. B. Cunningham Grahame. 'This seems to be a very fine subject for the sculptor and ought to result in a beautiful thing.'[2]

In Hudson's popular novel of 1904, *Green Mansions*, Rima, the mysterious heroine, a wild and beautiful woodland creature who is half bird and half human, represents the spirit of nature. The book appealed to Epstein's imagination; he was passionately involved with Kathleen at the time. But the practical challenge of translating the poetical Rima into stone was a difficult one. Epstein's allegorical figure was to stand as a bas-relief above a shallow pool with a raised base where birds could safely drink and bathe. He had to carve his allegorical figure in outlines clear enough to be visible some seventy feet away. *Rima* was formally commissioned on 15 February 1923, and five weeks later committee members visited Epstein's studio in Guilford Street to view his new drawings and a miniature clay model showing Rima springing from a tree, with a flock of birds in flight above her head. Muirhead Bone made a deft bird's-eye-view drawing of the memorial which, it was hoped, would persuade the Office of Works to adopt the project. When they viewed the designs, drawings and model, the official reaction was disapproving and disappointing. Sir Lionel Earle wrote to the Hudson committee,

> The Site Committee are very attracted by the idea of a bird bath . . . but they could not recommend permission being given for the stone as designed. They feel that the sculptured stone would evoke wide and bitter controversy and that even the setting leaves much to be desired. They fully recognise Mr Epstein's genius but they do not consider that his present design is either worthy of his talent or of the site upon which it is intended to place it. The first Commissioner reports that he feels unable to recommend it to His Majesty [George V] as Ranger to agree to its erection in Hyde Park.[3]

Clearly Epstein's work was too unconventional for the official mind. Cunningham Grahame, the chairman of the Hudson camp, a bluff Scot, a traveller and writer who admired Epstein and had had his own head modelled by the artist that spring, tried to retrieve the situation. By return of post he suggested that Epstein should modify his *Rima* with 'the neck less long, the arms shorter, the face prettier', but Sir Lionel Earle was adamant; it seems doubtful whether Epstein would have agreed to such prettification in any case. The Hudson committee were distinctly uneasy with their sculptor, and Mrs Pamela McKenna proposed in a letter that Sir Edwin Lutyens should be invited to design a memorial, with a bird bath, an inscription to Hudson but no sculpture. The loyalty and tenacity of Cunningham Grahame and Muirhead Bone won through and, rather surprisingly, Epstein was commissioned by the Hudson committee. For the third time he immersed himself in the story and produced a series of bold and exuberant drawings in a handsome album, eighty-six of which still survive.[4]

Epstein's studies follow the narrative closely, revealing Rima in different poses, stalking through the trees, propped against a tree, with large birds always close by. The drawings were circulated among the members of the Hudson committee in the autumn of 1923. If they had analysed them closely, they would have realized that Epstein's harsh poetry had seized on the strangeness of the sacred forest and the primitive figure who resided in it, and therefore he was unlikely to create a soft or pretty image.

Epstein's final choice of pose for *Rima* was based on *The Ludovisi Throne*, an ancient Greek masterpiece showing a woman naked to the waist with two attendants (Epstein acknowledged the debt later). But Epstein's *Rima* is an archaic, powerful figure with broad shoulders, large angular arms and pointed breasts, flanked by two aggressive-looking birds – a wood nymph perhaps, but not a graceful Greek nymph, with nothing of the English rose about her. By February 1924, over two years since the original figure had been commissioned, Epstein's final design was accepted both by the Hudson committee and by the Office of Works. Time and money had been spent in the effort and another appeal for funds was launched in 1924 in *The Times*. The newspaper commented that *Rima* was 'pretty sure to be one of the most beautiful memorials in the country'. The *Manchester Guardian* and *Country Life* also appealed for funds, and as a result of all the efforts an extra £1,150 was donated, enabling the work to continue.[5]

By May 1924 a block of Portland stone some two metres wide was delivered to Epstein in his tiny cottage in Epping Forest. He preferred the space and solitude of the country to work in; and he had his studio shed enlarged and lined with felt so that he could use it in the winter. In September, Cunningham Grahame visited and reported to his committee that 'Epstein was starting work with great enthusiasm'. Thanks to Grahame's friendly interest, the committee granted Epstein extra funds for the improvements. From September until April, Epstein worked, 'solitary, surrounded by the silent and often fog-laden forest' in the winter. Eric Gill was commissioned to carve the inscription with the words: 'This sanctuary for birds is dedicated to the memory of William Henry Hudson, writer and field naturalist'.

Finally, on Tuesday, 19 May 1925, a day of bright sunshine, a crowd gathered beside the railings of an enclosure surrounded by trees on the north side of Hyde Park. Inside the enclosure, the Prime Minister Stanley Baldwin and Cunningham Grahame made their speeches. Baldwin praised W. H. Hudson's role as a protector of wildlife and Cunningham Grahame likened the naturalist to St Francis of Assisi. The mood of the crowd was gently nostalgic, heightened by the music played by the band. Then the Prime Minister pulled the cord of the covering sheet. There was dead silence, followed by a gasp of horror, as the crowd viewed Epstein's wild, fervent *Rima* clamped into a small space. Cunningham Grahame would relate with some humour how he saw a shiver run down the spine of Stanley Baldwin. 'Immediately after, a "hullabaloo" unequalled for venom and spite broke out in the press,' Epstein wrote. He did not exaggerate. The campaign to discredit Epstein lasted for years and proved extremely damaging. His 'transgression' was to turn his back on the establishment's love of sentimental portraits of pretty English maidens and little birds and to illustrate the book of the South American-born author with a wild creature from the jungle.

The *British Guardian*, the fascist weekly, was predictably anti-Semitic, its comments part of an orchestrated response: 'The public will probably remember that the agitation against the hideous and disgusting monstrosity . . . which is now exposed in Hyde Park is not the first occasion on which objection has been raised to this Jew being commissioned to execute work for British public memorials.'[6] But the tone of more mainstream dailies was equally intemperate. 'Take this horror out of the Park,' screamed the *Daily Mail*. '*Rima* is hideous, unnatural, unEnglish and essentially unhealthy,' pronounced the *Morning Post*.[7] A letter from Margaret, Maharanee of Sarawak, to the Hudson committee, three days after the sculpture was unveiled, reveals the indignation of her class: 'What can be done about that ignoble monument in our dear Hudson's bird sanctuary . . . the dreadful naked, coarse-looking creature with hands so terrible that no nanny would own.'[8]

The mood of anger reached Parliament, and on 4 July the Tory MP Basil Peto asked the Under-Secretary of State for the Home Department, Commander Oliver Locker-Lampson, whether he had arranged for the early removal from its present site in Hyde Park of the Epstein bas-relief; and whether he would 'see that it is not re-erected in any other place in this country'. Locker-Lampson replied, 'The answer to the first part is in the negative.' At this there were Labour cheers. He added, 'The second part does not therefore arise.' Basil Peto remarked, 'May I ask the Honourable Member whether this so-called work of art belongs to the nation, and if so, whether he will consider the advisability of removing this specimen of Bolshevik art?' The Speaker ruled the question out of order.[9]

Removing *Rima*, a small panel in an obscure corner of Hyde Park, visible only from a few yards away, became an obsession among those who loathed the 'intrusion' of modern art. *Rima* often featured in the headlines. She was the subject of after-dinner speeches and of caricatures and skits in music hall and theatre. One evening Dolores and another Epstein model, Anita, visited the Aldwych Theatre to throw rotten tomatoes at a caricature of *Rima* on stage in an embarrassing display of loyalty. Epstein relates how in Hyde Park a 'shabby gentleman' drew crowds on to the grass in front of the monument with his passionate protests against the sculpture. 'Would you', he asked the excited audience, 'want your sister depicted in this manner?' One day Epstein's detractor set himself to speak for twelve hours in the open air, rewarded by snacks and drinks from the audience and a welter of publicity from the newspapers and even the cinema news.

The press comment, which began in May immediately after the memorial was unveiled, lasted all year. Sometimes the comment was light-hearted and witty:

> There once was a sculptor of mark
> Who was chosen to brighten Hyde Park
> Some thought his design
>   Uncommonly fine
> But most like it best in the dark

quipped *Punch*.[10] But other comments held uglier undertones. 'Mr Epstein's work in Kensington Gardens is so far from being an object of admiration that, were not the English a tolerant people, it would long ago have been broken into pieces,' remarked the *Morning Post* on 7 October 1925. Fortunately, the panel was fairly inaccessible, but by mid-November the paper was able to report, 'The inevitable has happened to Mr Epstein's *Rima*. She has been ingloriously daubed with green paint.' Four days later the *Post* observed, 'There is some quality in the memorial in Hyde Park which revolts the public . . . The sentiment has already found expression in the youthful foolish and rather hooligan dose of green paint.' On that same day, the paper printed a letter from prominent right-wing figures in the world of the arts demanding the removal of the memorial as quickly as possible. 'It would be a reproach to all concerned if future generations were allowed to imagine that this piece of artistic anarchy in any way reflected the true spirit of the age.'[11]

The signatories included Hilaire Belloc, Sir Arthur Conan Doyle, Sir Frank Dicksee (President of the Royal Academy), Alfred J. Munnings (a future President of the Royal Academy) and Her Highness the Ranee Margaret of Sarawak. It was only at this stage, six months after a vicious campaign against *Rima*, that liberal opinion intervened. Muirhead Bone could barely comprehend the enormity of the suggestion. He gave an interview to the *Observer* and wrote a dignified letter to *The Times* on 25 November 1925: 'Opinions will always differ about the artistic merits of works of art and they are likeliest to differ about a work so modern in style as Mr Epstein's Hudson Bird Sanctuary panel in Hyde Park . . . I have the agreement of the following signatories against any proposal to remove so completely authorised a work on the demand of a mere section of the public.'[12] The signatories defending Epstein included Arnold Bennett, George Clausen, C. B. Cochran, Samuel Courtauld, the Rt Hon. Ramsay MacDonald, George Moore, Henry Nevinson, Sir William Orpen, Professor William Rothenstein, C. P. Scott, George Bernard Shaw and Hugh Walpole. Five other professors signed the protest letter as well as Campbell Dodgson, the Master of Downing College, Cambridge. *The Times* also reported that they had received 170 letters of protest against the proposed removal of *Rima* from students of the Royal College of Art and from eighty-five students at the Slade.[13]

Quite apart from the merits of the case, if the principle were established that properly authorised public works of art could be dumped by a manifesto signed by thirteen people and backed by a newspaper, then the possibilities for endless wrangling and rebellion would threaten government departments and artists alike.

Although 'Rimaphobia', as Epstein dubbed it, did not stop at the end of the year, Muirhead Bone finally scotched the efforts to remove her with a carefully argued eleven-page memorandum to Lord Peel, the then First Commissioner of Works. Bone pointed out that the Hudson committee had, at every stage, complied with the requests of the Office of Works. In his measured way he was firm and clear. As a Trustee of the National Gallery he felt able to remind the commission of the stoning of Michelangelo's *David* by the Florentine public at its unveiling, adding that, since English sculpture lagged behind that of other nations, it would be extremely unfortunate if it were established that no bold or unconventional work could ever hope to secure official permission for its erection. 'I think that the claim of the younger, unacademic artist to represent contemporary artistic thought . . . is not an altogether unreasonable one.'

In the growing anti-Semitism of the 1930s *Rima* became a target again. She was daubed with swastikas, and the initials IFL (International Fascist League) were painted on the panel.

Epstein was genuinely amazed at the ferocity of the attacks on *Rima*. Fortunately his concentration and energy were always engaged on the new piece, the next project, and he rarely reacted to the extreme criticisms of his work. But he did say publicly that much of the *Rima* criticism was dishonest, with no solid argument raised against his relief, 'only jokes about cruelty to birds'. Some five years after the memorial was erected, he walked across Hyde Park to look at his small carving. 'I tried to view it as impersonally as possible. The wind was blowing and the leaves falling. It seemed just right. I really cannot understand what all the fuss was about.'[14]

Throughout the years spent battling over *Rima*, Epstein had to take commissions when he could and exhibit his work in order to make a living. In January 1924 the Leicester Galleries, sensible of the huge crowds that Epstein's name attracted, put on a third exhibition of his work. No less a critic than Roger Fry was sent by the *New Statesman* to review the show, apparently with the aim of cutting Epstein down to size. Since the days when Fry and Epstein had been on opposing sides in the wrangle over Fry's Omega Workshop they had distrusted each other. Nevertheless Fry, who wrote, lectured and painted himself, was highly respected as the most authoritative voice on modern art. One has the sense of the author licking his lips as he went round the Leicester Galleries gazing at the Epstein bronzes. First he built up an expectation:

> We are brought up to a pious belief that sculpture is an altogether noble and reputable affair . . . yet sculpture has always bored us – till now – and now comes Mr Epstein. As we passed round the Leicester Galleries where his work has been on exhibition, each bronze head gave us a new and distinct sensation, a thrill of wonder, surprise, recognition and, as a result of so pleasant a shock, admiration and gratitude. What miraculous gift was this which could make bronze reveal to us definite, singular, vivid human beings – human beings more definite, more emphatically personal, more incisive in the accent of their individuality, more invasive at a first glance, of our own consciousness than the individuals of actual life.

The critic was laying it on disturbingly thick.

> Mr Epstein started from the first with remarkable gifts, but in his early work he was an experimentalist in styles . . . Now at last he has found himself; when we realise the astonishing assurance, the indisputable completeness and efficacy of these works, the brilliant resourcefulness and certainty of technique, we must call Epstein a master.

Then came the *coup de grâce*:

> But a master of what? Of the craft of sculpture, undoubtedly
> of vigorous characterisation . . . even so one can imagine a
> finer, more penetrating, less clamant kind of interpretation of
> character. One might tire, perhaps, of the element . . . One
> would prefer to live with something less vehement in its
> attack, rather more persuasive . . . If I examine my own sensa-
> tions and emotions, I am bound to confess that they seem to
> be of quite a different nature when I look at good sculpture
> from what I feel in front of Mr Epstein's bronzes . . . They
> come from the recognition of inevitable harmonic sequences
> of planes, of a complete equilibrium established through the
> interplay of diverse movements, and a perfect subordination
> of surface and handling to the full apprehension of these and
> similar qualities.[15]

At his best in his bronzes, Epstein penetrates to the core of his
subjects with his intense empathy and understanding; at his worst
he can be overblown and emotionally self-indulgent. But his
grandeur, both as modeller and carver, lies in his involvement with
the fundamental elements of human experience. Epstein saw Fry
and his 'Bloomsburies' as dilettante and effete, but he was no
match for them intellectually, and Fry's attack was very damaging.
Although the *New Statesman* reached only a minority readership,
they were people influential in the arts, and Fry himself was
widely respected. The article was twice reprinted.

A month after Fry's article a more disturbing attack appeared in
the *New Age*. This was the journal that had championed Epstein
and printed T. E. Hulme's influential essays on his art. But A. R.
Orage, the editor, had left the paper in 1922; under a new editor the
politics of the paper were reflected in the criticism of Epstein's
exhibition:

> Puzzled, vaguely uneasy, you wander round closely inspect-
> ing each head in turn. Wonderfully moulded, they are the

work of a genius. They grip you. They will not let you go. But a sickening disgust gradually conquers you. The intensity of repulsion aroused by them cannot be explained merely on the ground of their Semitic cast – their high cheek bones, their half-eyes, their prominent noses and their full open lips. There is something more . . . They are instinct with evil . . . We recall the poise and balance of the Greek gods and feel that we are surrounded in their stead by Circean beasts. Where is man's power to erect himself above himself? How loathsome is the species when deprived of nobility and dignity! Even the charming studies of Peggy Jean, the baby laughing, grave, asleep, are touched with horror.[16]

This offering, signed 'Rusticus', represents something more than art criticism. As Epstein wrote in 1940, 'This astonishing tirade might have been written in the Germany of today.' Epstein was rarely angered by criticism, but he was stung by sneering remarks about his sculpture of Peggy Jean. She was five and a half at the time and he had made ten busts of her, asleep, awake, pouting, laughing, looking sad, in a record of delight in her development.

There were few sales at the Leicester Galleries in 1924; and after the show closed in February Epstein was as usual badly in need of money. Again it was Muirhead Bone who arranged a congenial commission for him. Since his childhood in New York, Epstein had admired the stirring stories of Joseph Conrad, and he was delighted when Conrad, now in his sixties, agreed that Epstein should model his head for an official portrait commissioned by the Polish government.

He arrived at Conrad's home, Oswalds, near Canterbury, towards dark, with snow falling. Epstein stayed near by in the village of Bridge. He hated the constraints of living in other people's houses but found the inn cheerless and cold. The next morning he began, but by the end of the day's work felt despondent. He was evidently feeling lonely too, and autocratically wired for his five-year-old daughter to come to stay with him. Peggy Jean always raised his spirits, and after her arrival 'things looked better'.

Epstein soon became deeply absorbed in the study of Conrad. The writer took the sittings seriously and would pose until one o'clock, when they lunched and talked. With Conrad, whose work he so admired, Epstein was at his best, and the writer treated him with sympathy and goodwill. 'It may have been because of my meeting him late in life that Conrad gave a feeling of defeat; but defeat met with courage,' he said. Conrad had

a demon expression in the left eye, while his right eye was smothered by a drooping lid, but the eyes glowed with great intensity of feeling. The drooping weary lids intensified the impression of brooding thought. The whole head revealed the man who had suffered much . . . My bust of Conrad brought out his fierce, almost demoniac energy, but I did not try to read into his psychology – I went entirely by what I saw.

After three weeks' work the bust was complete, and Epstein wired his moulder to come and take the head away to be cast.

Conrad, who died five months after the head was made, wrote to his biographer Richard Curle, 'The bust of Ep. has grown truly monumental. It is a marvellously effective piece of sculpture with even something more than a masterly interpretation . . . It is wonderful to go down to posterity like that.'[17] In spite of his achievement, Epstein's bust was not purchased by the Polish government, and when Muirhead Bone offered the bronze to the National Gallery it was again rejected.

Since the sculpture for Hyde Park suffered so many false starts, Epstein was forced to take on other commissions. His sense of irony saw him through an extraordinary stay at Blenheim Palace in the spring of 1924. He had been invited there to create a bust of the Duke of Marlborough by his friend Gladys Deacon, now Duchess of Marlborough, a cultivated American who was finding country-house living somewhat irksome. Epstein enjoyed playing the *enfant terrible* among the aristocrats. When walking in the parkland surrounding the palace, wearing shabby clothes spattered with plaster, he was often called upon by the gamekeepers to explain his presence. Epstein's reply that he was a guest 'always produced a comic forehead salute of flunkeys, and apologies . . . I think I've been the terror of this place for the last 7 days,' he bragged to Kathleen on Blenheim Palace paper. 'I break in on tea parties in the rudest fashion and have given my host and myself no rest.' Epstein and the Duke did not appreciate each other's company. 'One day the Duke asked me to see the Chapel of Blenheim. We entered a building totally devoid of Christian symbolism or Christian feeling. I said, "I see nothing of Christianity here." The Duke replied, "It is the Marlboroughs who are worshipped here."'[18]

The Duchess had tried to create an atmosphere conducive to creative work by arranging for an organist to play Bach for an hour in the morning before Epstein began his work, but the Duke complained that the music was boring and asked why they didn't play jazz or nightclub music instead. Epstein found the art in the palace disappointing. He thought many of the paintings were mediocre, with a 'large and vulgar Sargent' dominating one room and a 'flashy Boldini' in place of honour in another. The question of taste bedevilled the sculptor and his sitter. The Duke wanted to see himself as a Roman senator in a toga with bare shoulders; Epstein wanted the bust, which was to decorate a niche in the entrance hall of the palace, to be in contemporary costume. The Duchess sided with Epstein, and after an ill-tempered argument the head was left uncompleted. Epstein also made a striking study of the Duchess but never finished it.

It was not only the strange and alien atmosphere of Blenheim which made him long to be home, but also his need to be near Kathleen.

The place is of course beautiful, there are wonderful cedar trees, but I cannot see myself living here for any length of time . . . how much I want to see you, how much I want to be with you, talk with you. I think of you all day . . . I love you

my darling girl and lie and think of you many sleepless hours
and imagine myself holding you as I often have. What happiness beside you, you and I embraced, made god-like in the
intensity of our joy. I have had nothing in my life to equal my
happiness with you and never will have, that I know.[19]

Epstein returned home to Guilford Street soon after he wrote that
letter and, two years later, in 1926, the Duchess of Marlborough
found a compromise solution for the unfinished bust. The Duke,
resplendent in his Garter robes, 'encased in aristocratic pride', sat
for Epstein in London; this was the version that went to Blenheim.
The photographs of the earlier study indicate that the personality
of the Duke emerges more strongly with the addition of his regalia.

Throughout the 1920s Epstein's name was prominent in the press,
the man and his work synonymous with scandalous sculpture and
beautiful models, a combination which made officialdom
distinctly nervous. In January 1924 an unexpected vacancy for a
Professor of Sculpture at the Royal College of Art had arisen when
the incumbent suddenly resigned. Both William Rothenstein, who
was principal of the college, and Henry Moore, who became assistant professor, claim to have proposed Epstein to fill the post. But
the mere suggestion of appointing such a controversial artist
caused the Permanent Under-Secretary at the Board of Education
to react nervously: 'To appoint Epstein would be a very perilous
experiment and might cause considerable embarrassment. For a
Professor we would want not only a genius (as to which I am no
authority) but also character: and I am not sure that character in a
place of this kind is not of greater importance.'[20]

Epstein needed the extra money that year to cope with his new
responsibilities. On 1 July 1924 Kathleen Garman bore him a son,
Theodore. During her pregnancy Epstein had been in Epping
Forest working, and was only occasionally able to be with her. He
missed her ferociously when she was away.

I've so longed to see you that my whole day & night is conditioned by my great longing . . . were we together it would only be to kiss and embrace; you are right when you speak of our mysterious happiness . . . last night I believe I spent almost the whole night thinking of you . . . I am not with you my arms that wish to hold you haven't [sic] you my hands that want to feel you miss you: yours are the kisses I want.[21]

He wrote that letter when Kathleen was away in Martigues in the south of France with her sister Helen. When she was at home Helen often acted as go-between for the lovers. This undated letter must have been written in late June, just before Kathleen gave birth:

I have both your letters – one of yesterday and that given me by Helen. I am glad you are feeling well and if you are well enough we can meet. Oddinios [sic] on Saturday evening at 7. If you don't feel well let me know and I'll come to your place.

I have been working hard and am reduced to a jelly this afternoon. The shed is so big. Outside all is wonderful and I think of the wonderful cool green of the forest. You write as if my figure is already finished. It is altogether in an embryonic stage and I can only just see it coming [Epstein seems unconsciously to be reflecting Kathleen's pregnancy in his imagery]. I must have time to work it out – time is the only thing I fear I will not have. Time and peace to work at it. The Hudson people worry me weekly . . .

Sweetheart I long to be with you again. Wait for me and we will enter the Heaven on Earth which is ours when together. I imagine you now in Regent Square. London must be stifling for it is hot here. I work in my shed before what I hope will be an image of loveliness [he had deleted holiness]. Whenever it is finished you will see it . . . May it be worth your gaze.[22]

Epstein's letter reveals a reverence for Kathleen, pregnant with his child – a reflection of his feelings of awe for the act of generation as well as for the woman who had given up so much to be with him.

Epstein's life was unusually episodic in the twenties. At home he lived in a crowded house in Bloomsbury with his wife and daughter and sundry models. Peggy Jean remembered a goat in the basement,[23] which might have accounted for Epstein's 'smell' which some contemporaries remarked on. For his grand commissions he might stay temporarily in a palace or a country inn. At least two evenings a week he spent with Kathleen and at weekends he often went to the cottage at Loughton in Epping Forest.

In the summer of 1924 Epstein visited the British Empire Exhibition at Wembley. He was struck at once by the unusual looks of Miss Wembley, the beauty queen of the exhibition, a statuesque Indian woman, almost six feet tall, known as Sunita. She had a grave, brooding, maternal authority in her looks, which particularly appealed to Epstein, as well as a sensual grace. Sunita was accompanied by her small son and her sister, and together they ran a stall selling Eastern artefacts at the exhibition. For Epstein the trio were irresistible.

The Indian sisters were in their way as modern and remarkably free from convention as the Epsteins. According to family legend, Sunita joined Diaghilev's Russian Ballet during her travels in Europe; this is unlikely, since she was almost six feet tall, but it gives an indication of the glamour that clung to her. Her real name was Amina Peerbhoy and she was the daughter of a doctor from a well-connected family in Kashmir. Her mother had been murdered by a servant when she was a small girl and she and her sister were married off in their early teens. Amina's husband was a Chief Justice, and she had a son by him. Both girls were unhappy in their marriages and they managed to slip the marital yoke and travel to Europe with Amina's small boy in tow. In Europe, the three westernized their names: Amina became Sunita; her son Anwer became

Enver, and her sister Mariam became Anita. In 1924 Sunita had already begun to model in Paris, where the painter Matthew Smith made a drawing of her, and, according to her family, she was involved in a love affair with him.[24] Once Epstein met the sisters they were swept into his circle. He expansively invited the whole family to live with him in the Guilford Street house. Dolores had moved on by then, and Margaret accepted the new necessities for Epstein's art, hoping always that Sunita or Anita, or both, would supplant her rival Kathleen.

Rivalry for Sunita's affections may have affected Matthew Smith's attitude to Epstein. On the surface, Smith had reason to be grateful to the sculptor. It was thanks to his influence that Smith's work had first been shown publicly in London at the London Group's 1916 winter exhibition.[25] Epstein bought Smith's still life *Lilies* and had begun to amass a Matthew Smith collection by the 1920s. But Smith felt that Epstein was too importunate and bought too many of his paintings – 'just the ones I don't want him to have'. Smith's sensuous, glowing still lifes of flowers and fruit and his sculptural nudes appealed to Epstein, and his friend led just as unconventional a life as Epstein himself, yet he appeared retiring and hesitant, dressed in well-cut tweeds and wearing thick glasses. According to a friend, Matthew Smith felt 'he was too weak and Epstein too strong, just like a cat playing with a mouse'.[26] The tension between them may have originated with Epstein annexing Sunita.

Sunita was a magnificent model and Epstein made scores of drawings of her, and several portraits in bronze of Sunita, her son and her sister. Each of the trio became important subjects in Epstein's art from 1925 to 1931, and Sunita and Enver were to be the models for a *Madonna and Child*. How the Indian family fitted in with the Epsteins remains a mystery, but that they stayed so long and remained on good terms is surely a tribute to both sides.

In 1926, in his shed in Epping Forest, Epstein was modelling a life-sized portrait of a troubled young woman in the early stages of pregnancy. It can be no coincidence that at the time Kathleen was pregnant with their second child, Kitty, born on 17 August 1926. Epstein's vulnerable figure hangs her head down, and folds her hands limply in front of her. She is Epstein's most modest vision of generation, caught, as it were, unaware. He himself wrote that the figure 'expresses a humility so profound as to shame the beholder who comes to my sculpture expecting rhetoric or splendour of gesture'. He exhibited the figure at the Leicester Galleries in June 1926 and wisely titled the work *A Study* (the real title is *The Visitation*, but Epstein wanted to avoid controversy). The bust was bought by the Contemporary Art Society and given to the Tate Gallery.

George Gray Barnard, Epstein's former sculpture teacher at the Art Students' League in New York, who was passing through London, visited the Leicester Galleries with Epstein and was delighted with his former student's work. He pressed Epstein to send the figure to New York, where, he promised, he would ensure that *The Visitation* would have a place in the Metropolitan Museum.

9

Mr Epstein's Latest

B Y THE 1920s viewings of Epstein's exhibitions had become fashionable in London, with admirers and detractors equally fervent in their opinions. Among certain members of the upper classes, baiting Epstein had become a popular sport. In the autumn of 1926 the Walker Art Gallery in Liverpool invited the sculptor to send in examples of his work to their exhibition. He sent two bronzes, *Mrs Epstein* and *Anita*. Lord Wavertree, the son of the founder of the gallery, used the official opening as an excuse to insult Epstein. 'If these are Mr Epstein's best, then a poor artist would have done better if he admitted his worst.'[1]

The remarks were widely reported in the provincial and national newspapers and Epstein decided to withdraw his figures from the exhibition, but the committee apologised for Lord Wavertree's rudeness and persuaded Epstein to allow his work to remain on show. Wavertree, however, remained unrepentant and revelled in the notoriety, inserting an advertizement in *The Times* thanking the large number of people who had written to congratulate him for his remarks. Epstein himself revealed how damaging the 'bullying newspapers' were to his sales. In Liverpool anti-Epstein feeling extended to church architecture, and when the new Roman Catholic cathedral was being built Archbishop Downey said in an interview, 'It would be a calamity if anything Epsteinish were to be found in the new building.' Epstein retorted brashly, 'Where else could be found a sculptor to do justice to the spirit of Christianity today, in a world almost wholly bereft of Christian action?'

By now it was easy to personify Epstein, so obviously un-English, as one face of the 'Bolshevik/Jewish conspiracy' of fascist propaganda. Six months after *Rima* was unveiled, the *Evening News* had claimed that the Hudson memorial was 'a dramatic and concentrated piece of evidence of the spirit of anarchy . . . so constant a factor in modern life that it links [with] the Red Flag . . . leading us backwards to barbaric conceptions of life'.[2] So its author was credited with helping to bring about the destruction of Western civilization, and supplanting it with a noisy primitivism.

If any of the right-wing gentry had penetrated Epstein's household in Bloomsbury, all their worst fears would have been confirmed. Here, living in glorious disarray, were husband and wife, models, mistresses and children, legitimate, illegitimate and racially mixed. Here amid the chaos Epstein contrived to work while Margaret struggled to maintain order. A visitor, James K. Feibleman, remembered her as a large woman with many skirts making a supreme effort to estimate their income over the past ten years while Epstein talked to him about art. The couple had kept no records. Feibleman, a philosophy graduate, was the son of a wealthy New Orleans businessman, who had sent along a companion, David Cohn, as his business representative. Young Feibleman, eager to sample European culture and sophistication, was immediately impressed by Epstein's warmth, sympathy and sheer physical presence. He enjoyed the 'confusion of eccentrics, hero-worshippers, models and critics. And through this tempest Epstein always walked calmly, as though the madness was none of his making, the people none of his seeking and himself the most conventional of men.'[3]

Feibleman commissioned a head of himself and, although he found sitting still a trial, he enjoyed the sculptor's 'brilliant conversation' and remarked on his catholic taste in reading. Epstein dipped frequently into the Bible, and was as likely to be found reading the newly published novels of D. H. Lawrence as a textbook on entomology or a history of the Chinese people. At night Peggy Jean, who slept at the foot of the bed, heard the murmur of Margaret reading to Epstein in French, from the classics: Molière, Maupassant and Baudelaire, a particular favourite. Margaret herself subscribed to Mudie's lending library and Epstein had a friend who was a second-hand-book dealer, so the supply of books was almost inexhaustible.

Epstein was an autodidact, always eager to learn more. Feibleman was flattered to be accepted so readily into the home of a well-known artist and he wrote at length about Epstein in his autobiography.[4] He was a young man of taste as well as wealth, and, when Epstein told him that the Polish government, which had commissioned his bust of Conrad, were two years late in paying the fee, Feibleman eagerly offered to buy it for himself, paying cash.

For a year Epstein had been working on a *Madonna and Child* with Sunita and her son Enver modelling for him. 'The model was of the Eternal Oriental type which seemed to me just right for a work of this religious nature.' Epstein's life-sized *Madonna and Child* has none of the ethereal innocence of Western icons. She is instead an immensely tender, immensely wise mother, her face lined, her hands practical and protective. Although naturalistic, the figures possess an arresting grandeur and dignity which elevate them into archetypal beings. Lord Duveen, the great art collector, asked Epstein whether he could see the work when it was still at the foundry, and they drove to the workshop in Fulham. After studying the *Madonna and Child* carefully, Duveen turned to the sculptor and asked, 'If you had in mind to do a Madonna and Child why did you not choose a beautiful model?' Epstein turned away in disgust.

Perhaps it was the lack of understanding of his vision and the hostility that he had met in England which led Epstein in 1927 to risk holding his first exhibition in New York, where his work was little known. Friends had promised to help him, Feibleman and George Gray Barnard in particular. An exhibition was arranged, to be held at the Ferargil Gallery on West 47th Street. Margaret was delighted. They would be out of England and therefore out of Kathleen's way for some months; and they gave up the lease on the house in Guilford Street.

Before the move, Epstein spent much of the spring and summer at the foundry. He was to take some fifty works to America, including of course *Madonna and Child*, a head of Rabindranath Tagore, the Bengali poet who was a cult figure in the twenties (Epstein found the poet aloof and cold and modelled him as a remote figure with a luxuriant beard), Daisy Dunn, a jazz musician from a hit musical, and the Duke and Duchess of Marlborough. Everything Epstein did seemed to make news then, and the press suggested that he was leaving England because of the shabby treatment he had received. James Bone, London editor of the *Manchester Guardian* and brother of Muirhead Bone, remarked in his newspaper that 'England had been a bad stepmother to him'. Although engendered with the kindliest of intentions, the publicity, like most publicity about Epstein, was damaging to him. It gave the impression that he was leaving England for good – which might have prejudiced English buyers against him on his return.

Yet Epstein arrived in New York full of optimism. Twenty-five years had elapsed since he boarded a ship bound for Europe in 1902, and he was now a famous sculptor. Journalists met him at the harbour; his iconoclastic reputation had preceded him. One asked him whether he had come to America 'to debunk sculpture'. Epstein, amused by the question, replied that he had come simply to show some of his pieces. Nevertheless, 'a leader in one of the papers cautioned me that the warmth of my reception depended upon my attitude to American art!'

When Epstein saw the gallery where his sculpture was to be shown he was deeply disappointed. The gallery looked mid-Victorian to him, with curtained walls and chandeliers, cluttered with plants, and poorly lit. He found that he was looked upon by the gallery owner 'as just another fortnight's exhibition in the yearly round of exhibitions and my tremendous struggle and expense in coming to New York was a matter of just casual interest to him'. After the fortnight the dealers wanted to send his works on tour all round the country in hundreds of towns and cities, and Epstein heard from another artist that the works could go on 'touring' for years and never come back. He had to hire a lawyer to change the conditions of his contract with the gallery.

Throughout his stay in America he wrote impassioned, caring and increasingly anguished letters to Kathleen. He had to keep the correspondence secret, and because of the delays and distance there were, inevitably, misunderstandings. With Peggy Jean and Margaret he arrived in New York on 1 October, and on 11 October he replied to the first letter he had received from Kathleen, who as the mother of two small children was feeling worried and insecure at their separation:

My own darling one, I have your loving letter in which you say you've none of mine yet. Posts take long but I imagine you must have my first letter by now and I wrote you again last Friday; also I sent a photograph of the wonderful Rembrandt portrait which is in the museum. It's quite as fine as the self-portrait in the National Gallery. By cable I sent off three times $15 which is about £3 and yesterday I sent 25 dollars – about £5. Wish I could send you more I will as soon as I can. I long for you as much as you do for me and I brood and think over the past and every detail is beautiful. I forget and see how small our bad times were: they are nothing and only our happiness remains in my mind . . . This is a barren time for me. Be patient my little sweetheart, so that I can get this exhibition through.

My first delay is in having the show postponed until the 14th of November. Now that we are so forcibly separated, I feel more than ever that my life is inevitably with you . . . I have had such bad hours that could I manage it, I would have taken boat and come straight to 13 Regent Sq., and lived with you from then on. I had hardly known what I let myself in for when I . . . gave up my works to these damnable people [the Ferargil Gallery]. I found on arriving here that I was supposed to show in a sort of basement place, badly lit, a commission of a third imposed on the works and only a 2 week show. I have forced on the gallery now these terms: a 2 weeks show in their upper and best gallery and the show to be extended beyond that for at least two weeks longer – possibly 4 weeks longer . . . Also as agreed, 25 per cent commission.

There is a terrible lot of balderdash written in the papers here as preliminary publicity. My friends from New Orleans [Feibleman and Cohn] will be here in a few days and they will see that I get fair play. I have taken a flat near the gallery for convenience . . . it's too expensive for me really and the success

or failure of my exhibition will determine what I do next. I
certainly will not travel, that does not appeal to me at all. How
I wish I could get back into real life. I sometimes imagine I'm
in a sort of nightmare and nothing is genuine here. I think
constantly of you darling and your letter will wring my heart
as I read it over by myself on lonely walks in the park or in the
coffee house where I am writing now. I row on the lake in the
morning early when no one is on it. It is in the midst of the city
in Central Park . . . There I can take out your letters and read
them. I look forward to the future; it holds my happiness again
with you. I have much to write but no paper. Tell me if you
received the $9 and the 5. I love you sweetheart.[5]

At first Epstein, Margaret and Peggy Jean stayed with his eldest
brother Louis, but they soon found the demands of relatives too
trying. 'My family were terrible and ready to tear each other to
pieces for me,' he wrote to Kathleen, and, when he searched for his
early drawings which his mother had packed away in a trunk, to his
distress he discovered that they had been thrown away when she
died.

Kathleen was missing him badly, tormenting herself by imagining
all the beautiful models and other American women he would meet.
Epstein did enjoy New York, perhaps more than he admitted in his
letters to Kathleen. He and Margaret rented a fifth-floor flat overlooking Central Park, with a wonderful view at night across the
wintry landscape: Epstein never tired of the spectacle of the city,
with its giant buildings, bridges and little ships, lighting up at dusk.
But he preferred watching the huge skyscrapers from the outside
and never felt quite comfortable riding high in the elevators to the
countless offices inside. He liked eating out in the restaurants where
Southern food was served by 'beautiful mulatto girls'. A brisk walk
from his home was the Metropolitan Museum, where he refreshed
himself with the 'wonderful Rembrandts' and the fine collection of
Cézannes; occasionally in the afternoons he went to the Museum to
hear a symphony concert.

Epstein went back to explore the places he had loved as a boy, before the skyscrapers dominated the city, and was inevitably disappointed. The docklands along the Lower East and West Side of the city had been modernized. The wooden piers jutting out into the river, where he had stood as a youth watching the great three-masted sailing ships glide into harbour, had disappeared. Gone too were the old warehouses with their pungent, spicy smells and the ships' chandlers. In these days of Prohibition, the Bowery, with its saloons and drunks, was hardly recognisable. Men and women going out to parties in the evening carried bottles discreetly wrapped under their arms. He was befriended by Frank Crowninshield, editor of *Vanity Fair*, who took him to formal gatherings, lunches and dinners. But he had to dress up for these occasions and was often expected to give a talk, which he disliked. Everyone who was interested in his work wanted to give him advice and tell him what to do next, in great detail.

He met one or two painters whom he greatly liked but was unimpressed by artistic standards. 'I saw nothing of a sculpture that would be the equivalent of *Leaves of Grass* [Whitman's collected poems] even in intent . . . nothing that was native, inspired by the soil or even the vast commercial enterprises of America. At present perhaps the great works like the Boulder Dam or the Panama Canal or the sky-scrapers come nearest to an impression of the American soul. Sculpture has to wait.'

There were three partners in the Ferargil Gallery and Epstein was on difficult terms with them all. The head of the firm, who prided himself on his skill as an art critic, wrote a preface to the catalogue, 'a strange mixture of illiterate jargon about my aims and achievements' which Epstein refused to allow. Another partner had hired a press agent (at Epstein's expense) who came up with wild schemes, suggesting that he should write an article damning all art in America to draw attention to his exhibition. Epstein was indiscreet enough in private but he saw the stupidity of that idea. The press agent also wanted to advertize his work in a beauty magazine. He dispensed with her services so that by the time of the opening date, 14 November 1927, the owners were thoroughly ill disposed towards him. For Epstein's forty-seventh birthday, four days before the exhibition opened, Kathleen sent him a blue ring. She also arranged for a bunch of red roses to be delivered to the gallery for the opening of the show. Epstein disliked the crowds and the overheated atmosphere of openings so did not go, but admitted later that he had been wrong. 'I made the mistake of not going to my private view or as the Americans call it preview. Americans want to see *you*. I thought the works were enough.'

'My show opened with a private view on Sunday,' he wrote to Kathleen.

> Crowds were there but of course I didn't show up. On Monday I came over. I will say the exhibition looks well although I haven't had one single happy hour over it . . . I am getting to hate this country and all its crude ways and only want to get away from it. My two N Orleans friends [Feibleman and Cohn] have failed me badly. They have done nothing for the show. And are leaving this week. Oko [an old friend from his boyhood who had promised to arrange for a group of people to purchase the *Madonna and Child* for the Met] has not turned up and I will have to do without him. If the *Madonna and Child* does not find a place here I shall send it back to London and show it there somewhere. There has been no notice in the papers as they are never admitted during the week. The newspapers here only print news of murders, local politics, football scores, prize fights and finance during the weekdays and Sunday is left for art and literature. There is already a set against me but I'm not troubled about them much. They are the 'decorative' sculptors, stylists and abstractionists of all kinds . . . How I wish I had given you one or two pieces, particularly the *Meum* mask which I think you like. When I see how my things have been treated here I am filled with fury. I have—[6]

Epstein was probably interrupted at that point – he did not finish the letter. But it seems striking that he should offer one mistress, Kathleen, his deep love, a portrait of another. Whether Kathleen was aware that Meum had been his lover, was the mother of Peggy Jean and was still a close friend of the family we cannot be sure – probably not. But it feels as if Epstein took his own diverse and unorthodox love life so naturally that he expected everyone else to do so. Epstein sent money for Kitty whenever he could and she was able to buy the piano she so badly wanted on an instalment plan. Her family, particularly her brother-in-law Roy Campbell, tried to make mischief between them, increasing the doubts she felt about Epstein's future intentions. She wrote to him about an evening at the Gargoyle club, and a visit from his friend, the painter Jacob Kramer, which aroused his suspicions. For both of them the separation was tormenting.

'Sweetheart,' he wrote two days after the letter about the opening of his show, 'I have your unhappy letter written from Blackhall.' Kathleen had gone to Herefordshire, to the hamlet of Kings Pyon, for a week, to stay with her mother, who had informally adopted her delicate fifteen-month-old granddaughter, Kitty.

> It must seem more and more tiresome to you. I can see that. I ask you to wait and yet now I can put a term to your and my waiting. Even that must make you impatient with me and you will blame me. To get a passage I must wait until the 17th [January] and I have booked for that. How I want to be with you and more than 'play' with you. I cannot imagine two persons who can be more with each other in spirit than you and I . . . when I ask you how our little girl is you will just say 'damn his impertinence' and that you no doubt think serves me right. I have no intimates here and I guard to myself my impatience to get away.[7]

Epstein was never to meet Kathleen's mother, and for the early years of her life his daughter Kitty had little contact with him. The Garman family were understandably wary of the American sculptor with a scandalous reputation and a fearsome wife who could barely support his own family yet monopolised Kathleen and spoiled her chances of marriage.

In his letters to Kathleen, Epstein often addressed her as 'Kitty' but from the context it is always clear when he is writing to his lover. In this undated letter from New York he reassures Kathleen that he is disillusioned with the New York scene and longing for her.

> You cannot imagine Kitty what rubbish they deal in here, pretentious 'decorative' sculpture, all imitators of each other. I sometimes wish to god I had never come here and placed all my hopes of making money in this country . . . I have got a fine collection together and if all would go well I will sell and make money & at least for my sweetheart I would be able to get those beautiful clothes which I have always wanted to get her. How are you darling . . . I think often terrible things of you but will not write them, they are caused by separation, a life altogether apart. I can neither see you nor touch you nor hear you . . . It is somewhat as you prophesied, the gallery people are & will be a trial to me. If only I could get my things decently on show I know purchases would be forthcoming. There have been notices in the papers somewhat sensational, well-meaning but badly written . . . I am filled with longing for you & a word from you will console me . . . Your lover your sculptor.[8]

He could certainly make love in his letters.

Despite the poor setting, Epstein's bronzes sold well; two, *Selina* and a beautiful head, *Girl from Senegal*, went into public collections. Although he had been asked to sculpt heads of businessmen and academics early in his visit to America, after the exhibition he found that he had more interesting commissions offered to him. He warmed particularly to Professor John Dewey, the educator and sculptor, because Dewey's students had each put $5 towards the $500 fee for the sculpture, which would be a presentation to Columbia University. The students would accompany Dewey to Epstein's apartment, and one of them, Joseph Rattner, stayed and kept up a 'running philosophic conversation . . . and made coffee for the three of us. I enjoyed making this bust and I recall the event with pleasure . . . He was a man absolutely straightforward, simple and loveable in character.'[9]

Through Dewey, Epstein was taken to see the remarkable Barnes collection of art housed in a suburb of Philadelphia. Dr Barnes, the patent-medicine millionaire, who had employed an American painter to go to Paris after the First World War to buy up Impressionist and Post-Impressionist paintings, had a reputation for boorishness, but Epstein found him extremely courteous. Pupils and teachers studying the collection were dismissed for the day so that Epstein could view the wonderful examples of Cézannes, Renoirs and the rest in peace.

After the exhibition ended at the Ferargil Gallery, Epstein's old college, the Art Students' League, asked him to exhibit some of his work there. Although he sold nothing, Epstein was not sorry that American students had the opportunity of seeing his work. He was astonished to find that all the work of the students was abstract and Cubist. He overheard one student remark to another, 'Epsteins are dull. They bore me.' But that did not irritate him so much as the remarks of George Gray Barnard, his old teacher from the League, who visited on the last day of Epstein's exhibition and declared that 'Epstein had succeeded in doing what Donatello had failed and that [his] work should tour the States'. Epstein disliked fulsome praise. 'What humbug,' he wrote to Kathleen.[10] He was not an easy man to please.

However reactionary he might appear in his pronouncements on abstract art, Epstein was generous and loyal towards the modern sculptors he admired. During his stay in America, the US government was seeking to levy a heavy import duty on Brancusi's *Bird in Space*, claiming that the sculpture was not a work of art but a piece of manufactured metal and as such taxable at 40 per cent of its commercial value, and that the maker of the piece was not an artist but a 'mechanic'. Epstein, called as an expert witness to counter the customs authorities' claims, won plaudits for his dress sense for the only time in his career. The *New York Evening Post* described the 'famous American sculptor and one of the most embattled of the moderns' as 'dressed harmoniously in a suit of warm brown and a lavender shirt', before reporting how Epstein 'smiled helpfully and expansively as he tried to make the justices and a government counsel understand that a mechanic can't make a work of art, "because as soon as he does so he becomes an artist"'.[11]

To convince the court that Brancusi's work was in the tradition of ancient art, he produced a piece of stone as evidence, which he assured the court was Egyptian sculpture dating back three thousand years and representing a hawk, although, like Brancusi's *Bird*, it lacked realistic detail. When a sceptical government lawyer asked, 'This is a bird to you?', Epstein replied, 'It is a matter of indifference to me what it represents, but if the artist calls it a bird so would I. In this there are certain elements of a bird. The profile suggests perhaps the breast of a bird.'

'It might also suggest the keel of a boat or the crescent of a new moon?' asked Justice Waite.

'Or a fish or a tiger?' chorused the lawyer.

But Epstein, who wrote about Brancusi as the 'modern artist who brought the greatest individual touch to sculpture', was not to be drawn. His evidence was important, and after two more years of legal wrangling the customs authorities were eventually forced to classify Brancusi's beautiful *Bird* as a work of art. Epstein enjoyed the experience and for once it brought him useful publicity.

Epstein made only three portrait busts in America, although he could have accepted many more commissions. He was interested in the battle-scarred face of the eminent anthropologist Professor Franz Boas, 'criss-crossed with mementoes of many duels of his student days in Heidelberg'. But Epstein found the man 'as spirited as a fighting cock' and admired the mental and physical courage he perceived in his sitter.

Early on in his four-month stay in America, Epstein met Paul Robeson, the left-wing singer and actor who was also a campaigner for black civil rights, at a cocktail party. The two liked each other at once and Robeson took the sculptor to Harlem, where they made the round of black dance halls and clubs, taking their own drink with them. Through Robeson, Epstein occasionally escaped the starchier literary functions attended by art critics and academics to visit more casual parties, where artists and writers met and Paul Robeson sang. It was not until the last week of his stay in New York that Epstein realized he badly wanted to sculpt his new friend. Robeson was playing the lead in the musical *The Emperor Jones,* and Epstein went to see the show and to talk to him afterwards. On his visits to Epstein's home for sittings, Robeson sang lullabies to Peggy Jean and she never forgot them.[12] Epstein completed the sketch of his friend with 'the splendid head' in less than a week, wishing he had had more time. His sympathy with the sitter is apparent in the yearning expressed in the noble head, now at the Festival Hall. The families remained friends and in later London years Epstein made a study of Paul Robeson junior. Robeson said later in a radio tribute to Epstein, 'I thought he was fine, just a fine human being . . . he caught the whole meaning and his feeling for my people.'[13]

Throughout Epstein's stay in America, one can gauge his anxiety about Kathleen from his replies to her letters. Kathleen apparently needed to show him how insecure she felt and could not resist feeding his jealousy. She told him, for example, that her sister Helen wanted her to put up a Russian man friend in her little studio room in Regent Square, knowing how much this would alarm Epstein. But he knew he had no right to protest. 'Does [Helen] imagine you would like to see him toasting his toes in front of our fire? In our place shall I say . . . The place is yours only and you will have whom you please. I am preparing to leave and haste the day of my leaving. There are so many things to say to you and so many to do – together. I love you darling.'[14]

Epstein's four months in New York might have been more fruitful had he not been torn between his two families. Kathleen's letters had become more and more despairing. Epstein's sister Sylvia even suggested that she had attempted suicide.[15] But only Epstein's side of the correspondence remains. His last letter to Kathleen from New York, dated 21 January 1928, is once again a reassuring message of love:

by the time you get this I will be most joyfully on my way to you. You have said I should know where my place is . . . With you I am glad to be alive & I worship with you. Never mind about the splendours of New York, my ideas . . . are quite apart from such things as shop windows & stupid social doings which seem to fill London papers as well as New York ones. We have known happiness together & with little or no money at all . . . Why cannot I be your lover & why must you think of fine clothes for me. You are beautiful and I've shown it in studies of you & I've seen such lovliness [*sic*] in you Kitty as would take me a lifetime to reproduce. You will, I know in your heart, accuse me now of insincerity or cowardice for saying things or feeling them without suiting action to thoughts . . . what you write about living away from the Bloomsbury district I agree with & I suggested that if I work in the studio I have now you come & live nearby in some comfortable flat where you can have all your things and I can easily come and see you.

Epstein had been loaned a house in St Paul's Crescent, near King's Cross, as a temporary home. He wanted to distance Kathleen from her family, since they always made trouble.

If you live near your sisters most likely you will have sudden descents of people you may or may not want to see and invasions . . . My plans for work are not very clear yet. I first want to get back & be with you. That is the great thing. I dream of being with you for lengths of time . . . I anticipate the shirt you are saving for me and as you have shirts of mine you ought to know the right size . . . I am giving all my affairs with the gallery into the lawyer's hands & he will be able to collect what is owing to me . . . of course those who know I'm going beg me to stay, promise me everything in the way of commissions, portraits, anything to keep me, but what they do not know is my happiness in London with you sweetheart. I'm feeling anything but well but on board the vessel. I'll get all right again & then to be with you lovely girl, the thought makes me impatient. Time & distance are not for us two Kitty . . .

The Metropolitan is run by old fogies that seems well known

. . . Its collection of modern sculpture is disgraceful. I've met no artist here who did not seem suspicious and business-like. Concerning me the most absurd reports were spread; that I came over with a press agent was one, this because of the great attention my sculpture attracted. The painters are poor, thin, copying French work or working in an absurd naïve manner they think is American. The sculptors are either stylistic or abstract or stupidly realist but no one with real sensitiveness or power. How I would like to go away somewhere to see the fine things with you, to Toledo & Madrid or the great Grünewald altar at Colmar.

Epstein ends his letter with bitter longing. 'Oh to work on something that was more than a portrait: to do a portrait seems my chief use to the world. May this next week and the following go quickly. If I get in on the Friday night, I'll be with you the following day. Saturday night may it come with its joy.[16]

While Epstein returned to London, Margaret stayed behind with Peggy Jean – to clear up the New York flat, supervise the lawyer who was collecting Epstein debts from the gallery and look after the exhibition in Chicago. Sailing home aboard the *Aquitania*, Epstein was treated as a celebrity: Lord Rothermere, the newspaper magnate, gave a dinner where the guests boasted about their millions. Charles Schwab, the steel millionaire, said solemnly that 'he really couldn't compute' his fortune; P. G. Wodehouse discussed stocks and shares. 'I was, of course, referred to as the "greatest sculptor in the world",' Epstein observed; 'in the eyes of these moneyed men that meant the sculptor who made the most money.' The shipboard meeting did, however, lead to a lucrative commission to make a bust of Rothermere.

Back in England, Epstein's loving reunion with Kathleen was brief, interrupted by the news from America that a tiny steel fragment had blown into one of Peggy Jean's eyes, temporarily blinding her in that eye. Margaret came straight home so that the child could be treated in England. When she was convalescent, Epstein sculpted his ten-year-old daughter, her head drooping, her rounded arms resting on a table that was too high for her, her fingers playing with an imaginary toy, a weight of sadness in the little figure. This, one of Epstein's most personal works, is tender, yet unsentimental. The critic R. H. Wilenski, writing in *The Meaning of Modern Sculpture*, remarked that 'modern sculptors regard *The Sick Child* as a masterpiece but not as a work of sculpture. They regard it as a pictorial masterpiece of the character of a genre portrait by Rembrandt.'[17] In the late 1920s and early 1930s it was becoming unfashionable among avant-garde sculptors to produce portraits of individuals. Henry Moore, with his timeless symbols of womanhood and fertility, was to become the sculptor who bridged the gap from realism to abstract art. Epstein, described by Wilenski as the 'individualist giant', resisted classification.

With two families to support and no large commission in prospect, the financial future looked as uncertain as ever for Epstein, and he was always unrealistic about his spending. The family stayed temporarily in St Paul's Crescent, while Margaret scurried round London looking for a suitable house for them to live in. In the spring of 1928 she finally found a house for sale that seemed to answer all their needs, 18 Hyde Park Gate. The narrow cul-de-sac in Kensington, with its solid houses, held what Virginia Woolf, who had grown up in No. 22, described as 'a whiff of the past; it was definitely gentlemen's territory'.[18] All the houses were of different design, private worlds built to accommodate a family and servants. A small iron gate from the street led into a tiny garden and at the top of a flight of white stone steps a heavy front door faced the visitor. Built out at the back of the five-storey house was a large room with a glass ceiling, a former ballroom, which would make an excellent studio. The studio was spacious enough to hold Epstein's London work. He still rented the cottage at Loughton, but until he moved into No. 18 he had pieces stowed in sheds and workshops all over Bloomsbury.

Jacob and Margaret slept on the second floor in a large double bed, and in the room opposite Margaret kept trunks, costumes and jewellery for Epstein's models, as well as her own possessions. Peggy Jean at last had her own room on the second floor, and there was a spare bedroom beside hers. Up in the gabled room there were separate living quarters, equipped with an ancient gas cooker and sink, a useful space for a servant or visiting model. There was ample room too for Epstein's growing collection of primitive art, which seemed to be scattered all over the house, although the owner could put his hand immediately on any piece he wanted.

The spacious living room, where the family ate and visitors were entertained, was the heart of the house. Epstein's bronzes of his family – a head of his wife; some studies of Peggy Jean as a baby; and a mask of Meum, Peggy Jean's natural mother – were placed around the room, and through glass doors two large Marquesan idols could be seen. Before long the studio was peopled with sculpture, heads and limbs of half-finished work, most of it shrouded, piles of clay, blocks of stone, pieces of wood and stacks and stacks of old newspapers. The studio was Epstein's domain; he kept the keys, and no one entered without permission, except occasionally Peggy Jean. The separate entrance in Queen's Gate Mews, almost opposite Hyde Park Gate, was useful to Kathleen, who had moved to Sydney Street, Chelsea, to be nearer to him. Epstein's life, geographically at least, seemed to have become more cohesive.

In July 1928, not long after the family had settled into their new home, Epstein's sister Sylvia arrived for a visit, and she wondered at the lovely house in a fashionable part of London. 'There was art everywhere,' she commented.[19] Even the bedrooms, she noticed, were stuffed with art, and alongside the art were cats. Her sister-in-law filled the house with them. Sylvia was struck by the exotic life her brother led in London. She recalled a Japanese butler hovering, and the open house at teatime at the weekends. Both Jacob and Margaret were naturally hospitable, and it was pleasant as well as practical to invite clients as well as friends to Sunday afternoon tea. Margaret, 'looking like a great Buddha', served tea and cakes, while Peggy Jean handed round the bread, butter and jam. Actors, politicians, aristocrats and financiers turned up as well as dealers, art students and models. One of the visitors was Betty Joel, a furniture designer, whom Epstein sculpted as *La Belle Juive*.

To celebrate Sylvia's arrival, Epstein took a party out to dinner at the refurbished Café Royal, including Betty Joel and her husband, and Godfrey Phillips, an industrialist who owned an art gallery in Piccadilly, with his wife Dorothy, frequent companions that year. Dorothy Phillips was extremely knowledgeable about the arts and Epstein made one of his most worldly and beguiling portraits of her with a sleek, fashionable fringe, her slender features framed in a sweeping upturned neckline. The bronze, entitled simply *Portrait*, was shown at Godfrey Phillips's gallery at 44 Duke Street, St James's, in October that year with an exhibition of seventy-five fine Epstein drawings, mostly life studies of Sunita and Amina, which were published in book form the following year. Mrs Phillips's bust was bought by the National Gallery of Millbank, now the Tate.

Epstein needed every sale he could get. All his life he seemed able to shrug off the most daunting financial commitments. He had borrowed heavily to secure the thirteen-year lease on his new house from an Irish dealer, Philip Sayers. That year he also moved from the small cottage he rented on the edge of Epping Forest to a larger house, Deerhurst, a few doors away. To add to his responsibilities, by the end of the year Kathleen was pregnant with their third child. He was counting on a lucrative commission: his old friend and colleague, Charles Holden, now a highly successful architect, had designed a new headquarters for the London Underground Electric Railway. Early in the year Holden had told Epstein about the project privately and asked him to make models. Despite the rumpus that employing Epstein always caused, Holden was adamant that Jacob must be the man to make the principal sculptures for his new building. It seemed almost as though the architect wanted his sculptor to act as his alter ego and take the risks for him.

10

A Respectable House

L ONDON IN THE late 1920s was changing. The old Café
Royal, demolished to conform with the rebuilding of
Regent Street, was re-created piecemeal over several years
and officially reopened in 1928. The new Brasserie, with its smart
modern décor, lacked the opulent nostalgia of the old Domino
Room it replaced, but models still used it as an employment
agency and writers and artists still dropped in. London's Bohemia
was moving outwards to Soho, to the cosmopolitan, sawdust-
strewn Fitzroy Tavern and to the more elaborate and pretentious
Restaurant de la Tour Eiffel. And the city itself was expanding,
linked by new Underground stations.

The architect Charles Holden – who in 1907 had worked with
Epstein on the BMA building in the Strand – had already been
commissioned by Frank Pick, the talented managing director of
the Underground Electric Railway Company, to design several
new stations, including Clapham South and Piccadilly Circus. In
1926 they turned their attention to a new headquarters for the
Electric Railway Company at St James's Park station, 55
Broadway, Westminster. The building was to combine a multi-
storey office block with access to an Underground station, and
Holden produced a plan of a modern, cruciform, stone-faced
tower. Muirhead Bone once again made the presentation drawing
of the design.

Charles Holden, now confident of his ability, always wanted to
imbue his buildings with passion and excitement. He privately held
talks with Epstein early in 1928 about the project, and, although no
sculpture had previously been planned, he asked Epstein to make

some models of figures for the new building. In light of the public outcry over *Rima*, this took great courage. At first Frank Pick was reluctant; he disliked the sculptor's 'ugly women'. But Holden managed to persuade the railway magnate to visit Epstein's studio and see his models, and Pick was convinced. Holden also obtained Pick's permission to employ six other modern sculptors to carve figures for the buildings, including Eric Gill and the thirty-year-old Henry Moore. Epstein almost certainly advised Holden to employ the young and relatively unknown Moore on the project. The enterprise was daring: 'the first example of an important building decorated by a group of well-known artists commissioned for the purpose', commented *The Times*.[1] Epstein was given the two prime sites, above the doors of St James's Park station on the northwestern and eastern façades of the building, high up above the sixth floor. The other sculptors were to carve eight flying figures representing the four winds on a band of Portland stone running round the four wings of the building.

Epstein, free to choose his own theme, had the most challenging task. He had to invent a new sculptural language to represent a modern building used for organising the movement of great crowds by the latest means of mass transport. At first he considered sculpture symbolizing the movement of traffic, the crowds passing through the station and the trains hurtling in and out. He eventually decided on the more universal symbols of Night and Day. Holden gave explicit instructions that the sculpted figures were to be 'carved direct in the stone without the use of the pointer or any mechanical means of reproduction from a preliminary clay or plaster model'.[2] He was an architect who shared Epstein's passion for direct carving, aiming in his buildings to combine functionalism with a sense of drama. The architect and the principal sculptor had come a long way since Epstein had employed a firm of architectural carvers to translate his models into stone. Holden wrote that he wanted 'to preserve all the virility and adventure brought into play with every cut of the chisel, even at the expense of some accuracy'. He might have been describing Epstein's work.

After the *Rima* scandal, neither man had any illusions about the reception that another public work by Epstein might provoke. When they first visited the site together, Holden told him he insisted on a policy of secrecy, and Epstein was introduced to the Clerk of Works simply as 'the sculptor'. Holden explained afterwards that it was better if Epstein was not named until he was actually working, since 'Dark forces might upset things.' So the chief sculptor of an important London building was, as Epstein puts it, 'smuggled in'.

Epstein welcomed the opportunity to try to achieve the perfect alliance between sculpture and architecture, which he so much admired in the art of ancient Egypt. He designed two powerful, simplified groups to complement the tall, imposing building. *Night*, the brooding figure of a seated woman looking down hypnotically on a youth lying in her lap, was based on a sketch for a *pietá* that Epstein was working on at the time. The female figure, square headed with broad cheekbones and large limbs, predictably makes no concession to the Western ideal of womanhood but, with its flowing draperies and downward rhythm, *Night* evokes an atmosphere of peace and repose. *Day* does not quite achieve the authority of *Night*. A flat-headed man of Mongolian appearance holds his naked son between his knees as the boy reaches up playfully to touch his father's beard. *Day*, carved above the eastern entrance to the station, caught the sunlight; *Night*, facing north, was permanently in shadow, so Epstein incised the lines of the carving more deeply to make them stand out.

Epstein began his work in October 1928, carving direct in stone, with the building above him an open framework of steel. For the first few months he was able to work in comparative peace, although the conditions were arctic. The building was being erected as he hammered, and he had to try to ignore the tons of stone being hauled above his head on a chain. He worked in the open in a draught that whistled down the narrow canyon of the street. 'I invariably began work with a terrible stomach ache brought on by the cold,' he recalled. He ate his packed lunch on the site and his daughter Peggy Jean remembers him coming home with 'frost-bitten fingers'.[3]

As the figures took shape, Epstein's peace was disturbed when the navvies on the building began to snigger. He had a lean-to shed erected around the sculpture to protect his privacy but arrived one morning to find that the shed had been broken into and surmised that journalists had bribed the watchman to let them in. By March 1929 the popular press were revelling in the game of hunt-the-sculptor. The *Daily Mirror* pounced on Epstein's bright red jersey, and the *Daily Graphic* displayed a photograph of the sculptor 'muffled and mysterious, entering the locked hut on the new Underground building where he is working in extreme secrecy'.[4]

By the third week of May the scaffolding was removed from *Night* and Epstein remained on site, to complete his work on *Day*. Both groups of figures received storms of criticism. A reader of the *Daily Express* described *Night* as 'a prehistoric blood-sodden cannibal intoning a horrid ritual over a dead victim'. The naked boy in the group was too much for Establishment taste, and, as Epstein remarked, 'Even the *Manchester Guardian*, usually very sensible and even-tempered in matters of Art, saw fit to bowdlerise the photographs they reproduced.' At a meeting of the Underground board in July, members, worried by angry letters from shareholders, wanted the sculptures removed from the building. Lord Colwyn, the cotton and rubber magnate, even offered to pay the bill personally and to replace the offending figures with sculpture 'more acceptable to the people of London'. Muirhead Bone managed to have the decision to remove the figures postponed and Holden spoke to Epstein, who very reluctantly agreed to shorten the boy's penis by an inch and a half, in an operation that was performed behind protective scaffolding.

The campaign against Epstein and his work continued until well into the autumn of 1929. The leaders, including the *Daily Telegraph*'s art critic, R. R. Tatlock, Sir Reginald Blomfield, a former President of the RIBA, and Sir Reginald Frampton, the sculptor of the Nurse Cavell Monument, fanned the sensationalism of the popular press. By the first week of October, *Rima*, Epstein's panel in the bird sanctuary in Hyde Park, had again been smeared with tar and feathers. The following week a party of hooligans travelling in a car hurled glass containers with liquid tar in them to disfigure the group of *Night* over the underground entrance. Fortunately they missed their target.

That the figures were howled down by some as ugly, primitive and too Eastern was only to be expected, although Wilenski described them as 'the grandest stone carvings in London' and Charles Aitken, director of the Tate Gallery, remarked, 'Mr Epstein's *Night* and *Day* give the right accent to the reticent mass of Electric House. A great achievement.'[5] Epstein had intended his groups to be seen as an integral part of the building and in this he unquestionably succeeded. The lines of the figures echo the verticals and horizontals of the doorways beneath them. He partly explained the unpopularity of his carvings himself: 'I used no model and I had in mind no particular race though people have always called the figure Mongolian. It apparently always strikes people as unpleasant and peculiar to portray a being so alien to the appearance of the Briton.'

But the opprobrium clung to Epstein. When in 1938 Charles Holden, appointed architect of London University's new Senate House, asked for Epstein as the sculptor to decorate the façade of his building, he was told that a condition of his employment was that Epstein must not be involved in the project. For twenty years after the scandal over the Underground headquarters, Epstein, who had shown such understanding of the needs of architectural sculpture, was effectively barred from decorating public buildings. Another damaging consequence was that in the future the scandal factor entered into judgement of Epstein's work, and critics aligned themselves not so much on an artistic basis as on political and racial grounds.

Although the virulent racist attacks on both *Rima* and *Night* and *Day* rankled all his life, Epstein was not professionally deterred from his course. He retained his enthusiasm for Henry Moore, having recommended him for the work on the Underground headquarters, and praised his *West Wind* in an article in the *Evening Standard*. At that stage in his career the younger man was keen to follow what Epstein was doing. When Moore was working on the

Underground headquarters, he made a sketch on stone of Epstein's design for *Day*.[6] Epstein behaved handsomely towards Moore: he bought three of his carvings in the early 1930s; and in 1931, for Moore's second one-man show at the Leicester Galleries, he wrote the foreword to the catalogue:

> Before these works I ponder in silence . . . Henry Moore by his integrity to the central idea of sculpture, calls all sculptors to his side . . . What is so clearly expressed is a vision rich in sculptural invention avoiding the banalities of abstraction and concentrating upon those enduring elements that constitute great sculpture . . . For the future of sculpture in England, Henry Moore is vitally important.[7]

Epstein now had four children to support. Kathleen gave birth to their third, a daughter named Esther, in April 1929. With two families and two houses to maintain – the large house in Kensington, and his cottage, Deerhurst, at Loughton on the edge of Epping Forest – and the prospect of any large commission now exceedingly doubtful, Epstein behaved with Olympian disregard for the future. In April 1930 he paid £300 for eighteen lots at Sotheby's and throughout the 1930s he bought magnificent works of art, especially African art. 'There is a profound and genuine reason for a sculptor's interest in African Art,' he wrote, 'for new methods and problems are presented in it, different from those of European Art. African work opens up to us a world hitherto unknown.'

> Primitive work when it expresses the principle of sex does it in a manner which cannot be offensive. Firstly because it is frankly sexual and moreover is part of an attitude which can only be termed ritualistic . . .
>
> The modern sculptor without religion, without direction, tradition, and stability, is at a terrible disadvantage compared with the sculptors of previous periods. He has to invent even his subject matter and he has at last been driven into the cul-de-sac of pure form.

There is no doubt, from these extracts from Epstein's writings, that he saw his work as a calling. Since adolescence he had always regarded money spent on his art as justified. In primitive art he found comfort and inspiration and sometimes solutions to technical problems. He had to have his collection, and since his student days there had always been patrons ready to 'lend' or give him money.

In middle age as in youth he was a reckless man. His decision to carve an immense symbol of fertility, *Genesis*, in the face of the fierce hostility his work aroused, was surely a red-blooded response to the 'anaemic society' he despised. Before his visit to America he had bought a huge block of marble in Paris and had it shipped over. Great columns of stone excited his imagination, and they would often stand in his shed at Deerhurst, stimulating his desire to work. Since completing *The Visitation* of 1926, a bronze figure suggested by Kathleen's second pregnancy, he had been brooding on a more elemental and universal expression of motherhood. Epstein himself described *The Visitation* as 'expressing a humility so profound as to shame the beholder who comes to my sculpture expecting rhetoric or splendour of gesture'. Perhaps he had fashioned the figure that way in deference to Kathleen. *Genesis*, the massive, swollen figure that he began to carve in Epping Forest late in 1929, was conceived deliberately without the 'charm of what is known as feminine'. Epstein's figure, weighing three tons, represents a more elemental and universal expression of motherhood: the woman is cut off at the knees, planted in the earth, like Winnie in Beckett's *Happy Days*. Her African-mask-like head with a brooding face is reminiscent of Picasso's early Cubist work, which was hardly surprising, since the two artists were rival collectors of African art.

When it was exhibited at the Leicester Galleries in February 1930, nothing could have been farther from the idealized Western image of the mother-to-be. The strange, primeval head rests uneasily on the distended body; one arm lies across her belly and her other hand rests against her thigh. Although Epstein intended the statue as a symbol, the mother of mankind, and not as an individual pregnant woman, the effect is disturbing. The reaction was predictable. Epstein had a preview when he was finishing the work in his Hyde Park Gate studio. Two gardeners working near by stood staring through the window with their mouths open, rooted to the spot. When Epstein moved they fled.

The critics, even in the serious newspapers, ignored Epstein's other bronzes and fastened on to *Genesis*: MONGOLIAN MORON THAT IS OBSCENE, crowed the *Daily Express*, while the *Daily Mail* entitled their article MR EPSTEIN'S LATEST – AND HIS WORST. Their critic described the statue as 'this simian-like creature whose face suggests, if anything, the missing link'. The critic of the *Daily Telegraph*, R. R. Tatlock, an old enemy of Epstein's, argued that the statue should be removed from the exhibition as unfit to show. His response, conditioned by the attitudes of the time, found the statue lacking in 'the delicacy and reverence proper to the theme', which was understandable. That he devoted only a few lines of his review to legitimate criticism of the *artistic* merit of the figure was less so. 'Regarded purely and simply as a work of art, the statue appears to me to be uncouth. I mean by that I do not very much like the effect of the relationship of the forms. The ensemble is, or appears to me to be, far too heavy. The statue as a work of art lacks altogether that finesse and elegance and that lyrical quality invariably present in a first-rate creation.' For the most part Tatlock indulges in a diatribe against what he terms Epstein's 'gratuitous coarseness', revelling in his description of 'a woman with a face like an ape's, with breasts like pumpkins, with hands twice as large and gross as those of a navvy, with hair like a ship's hawser', and ending ominously, 'There are other details of the figure which one simply does not care to discuss.'[8]

By now an Epstein monumental carving rated the same amount of newspaper coverage as a major sporting event. Gossip columnists, humorists and indignant letters to the editor largely supplanted criticism. However, one journal, the *Week End Review*, employed the painter Paul Nash to review the statue with a psychological post-mortem. There was no hint of solidarity among artists in his comments: the gist of the criticism was that Epstein set out deliberately 'to shock and wound the minds of men'. Not the man to accept gratuitous insults from fellow artists, Epstein wrote to the journal the following week, on 25 April,

> I suppose I ought to be extremely flattered at the length of Mr Nash's so-called post-mortem on *Genesis* and myself, but . . . I am struck by the ready accusation that I want to shock and . . . to challenge even to hurt the minds of men. I might assert with as much authority that Mr Nash paints anaemic pictures in order not to shock or hurt people's feelings . . . We all know art critics are recruited either from the ranks of journalists or are disappointed failures as artists.

In his autobiography, Epstein suggests that 'to shock and wound the minds of men' might be a legitimate aim for an artist. What infuriated him was that Nash 'associated himself with that large body of journalists and critics who declare that I work with my tongue in my cheek'. In his work, Epstein was always sincere, although sometimes he chose to challenge the public. He was both sensitive and combative and could never resist a fight. But making an enemy of Paul Nash, who was prominent in the modern movement, was to prove costly.

The 1930s were a time of innovation for Epstein. He could not stay idle for long and one wet afternoon in Epping Forest he began to illustrate the Old Testament. 'It's raining all the time,' he wrote to Kathleen in an undated letter from this period. 'I have nothing to read except an old Bible. I keep reading Genesis and have made some drawings.' His autobiography reveals that it was in 1931 and that his sketches led to a series of extraordinary watercolours. 'I became so absorbed in the text and in the countless images evoked by my readings, a whole new world passed in vision before me.'[9]

For months he worked obsessively, creating primeval biblical heroes in all their drama. As the son of an Orthodox Jewish family, for Epstein the Torah, the five Books of Moses, had been braided into his daily life, at home, in Hebrew classes and at the synagogue. Although he had long fled from organised religion, his intimate knowledge of the text freed his imagination to respond to the grandeur of the Bible stories. Epstein exhibited his vision of the Hebrew giants in fifty-four large pencil drawings with bold splashes of watercolour wash which were shown at the Redfern Gallery in February 1932. Abraham, Absalom, Isaac, Noah, David, Solomon – passionate men caught up in supernatural struggles – come to life in the watercolours. *Moses Striking the Rock* is revealed as a mighty athlete whose arms and legs echo the strokes of the lightning beside him. He is, of course, a Jew, with a prominent nose, his stance dignified and heavy with conviction.

Although all the drawings, each priced at twenty guineas, were sold, in the growing racism of the thirties most critics fastened on the racial element. 'It seemed', Epstein wrote, 'that I had again committed some kind of blasphemy and countless jibes were forthcoming.' However, as with all his work, there were distinguished writers who recognized his worth. The young Cyril Connolly, writing in the *Architectural Review*, remarked on the 'sureness and simplicity, the power of the line, the extraordinary sense of drama . . . No one should miss this fine exhibition of beauty, of alien splendour.' It is as if, he continues, 'we see them as Blake would have drawn them had Blake been a Jew'.[10]

William Gaunt, writing in the *Studio*, tackled the issue of prejudice head on: 'The Epstein controversy seems to have become a sort of national institution.' The mere mention of the name Epstein was enough in itself to assure many people of an impending outrage. 'This type of criticism', Gaunt added, 'is neither fair nor even germane. It is not fair, because it makes Epstein the scapegoat of the whole modern movement . . . It is not germane, because it makes it difficult for the sculpture or drawings concerned to be calmly appraised . . . and relates them to a multiform prejudice, racial, religious and even political.' Gaunt then assesses Epstein's achievement:

He throws himself sympathetically into the spirit of this

primitive people, sensual, emotional, tortured, intense. With this he combines . . . something of the attitude of the ethnologist and the scholar . . . Epstein has used colour as a poignant and dramatic note, emotionally, that is to say, in key with that foreboding emotion of the Old Testament. He has used drawing similarly, not to give information but to interpret the psychology of Moses and Abraham. In this vivid transposition of the sentiments of an ancient race, I personally think he has been successful . . . The drawings are not, in the conventional sense, pleasant pictures; they are harsh with a patriarchal harshness. They may not be models of beautiful draughtsmanship but they have a living relation to their subject.[11]

Throughout his life Epstein lived in his imagination in the splendour and harshness of the primitive world and was attacked so virulently that it is hard to think of him leading an everyday life. He was combative, intense and focused on his work, but the impression that he made on the young Emlyn Williams, actor and aspiring playwright, in November 1931 – just as he was finishing those fiery Old Testament drawings – provides a useful antidote to the monstrous legend. Emlyn Williams had not yet written *The Corn Is Green* or *Night Must Fall* when a faithful patron commissioned a bust of him. Epstein agreed on a fee of £200 with the patron, Williams's former schoolmistress Miss Cooke, and Williams wrote a brilliant account of the encounter. When he turned up at 18 Hyde Park Gate the front door was opened by a coatless caretaker with sleeves rolled up who seemed to be engaged on some job in the shabby hall. The man smiled and bowed. 'Please come in.' Williams discovered that 'It was Epstein: a burly man with curly dark thinning hair, teeth ragged and discoloured, and a manner as diffident as his voice.' He followed Epstein down two steps into the studio.

'Excuse me while I walk round you.' He then took me gently by the elbow as if I were a breakable object and led me to a gnawed high stool in the middle of the studio. I climbed on to it and sat immobile, determined not to look at him. Straight in front of me, a criss-cross contraption had been knocked together from raw wood mixed with a shapeless grey mass pitted with holes: tiny snails of clay rolled and pressed together between finger and thumb.

He did as he had said, he walked round me. I could not resist quick sidelong looks and saw the shy host give way to a cool detached professional with narrowed eyes. He proceeded on his continuous circle on feet suddenly light; abruptly he would stop, squint, then dip his knees to scrutinize a new plane of my face from another angle.

He was even more of a surgeon than the actor is, as he felt his way towards an operation of the utmost delicacy. I felt that with every second my face was becoming more and more transparent, until there was no secret which was not known to him.

He took up a palette filthy with the stains of old clay and slapped fresh stuff on to it which he rolled briskly into more snails and slapped on to the mess on the stand. 'Relax, please.' After studying my face with the cold, absent stare of an adversary, he set to work with lightning dexterity, no sound but the rapid breathing I was to hear for nine more mornings. Alternating with the sharp unconscious grunts of creation.

Every morning Emlyn Williams witnessed the same metamorphosis from what he saw as 'the clumsy courteous host' into 'the absorbed implacable creator with the hands and even the toes of a dryad'. Williams's account continues,

We agreed that I should not examine the bust till it was finished and cast and he only spoke of it once. 'Strange,' he said, 'I have always found that the face of every male sitter has one profile masculine and the other feminine. I've rarely seen it so marked as in this one.' 'This one', as if he were discussing his work with someone else.

As the end approached, the hammer-gossamer hands took to hovering stealthily above the work, as if about to pounce and destroy it, while the eyes bored into my face and then into the clay, darting with increasing speed from one to the other. Then two fingers would slowly descend, stubby and yet feather-light, and flick the clay with the last touches. They would press it a thousandth of a millimetre to left or right: a stroking which, if it had not been professional, would have been a caress.

The rhythm of his movements – of the fanatical jerks of the head as he stared from me to the clay and back, of the airy touches – began to accelerate: the grunts grew sharper, the breathing more frantic, as if this were a sex ritual and an act of consummation were taking place. And that seemed splendidly right, for what is more physical than the phenomenon, as simple and mysterious as birth, of a pair of human hands, over hours, moulding clay into the eternal semblance of a mortal man?

After the very last brush of a fingertip coaxing a last edge of clay-flesh one hair's breadth into perfection, the hands rose slowly together from the work and turned back into the peasant hammers. Then came the long expulsion of breath as final as the end of life. It was done. 'I think that's all,' he said, striking a match with a timid smile which showed the broken teeth. 'You have been very patient.'[12]

For ten days Emlyn Williams had been observing Epstein as closely as the artist observed him. Epstein always spoke about the physical satisfaction he felt in sculpting, and this account illuminates the dynamic between the artist and his subject. His encounter with John Gielgud a couple of years later had a less successful outcome. Although Gielgud admired the sculptor at work, the portrait that Epstein produced is curiously impersonal. The great actor retained an impression years later of the artist's 'excellent manners'.[13]

Portrait sculpture became an increasingly important source of income for Epstein in the 1930s, and he was often approached by dealers who wanted him to model 'bric-à-brac nudes', mildly pornographic figures which would ornament a mantelpiece or a smoking-room table, reproduce in any number of casts and sell extremely well. But the proposition did not tempt him. He still harboured dreams of 'carving mountains', and in 1932, working in his shed in Epping Forest, he made two carvings, *Elemental* and *Woman Possessed*, in Hopton Wood stone, both obviously created to express his interest in the life-force.

In the first, *Elemental*, the figure of a man in foetal position struggles to emerge from the stone, his hands gripping his ankles, his barely formed face turned upward towards the light. Never exhibited in Epstein's lifetime, today this powerful image is highly regarded by the critics. In *Woman Possessed* a female figure lying on her back, fists clenched and body arched, is captured in a mysterious orgasmic trance.

That same year Epstein had his vast sculpture *Sun God* moved from the shed near his old Guilford Street house, through the roof of the Hyde Park Gate studio, and began to deepen the relief on his majestic block after a break of more than twenty years. When the large stone was standing free in the studio at Hyde Park Gate, he was tempted to carve on the reverse side of the stone. *Primeval Gods* depicts a strange male deity with flat features and hunched square shoulders, not dissimilar to the father figure in *Day*, bearing in his belly two infants suspended as though tumbling. The motif of the male carrying his progeny had cropped up before in *Rock Drill*. As a man Epstein was so intensely paternal that the notion of bearing children may have struck him as desirable. Not, paradoxically, that his own children saw a great deal of him.

He visited Kathleen every evening for an hour after he had finished his work. Twice a week, on Wednesdays and Saturdays, he came to take her out to dinner, at first without the children, but as they grew older they sometimes accompanied their parents. The passionate love affair allowed Epstein's romantic nature full rein. He always arrived in Chelsea with flowers, wine, records – the gifts of a lover, although not necessarily of a paterfamilias. Kitty

Godley, Epstein's eldest daughter by Kathleen, noticed her mother's 'extreme poverty' on her visits to the various houses in Chelsea where she lived. As a baby Kitty had been informally adopted by her maternal grandmother and lived a life of 'ordered frugality and peaceful routine' in the country in Herefordshire. She came to London to visit her mother and meet her father for the first time in the 1930s when she was five or six. The little girl had formed her ideas of a father from the novels of Frances Hodgson Burnett and was expecting to meet a bewhiskered gentleman in a velvet jacket. Instead she met a stranger with curly black hair and a pronounced American accent. Kitty found him haunting and rather frightening and, as a small child, she began to hallucinate, on hearing a man's footsteps. She was an observant girl and noticed, 'My father usually left money on her [Kathleen's] dresser which oddly was in the kitchen.'[14] In 1930 Esther, the baby, was a year old, Kitty was four and Theo was six. Kathleen complained bitterly that Epstein, who was prodigal with flowers and delicacies from Fortnum's, never left enough money for boots and shoes for growing children. Kitty remembered the striking contrast between the 'jars of apricots in brandy and Grand Marnier and slum-like bathroom in the basement'. In the early hours of the morning, when Epstein stayed over, Kitty would sometimes glimpse her father creeping downstairs in the sleeping household to go home to Hyde Park Gate.

By the 1930s Epstein was increasingly an isolated figure in the world of art. In 1926 the Tate Gallery had put on an exhibition of contemporary European art for the first time, including paintings and drawings by Braque, Picasso and Matisse; by the 1930s abstract art of various kinds was becoming more popular in Britain. Epstein would have none of it.

> I never saw the abstract as an end in itself and I do not agree with the people who would divorce art entirely from human interest. They argue . . . that the possibilities of pure form are

endless. That is not the case. They are limited like the patterns in a children's kaleidoscope . . . The discipline of simplification of forms, unity of design and co-ordination of masses is all to the good . . . But to think of abstraction as an end in itself is undoubtedly letting oneself be led into a cul-de-sac, and can only lead to exhaustion and impotence.[15]

In 1932 Arnold Haskell, a young critic, was visiting Epstein regularly, faithfully recording his views and collating the work in a book, *The Sculpture Speaks*, which was highly sympathetic to Epstein. But Epstein was increasingly out of step with younger sculptors who were responding to the new influences. The literary element in Surrealism, which aimed to release images from the artist's subconscious mind that mocked the world of reason, particularly appealed to British artists. The notion that any object could become a work of art if selected by an artist intrigued Henry Moore, whose collection of pebbles, shells and stones remained important to him all his life. In 1931 Moore, Barbara Hepworth and John Skeaping (Hepworth's husband at the time) went on holiday to Norfolk. They all collected large ironstone pebbles from the beach, and carved and exhibited them. They were a group with common interests and intertwined private lives. Moore and Hepworth had both studied at the Leeds School of Art. Hepworth married first John Skeaping and then Ben Nicholson.

For a time in the 1930s several leading British avant-garde artists lived in the modernist Isokon flats in Hampstead. The doctrine of 'truth to material' – direct carving, respect for the chosen material, the relationship between line and mass – became an almost religious tenet of modern sculpture; carving was considered superior to modelling in clay. Epstein regarded the attempt to extend the range of sculpture as leading to puerile experiment. He was even witty at the expense of modern art. 'I flirted with the maiden called Abstraction it is quite true, but it never came to marriage. I parted company with the lady a long time ago.'[16]

Epstein's flippant attitude to modern art made him unpopular with both critics and artists. He was pointedly excluded from Eric

Underwood's *A History of English Sculpture* on the grounds that he was 'alien' and that his work, though 'vigorous and dynamic', was not appropriate for inclusion. Together with Moore and Skeaping, Epstein had represented British sculpture at the 1930 Venice Biennale. After that, throughout the 1930s, he was not invited to exhibit outside Britain again.

Epstein's refusal to embrace the new non-figurative art soon saw him isolated and overtaken. Gradually Moore, who had been known as Epstein's protégé, began to overshadow him. In the early 1930s the popular press attacked Moore's powerful female forms as 'ugly, monstrous, or barbarous – like Epstein's'. EPSTEIN OUT-EPSTEINED, screamed the *Daily Mirror* in April 1931. The caption to the caricatures of Moore's art in the paper reads: 'A monstrosity . . . at an exhibition of Sculpture which surpasses even that of Epstein.'[17] Like Epstein, Moore was pilloried as a dangerous revolutionary by the right-wing press, but the comparison gave more prominence to Henry Moore as the coming man and put a strain on their friendship. A passing reference in a letter of Ezra Pound to John Drummond in May 1934 reveals how far Epstein's stock had fallen among avant-garde writers. Pound refers furiously to the 'peedling Tate Gallery refusing Epstein's Birds [*Doves*], which matter, and presumably buying his latest tosh [almost certainly his bronzes]'.[18] He had become known as a portrait modeller, definitely old hat. After his generous behaviour towards Henry Moore, Epstein must have found Moore's harsh verdict on him at the time as 'scarcely an innovator let alone a revolutionary' and 'a modeller rather than a carver' hard to take.[19]

Perhaps he wanted to re-establish his reputation as a carver and challenge the Young Turks in his 1933 exhibition at the Leicester Galleries. For the first time his show was titled 'Carvings and Bronzes' instead of simply 'Sculpture'. He included his reworked *Sun God* with *Primeval Gods* on the reverse as well as *Female Figure in Flenite* and *Doves* (second version), works that had won high praise from the moderns before the war. However, this time the press chose to ignore the pre-war work and concentrated on 'the scandal of *Primeval Gods* and on the portraits which were as usual, commended'. He exhibited two bronzes of Kathleen in the show and two titled *Isabel*, the second tremulously alive, with pert breasts, long corkscrew earrings and a challenging sensuality.

Epstein was in his fifties, full of vitality and still irresistibly drawn to beautiful women. Despite a tendency to be overweight and the false teeth that Peggy Jean remembers he carried in his pocket, he exuded an air of sexual energy. In the summer of 1932 Isabel Nicholas, a twenty-year-old student who had just resigned from the Royal Academy School, rang the bell at 18 Hyde Park Gate. Epstein himself answered the door and, when she told him she was looking for work as a model, he invited her into his studio. The daughter of a master mariner from Liverpool, Isabel was witty and spirited as well as good looking, and had had experience of posing for fellow students at Liverpool Art School when she was sixteen. Her father had died suddenly in 1930, and Isabel's mother and younger brother, Warwick, emigrated to Canada, but she stayed behind, determined to become an artist. She was accepted by the Royal Academy on the strength of eight drawings from the nude and began her studies in December 1931. After struggling for six months she resigned, disillusioned by the lack of commitment of fellow students. She was absolutely penniless and had been told that Epstein might hire her as a model. He enjoyed her story, which had some obvious similarities to his own, and sympathized with her criticism of the Royal Academy. On the spot he decided to employ her as a model and studio assistant. She would, he assured her, have time to herself to sketch and paint. Isabel went off to collect her belongings from her bed-sit in Holland Park and moved in. Margaret was delighted with the arrangement, hoping desperately that this ripe young woman would divert Epstein from his passion for Kathleen.

The Epsteins treated Isabel as a member of the family. They took her with them when they went out to restaurants and at weekends they all went to the cottage in Epping Forest. Isabel shared a bedroom with Peggy Jean, six years her junior, and made several portraits of her. She worked mainly in watercolours and recorded that 'Epstein was greatly interested in what I was doing.'[20]

Painting animals was an obsession with her. As a child her father had imported exotic creatures from South America to sell to English zoos, and she spent hours at the London Zoo painting the animals and in the London parks sketching swans. When the family went to Paris on an annual trip, where Epstein would visit his casters, scour the dealers for African figures and meet up with friends, Isabel came too, enjoying the life of Montparnasse.

In the hot summer of 1933, Epstein, Margaret, Peggy Jean and Isabel went to stay at Deerhurst. Peggy Jean loved to paint, although her father believed that her natural ability would be spoiled by art school training and refused to send her to study.[21] She spent the days outdoors in Epping Forest, sketching and painting with Isabel. Epstein sometimes went along with them, while Margaret remained at the cottage, enjoying the hours spent tending the large garden and the respite from the bustle of town life. Kathleen was in Martigues in the south of France, visiting her sister Helen, recently married to a fisherman. Although their affair was twelve years old and Kathleen had borne him three children, Epstein found her absence insupportable. This letter is dated simply 'Thursday':

Sweet Kitty
I came yesterday & no letter but today the weight of disappointment is gone with your note & I feel in touch with you slightly. I was quite anguished not hearing from you yesterday & hung round the post office until the last post. I sent off today £9.10s which I hope you will get, at any rate tomorrow morning. I read of your doings & a little of your thoughts. I can imagine perhaps I do imagine you doing much more than you write of, thinking much more also than you tell me. Nothing I do or think can be as real to me as when I am with you, that is reality, that is living & this week & next week will be only thinking & dreaming. I paint & paint which helps to pass the day. I paint daisies (marguerites) also dahlias & (God help Van Gogh!) also some sunflowers. I have thoughts of painting the marguerites for you. They are

difficult, but if you care for any they are yours. I'd like to go off into the woods for a walk but by myself thinking of you, that's too lonely & too harassing. Yesterday I walked through the forest to Epping with your letter in view. Apart from working, being with you sweet girl has been & is the obsession of my life & now you are hundreds of miles away . . . I hope you are getting the sun & health. I can see you are surrounded with loving friends but remember I am here & thinking daily & hourly of you . . . I am thinking of using my flower show here with a Woolworth [*sic*] & selling everything cheap to make money I long for you as I always have . . . I can only regret this parting & until I see you cannot be happy.[22]

Epstein painted over a hundred landscapes and flower paintings in two months, almost two a day, bold, exuberant paintings of trees dancing with movement and fiery-coloured flowers that fill the page. In his painting one senses the freedom he felt in a medium that yielded quick results. Back in London, Margaret, who assiduously tended all his business affairs, had arranged for Dudley Tooth, of Tooth's Gallery, to visit the studio in Hyde Park Gate. The gallery owner was enthusiastic and offered Epstein a Christmas exhibition. The exhibition was a sell-out, a huge success, and Epstein's Christmas flower exhibitions became an annual event in the social calendar. The irony of the situation did not escape him: he had spent his holiday painting watercolours for two months at very little expense and for a quick return, yet he could spend two or even twenty years working furiously to produce monuments for a relatively small fee and earn only condemnation at the end of his labours. 'Not', as he explained to a reporter from the *Lincolnshire Echo*, 'that painting is a hobby. Painting is wonderful. But sculpture is my life.'[23] He described to the reporter how he started to paint almost accidentally. In reality he had, of course, experimented with watercolours before, but never in so concentrated a fashion.

In 1933, his friend Edward Good (Moyshe Oved) – the

whimsical and charming proprietor of Cameo Corner, a jewellery shop near the British Museum – had written an esoteric parable in vindication of the Jews, showing them as creators of world harmony. Epstein illustrated his friend's work, *The Book of Affinity*, with seven watercolour illustrations. Edward Good was a loyal admirer of Epstein's work and often lent him exotic jewellery for his models to wear.

In the 1930s Epstein's reputation as a portrait sculptor was unsurpassed. In September 1933 Albert Einstein, who had been in Belgium sheltering from the Nazis, was warned of an assassination plot and flew to Britain for refuge. Epstein wrote to Commander Oliver Locker-Lampson,[24] who was in charge of Einstein's safety, and obtained permission to sculpt him. Epstein travelled to the camp where Einstein was staying, a wild, secluded spot near the seaside town of Cromer, and found his sitter delightful. 'Einstein appeared dressed very comfortably in a pullover with his wild hair floating in the wind. His glance contained a mixture of the humane, the humorous and the profound.' The sittings took place in a cramped hut and Epstein asked for a door to be removed, which was agreed. For two hours a day he was free to model his sitter. 'Einstein watched my work with a kind of naïve wonder and seemed to sense that I was doing something good of him.' The two men joked together, and Einstein told the sculptor of the one hundred Nazi professors who had condemned his theory in a book. 'Were I wrong,' he said, 'one would have been enough.' At the end of the sessions Einstein would sit down at a piano in the hut and play. 'Once he took a violin and went outside and scraped away. He looked altogether like a wandering gypsy, but the air was damp and the violin execrable and he gave up. The Nazis had taken his one good violin when they had confiscated his property in Germany.'

Epstein had only seven days – fourteen hours – in which to capture Einstein's complex personality. The head, which is little more than a mask, was dashed off at speed with the face wreathed in wrinkles and the clay roughly worked. Yet the overall effect of Epstein's portrait is of a profoundly humane, troubled man, looking into the future with rueful wisdom, reminiscent, as the artist intended, of Rembrandt's great self-portraits.

After a week Einstein was rushed off to make a speech at the Albert Hall before leaving for America. Epstein never forgot his remark about the effect the Nazis had on him: 'I thought I was a physicist. I did not bother about being a Jew until Hitler made me conscious of it.'

Perhaps a week away from his own tangled personal life was a welcome respite for Epstein. There were always upheavals in his anarchic house: servants who came and went – even at one point a butler and a governess – and a succession of beautiful young women. Isabel Nicholas became, perhaps inevitably, Epstein's mistress in 1933. In the open household, there could be few secrets. Peggy Jean, who was a teenager at this time, remembers coming into the bedroom that she shared with Isabel and finding Epstein's sock. 'Why', she asked her mother, 'is Daddy's sock in my bed?'[25]

By January 1934 Isabel was pregnant with Epstein's child. Margaret, now aged sixty-one, decided heroically that she would pretend to bear the child and bring it up as her own, the second of her 'children' by one of her husband's mistresses. For more than a quarter of a century she had devoted her life to Epstein, acting as his official wife and entertaining for him, as well as being his secretary, housekeeper and devoted friend. Kathleen, of course, knew nothing of the secret life at Hyde Park Gate. Peggy Jean helped Margaret to strap a pillow to her stomach and go through the charade of pregnancy, much to the annoyance of the governess, who disapproved of her charge's knowledge of the deception practised by her 'mother' and father.

Now a well-developed girl of fifteen, Peggy Jean was beginning to attract boys and to cause her parents anxiety. 'Do you think my way of life has influenced her?' Epstein asked his wife.[26]

11

Time and Eternity

ON 8 JANUARY 1934 a press photographer snapped Epstein and Isabel at a film première outside the Marble Arch Pavilion.[1] Wrapped in a fur coat, heavily made up with pale powder and dark lipstick, her glossy black hair in a fringe, Isabel personifies the young vamp, while the middle-aged Epstein in winter overcoat and Homburg hat looks furtively over his shoulder. With Isabel he was not only betraying his wife but also Kathleen, his beloved mistress and the mother of three of his children.

Isabel was ambitious and talented, determined to make her mark as an artist, so she was quite happy to fall in with the Epsteins' plans to bring up her child. She stayed in the country for a time during her pregnancy and, on 12 September 1934, gave birth to a boy, Jackie (Jacob), at Surbiton General Hospital. Isabel went off to Paris and that was the last she saw of her son. Unlike 'Auntie' Meum, who continued to visit the Epsteins, bringing presents to the adolescent Peggy Jean, Isabel made a separate life and was soon happily absorbed in the artists' quarter on the Left Bank, consorting with painters and sculptors. Later in life she became an intimate friend of Francis Bacon.

Epstein was enchanted with his baby son; he was good with children of any age – he listened to them and spoke to them without sentimentality – and there were always children's books in the studio for his young sitters. Margaret, who could no longer look after an infant herself as well as running the complicated household at Hyde Park Gate, hired a series of nannies.

That year Epstein returned to a specifically religious theme in his *Behold the Man* (*Ecce Homo*), the figure of Christ brought before Pilate. 'I wished to make . . . a symbol of man, bound, crowned with thorns and facing with a relentless and over-mastering gaze of pity and prescience our unhappy world.' He had an almost physical love for his material, in this case a huge block of 'noble stone', and carved his figure so as to retain a faithful impression of the original stone. The marble proved almost impossible to carve – 'the toughest, most difficult piece of stone' he had ever tackled – and he broke all his tools on it. Only after finding toolmakers who could supply a 'point' that would withstand the pressure was he able to make a start on carving the huge marble figure.

Epstein's son Jackie remembers that *Behold the Man* was one of the sculptures that was most important to his father throughout his life.[2] It is hard to resist the feeling that Epstein identified with the agony of Jesus, misunderstood and misjudged, yet comprehending mankind's suffering. The huge head crowned with thorns, a rough primitive form, dominates the squat body, as the figure sits erect, his hands bound, judging and pitying his tormentors. The statue was never sold, and Epstein would work on it at the Hyde Park Gate studio from time to time. He first exhibited *Behold the Man* unfinished, together with other works, at the Leicester Galleries in March 1935.

The timing of the exhibition gave its many detractors an opening shot. The *Catholic Times* fulminated,

Mr Epstein has chosen . . . Lent when Christians commemorate the death and sufferings of our Saviour to make known to the world his conception of Christ. We have looked, painful as the experience was, but . . . we see only a distorted reminiscence of a man, the debased sensuous features of an Asiatic monstrosity. We protest against the insult to Christ offered by the work of this artist who has genius and skill but who has not considered that experiments are only made on vile bodies.[3]

Some readers of the *Daily Mirror* were quick to applaud the newspaper's decision not to publish a picture of the offending figure. G. K. Chesterton, who apparently had seen it, wrote, 'It is an outrage and I admire the *Daily Mirror* for refusing to publish a picture of the statue. It is one of the greatest insults to religion I have ever seen, and will offend the religious feelings of the whole community.' Colonel Hamilton of the Salvation Army also congratulated the editor for his stand. 'It is grotesque,' he added, '. . . nothing more than sacrilege. Words almost fail me.' The rowdier newspapers outdid themselves in vituperation. But the *Daily Telegraph*, who now had a thoughtful critic in T. W. Earp, looked at the sculpture with an admirably cool eye:

Sculpture in England owes Mr Epstein a considerable debt of gratitude. He found it an exhausted art, devoted to academic exercise, conscientious portraiture and a small – almost codified – range of subjects. But Mr Epstein gave the art a new lease of life. He brought to it an enthusiasm and an impetuous imagination which broke its rigid mould.[4]

The critic added with disarming fairness that, although controversy raged, as usual, over *Behold the Man*, 'no photograph can give a fair conception of a figure so sculpturesque that in the limits of a gallery it is not seen under fair conditions'.

The *Manchester Guardian*'s critic, James Bone, rallied to Epstein's defence with a topical argument: 'As in all [Epstein's] work racial feeling is somehow there and one is aware of a further conception of the race of Christ suffering through the centuries and terribly in our day. It is the most impressive of Mr Epstein's great stone figures and seems a culmination of his carvings.' But it was Anthony Blunt's measured praise in the *Spectator* which proved prophetic. While pointing out that Epstein had invigorated European religious art by drawing on primitive sources, he found the statue not altogether successful because of the sculptor's over-simplification of expression, but added, 'In a sense however this extreme simplicity makes the statue the more suitable to be placed in a church, where it would be seen from a distance and would make its appeal instantly.'[5]

Epstein was asking 3,000 guineas for the figure, which was never sold in his lifetime. In 1958, towards the end of his life, the rector of Selby Abbey wrote to Epstein asking him whether he would leave the giant statue to Selby in his will. Epstein was delighted with the request; he travelled to Yorkshire to see the site and agreed to present *Behold the Man* there and then. But his hopes of placing his work in a fitting location were dashed by a petition of parishioners, who appealed to the diocese of York and overruled the wishes of the vicar and Church officials. At last, in 1969, *Behold the Man* found a suitable site amid the ruins of Coventry Cathedral, where it can be seen in all its power from a distance and in a setting that resonates with tragic history and 'the inhumanity of man to man' which had prompted *The Risen Christ* after the First World War.

At home in Hyde Park Gate, Epstein began to make a series of drawings and busts of his little son; while in Chelsea, only a mile or two away, Epstein's second family were growing up. In 1934 eight-year-old Kitty was still only a visitor at her mother's home, although her older brother Theo and five-year-old Esther lived with Kathleen. In the highly charged atmosphere of her mother's house Kitty felt intimidated and somewhat uneasy. Nevertheless she was excited when Epstein decided to draw her and remembers the occasion vividly. She was immensely curious and fascinated by her father and yearned for his affection, but to her disappointment Kathleen remained in the room with them during the session. Kathleen read aloud to her lover and their daughter from *The Arabian Nights*, the collection of Persian fairytales told by Scheherazade to her husband the king to keep him amused and thereby deter him from having her executed in the morning (as he had his other wives). No doubt the stories were intended to absorb Kitty's attention and stop her from fidgeting, but the sensitive girl felt that her mother was flirting with her father and distracting him from his daughter. In his bold drawing of her, reminiscent of Tenniel's drawings of Alice in *Alice in Wonderland*, Epstein captures the pensive quality and intensity of the child.[6]

Epstein was, within the limitations of divided loyalties, a devoted father who did his best for all his children. However, his children by Kathleen Garman grew up physically apart from him and suffered for what was in the 1930s the cruel stigma of their illegitimacy, while, because he was married to Margaret, their father was never accepted by the rest of the Garman relatives. The name of Epstein was so unusual and so constantly in the press that it made the Garman children's position even more raw and uncomfortable. Epstein had carefully compartmentalized his life, keeping the activities of one household secret from the other. One morning in 1935, however, at breakfast, Kathleen's eleven-year-old son Theo, who had recently started secondary school, read in the paper that Jacob Epstein had given a party for his small son Jackie.[7] The news of Epstein's other son came as a complete shock. Kathleen felt hurt and betrayed that her lover and the father of her three children had deceived her – and had kept her in ignorance about having a child by another woman. Theo, an artistic and highly strung boy, resented his father bitterly from that time on.

Peggy Jean, Epstein's first child, came off best. She was born in 1918 when her parents, her father in his thirties and Margaret in her mid-forties, were still full of vigour. Peggy Jean still remembers family life with affection: outings to the zoo, where Epstein was an honorary member and Margaret was knowledgeable about the animals (her pet name for her ebullient husband was 'buffalo baby'). Margaret was a motherly woman, with a flair for tending sick animals; she once brought home an injured bat and nursed the creature back to life.

As Epstein adored the theatre, the family often went to see Shakespeare and to the ballet. Peggy Jean's favourite outing was to the London Palladium, where occasionally after the show the family went backstage to the dressing rooms of black artists such as Paul Robeson or Eartha Kitt, with whom he was friends. Singers, musicians, dancers and film stars visited the house at

Hyde Park Gate. Peggy Jean remembers the tiny Russian ballerina Anna Pavlova, 'very conceited' in her opinion; as a young teenager she had a crush on the violinist Yehudi Menuhin, but her father considered him boring, since he only wanted to talk about baseball. When they were in London, the Budapest String Quartet always visited. As to film stars, Charles Laughton and Edward G. Robinson often came to tea or cocktails; Margaret mixed an excellent White Lady. Edward G. Robinson bought many of Epstein's flower paintings, and to Peggy Jean's delight they always went to see the star's latest gangster film. 'He was a very good actor, Daddy said.'[8]

The house might have broken chairs and worn linoleum in the hall, but it looked magnificent, with Epstein busts and extravagant displays of flowers in the living room. Since Epstein's watercolour exhibitions of 1933, a firm of Dutch dealers in Old Masters, Ascher & Velker, had commissioned a series of flower studies from him each year, and they sent him crates of blooms every week.

One afternoon in the 1930s Margaret and Epstein took little Jackie to the Crump, a kennel in Bishop's Stortford run by Meum, Peggy Jean's real mother, who had retired from her dancing career. They had come to choose a puppy for Jackie, and Meum's niece noted the event in her diary:

> Epstein had an imposing head but a squat, rather podgy body. Peggy [Margaret Epstein] sat like a menacing Buddha and said very little while dominating the whole room . . . her head was hennaed bright red and her legs so swollen with dropsy they looked as if they were going to burst. She breathed and walked with great difficulty but showed great tenderness to the child. I thought her terrifying, a primitive goddess, silent yet powerful. If the words 'old soul' mean anything at all, Peggy was one, very old.[9]

At the end of May 1936 Margaret made her will. She was sixty-three, with a baby of eighteen months and a teenager of seventeen to look after. She was obviously seeking to protect her 'children' in case of further complications. If Jacob were still alive on her death he would be left all her property and appointed her executor. If not, her friend Betty Joel would be the sole executor with the instruction that any assets be held in trust for the children, Jackie and Peggy Jean. She had very little to leave and yet wanted to do the best for those she loved.

Peggy Jean had grown into a beautiful but rather wayward young woman – hardly surprising considering the hectic household in which she lived. As she said later, she was expected to be both a well-brought-up young lady, chaperoned everywhere, and a madcap bohemian, looking out for suitable models for Epstein.[10] After her latest governess resigned, she celebrated by dancing all night in clubs with dubious reputations and sleeping all day. Epstein's newly married sister, Sylvia, had invited Peggy Jean to New York for a visit, and Margaret was anxious to pack her off, away from the heady atmosphere of Hyde Park Gate. 'Jacob feels when he comes home at 7 a.m. in the morning & sees Peggy Jean getting out of her taxi in front of him by half a minute that perhaps his life has influenced her. He feels this very much.'[11] At last Epstein was beginning to realize that his own anarchic behaviour had consequences for his family. He somewhat half-heartedly supported Margaret's plan to send Peggy Jean to America, although he could hardly bear to be parted from her. While Peggy Jean lodged with her aunt in New York, it was hoped that she would attend the Art Students' League, her father's old school. Margaret scraped together a little money for school fees and pocket money for the visit. In a letter to Sylvia, she confided her hope that Peggy Jean would marry 'perhaps some nice doctor, Jewish-Scotch or Jewish or Scotch, who would understand her & then she would be heroically good . . . Once she gets over the all-for-enjoyment period & see [sic] that the unselfish life is the life of greatest happiness come what may.'[12] Margaret could speak from experience on that topic.

Peggy Jean, however, was not ready for self-sacrifice. She loved New York and wanted to stay there, but did not want to attend the

Art Students' League or look for a job. She walked round the small apartment without clothes, just as she had done at home; this confused and excited her uncle and distressed her aunt. She stayed out late at night enjoying the city life. Understandably, her Aunt Sylvia felt a great sense of relief when she put her niece on a boat for home in October 1936.

In the rearing of Peggy Jean, as in other matters of conduct and belief, Margaret tried to act as the keeper of Epstein's conscience. She tried to instil into her an awareness of her Jewish heritage, although she was Jewish only on her father's side and therefore not accepted in Jewish law. She wanted Peggy Jean to learn the piano. 'All nice Jewish girls learn the piano,' she said.[13] In a time of growing anti-Semitism she even found a young Jewish woman, a refugee, to take Peggy Jean to the synagogue and explain to her the rudiments of Judaism.

On political questions Margaret was better informed and more politically committed than Epstein, and he relied on her judgement. The strong bond they shared in their left-wing politics and their attitude towards race helped to keep them together, despite the tortuous course of their marriage. In 1933, the year that Hitler came to power, the artist Arthur Lett-Haines organized an exhibition of contemporary British art at the Anglo-German Club and wrote twice to press Epstein to exhibit. Margaret suspected the motives of the club, and Lett-Haines enclosed a club prospectus with his second letter 'to assure Mrs Epstein that our constitution is entirely apolitical, if in any case art did not transcend those matters'.[14] Margaret was not reassured, and Epstein declined the invitation. His romantic temperament made him cling to the idea of the universality of art and shun all political action. Even in the 1930s, he stoutly declined to believe that 'the average unfavourable criticism of my sculpture or drawings could be put down to anti-Semitism'. Yet the climate of the times forced him into political action.

In November 1936 Professor Rudolph Hellwag, a German artist, came to London to try to organize an exhibition of British art in Berlin as part of a drive to forge ties of friendship between artists. He visited the annual exhibition of the London Group at the New Burlington Galleries in Piccadilly, and, despite the Nazi government's abhorrence of modern art, was genuinely impressed. He offered to transport the London Group's exhibition to Germany, with all expenses paid. The snag was that there were six prominent Jewish artists in the London Group, including David Bomberg, Mark Gertler and Epstein himself, who had been a founder member in 1913 and was credited with inventing the group's name. Hellwag's vision of artistic fellowship did not include Jewish artists, who could not 'for political reasons' be allowed to show their work. The London Group stood firm and officially rejected the offer. Epstein, as the senior and honorary member *and* a Jew, wrote a forthright letter to the *Evening Standard* on 2 December.

> Every decent-minded artist in England ought to reject the offer to exhibit. It is nothing more than an attempt to enlist the support of British artists in the cause of Nazi propaganda. The London Group of Artists have already officially rejected the invitation. They were invited to exhibit subject to the exclusion of certain works which could not be accepted for political reasons. The Germans have banned Jewish exhibitors and have badly treated German artists in exile. The works of several British artists on exhibition in Germany have been destroyed. Now they are attempting to disguise propaganda as a love of culture . . . all British artists should do their utmost to check the attempt.[15]

Other artists from the London Group, including Duncan Grant, Ethelbert White, Charles Ginner and Epstein's close friend Matthew Smith, publicly urged fellow artists to boycott the scheme. Despite an enthusiastic acceptance by many members of the Royal Society of Portrait Painters, the planned exhibition of British art in Berlin never took place. The Nazis held their notorious touring exhibition of degenerate art in 1937.

Epstein was still a pacifist, and in 1937 joined with other left-wing artists and writers, including Henry Moore, Eric Gill and David Low, to form a National Congress organized by the British section of the International Peace Campaign in an attempt to 'rouse the British Public to energetic action on behalf of World Peace'. When the Spanish Republican government invited members of the congress to Spain, the Foreign Office refused visas to Epstein, Moore and other artists, much to his chagrin.

When Epstein had been about to be conscripted during the First World War he said that an artist fights a battle every day. That was certainly true of his own life in the 1930s. His Strand statues, so vehemently attacked when they were unveiled in 1908, came under threat again when in 1935 the Southern Rhodesian government bought the building formerly owned by the BMA. The new owners found Epstein's figures undesirable and planned to have them removed. In May 1935 the sculptor wrote to the *Observer* to protest,

> The figures were intended to have a universal appeal, even perhaps [to be] understood in Southern Rhodesia. The High Commissioner has taken no trouble so far as I know to consult Mr Charles Holden, the eminent architect, or myself. The statues are an integral part of the building and are actually built into the fabric . . . (actually carved in situ) and to remove them would be risking damage to the statues . . . We think dynasties that destroyed and mutilated the works of previous generations are vandals . . . How is this different in spirit and intention?[16]

The battle for the Strand statues was a replay of the 1908 campaign to destroy them. Walter Sickert wrote amusingly to the *Daily Telegraph*,

> The 18 statues form part of the architecture of the former British Medical Association. Your phrase in brackets, 'although field glasses were necessary to view them

properly', should perhaps have run 'to view them improperly' . . . The whole building is planned to 'tell' viewed from the road. The convention of movement, life and growth is a miracle of genius and accomplishment. I can hear the flowers of rhetorical respect that would be draped, at banquets, on this work, if the sculptor were dead instead of alive and kicking . . . You must not ask of sculpture that it should be a shop-sign or trade-mark.[17]

An influential committee of museum directors circulated a petition for the preservation of the statues, published as a letter in *The Times*, and the grandees who signed included Eric Maclagan, director of the Victoria and Albert Museum, Kenneth Clark of the National Gallery and H. S. Goodhart Rendel, president of the Royal Institute of British Architects. When the president of the Royal Academy, Sir William Llewellyn, refused to add his name to the signatories, on the grounds that it was 'not an Academy affair', Walter Sickert resigned from the RA. The letter to *The Times* from the art grandees concluded, 'If the statues are removed, and still more if they are irreparably damaged in the course of removal, we find it difficult to believe that this generation will be acquitted by our successors of a charge of grave vandalism.'[18]

The statues were temporarily reprieved, and it took a coronation to destroy them. In May 1937 Epstein's statues in the Strand were draped with bunting for the coronation procession of George VI. When the bunting was removed after the ceremony, a fragment of stone from one of the statues was dislodged and fell to the ground, just missing one passer-by and slightly bruising another. Decaying stonework was a welcome excuse for the Southern Rhodesian government to get rid of the figures on safety grounds. They erected scaffolding to examine the statues and flatly refused the pleas of both Epstein and the architect Charles Holden that the sculptor be allowed to examine and report on the state of his work. As Muirhead Bone, the tireless campaigner on Epstein's behalf, pointed out in a letter to *The Times*:

Decayed stonework is no new or indeed difficult problem. The Colleges of Oxford . . . tackle the same sort of thing year in, year out . . . It is difficult to credit that entire destruction is the proposed solution by the present owners of this fine building . . . there must certainly be a better way, and the respect due to works of real genius – for these famous figures have been widely accepted as that – claims a serious attempt to find it.[19]

This time all the efforts of Epstein's supporters to preserve the figures were baulked. The sculptor was not even allowed in the building. Muirhead Bone did manage to arrange that plaster casts be made of the statues, but, when Epstein sent his expert plaster moulder along to assess the situation, the Southern Rhodesian officials refused to allow him access. The moulders approved by the owners of the building 'hustled through a wretched job', according to Epstein. 'They made moulds which were complete travesties of the original.' Epstein was prone to take offence easily and to magnify insults. But in this case his deep sense of grievance was fully justified. To see his work dismembered and the mutilated fragments of his statues left on the building was wounding and insulting. His 'thirty years war' had ended in defeat.

Yet throughout the indignities he endured prior to the Second World War he kept on working at a frenzied pace. In the face of public humiliation he carved huge monuments, still battling to 'carve mountains'. Painting flower pieces and landscapes became a valuable sideline, and of course he modelled outstanding portraits. He remained resilient and remarkably innovative.

By the beginning of the 1930s the art of ballet had travelled from Russia to Britain, and on stage British dancers dared to appear under their own names rather than adopting Russian pseudonyms. In 1930 Marie Rambert founded the Ballet Club in an old parish hall in Notting Hill, which in 1931 was rebuilt and embellished by her husband, the dramatist Ashley Dukes, into a fashionable little theatre, the Mercury. This was the first permanent home of ballet in England, with a company and a school of its own. The elegant Mercury Theatre, with its tapestry curtains, rare collection of nineteenth-century ballet prints on the walls and fine wines in the bar, was a popular society venue. Although the theatre seated only 150 people, they were an influential audience. Among them were leading figures from the worlds of cinema, theatre, politics and books, such as Anthony Asquith, Lady Violet Bonham-Carter, C. B. Cochran, Lady Diana Cooper and Rupert Hart-Davis, as well as the economist John Maynard Keynes and his wife, the Russian ballerina Lydia Lopokova – and Jacob Epstein.

Epstein was a keen and knowledgeable follower of ballet, influenced by his friend and admirer Arnold Haskell, who had become an important ballet critic and promoter of the art. In the autumn of 1935 he was invited to design the drop curtain for *David*, a ballet written by Poppoea Wanda with music by Maurice Jacobson. It was to be performed at the Duke of York's Theatre in St Martin's Lane by the new Markova–Dolin Ballet Company. Epstein tackled the new venture with characteristic enthusiasm. He took on the designs and painting of the large canvas curtain, 30 by 25 feet, working with Bernard Meninsky, an artist acquaintance who had designed the scenery, to produce an exciting preview of the ballet before the curtain went up.

In an interview with the *Daily Telegraph* in November 1935 Epstein described his excitement at the 'new departure'. He painted the work in bold primary colours – red, yellow, blue and orange. 'The figures and general design are monumental in force and scale. Perhaps I can best describe the effect as being like a Russian icon,' he said. He planned to place David at the centre of the curtain, wearing a breastplate bearing a huge Star of David. Two ferocious Lions of Judah guarded the king, and nine panels representing scenes from David's life framed the centrepiece. Epstein embarked on the huge painting with his usual vigour and had the curtain completed to show to the press by 7 January 1936, six days before the ballet opened. He had prophesied that his work would 'produce a very definite reaction in the beholder',[20] and for once the reaction was almost entirely favourable. 'It is one of the finest pieces of decoration ever seen in a London playhouse,' the *Observer* commented. 'The Epstein curtain sent hopes soaring high,' enthused the *Dancing Times*. 'Not only was it a fine picture in itself but its form was that of title-pages of books of a bygone age, in which, by means of engraved panels, the artist delineated the most exciting events that were to follow.' Arnold Haskell, by then ballet critic of the *Daily Telegraph*, considered the curtain 'the most striking feature of the production'. When Epstein's study for the curtain was shown at the Redfern Gallery to coincide with the performances of the new ballet, the *Telegraph*'s art critic, T. W. Earp, found the 'large water-colour of dazzling hue gave the impression of shimmering movement, already partaking of the triumphant rhythm of the dance it preludes'.[21] That January, not long after *Behold the Man* had been so viciously attacked, Epstein was the darling of the ballet crowd – more sophisticated, it must be said, than the mob of sensation-seekers who had crowded in to gawp at his monumental sculpture. Epstein's curtain was a great success and he enjoyed the exhilaration of working in the theatre; but he was never to return, and his curtain has long since disappeared.

Whatever other work he was engaged in, modelling portrait heads, painting or drawing, the large block of stone in his studio served to remind him, if that were necessary, of his commitment to carving in stone. In 1936 a huge block of alabaster lay prone on the floor calling Epstein to work. From time to time he would look at the golden-brown stone and consider how he should use it.

With Kathleen, a trained pianist, he had deepened his love of music. They frequently went to concerts together, and he would often bring her records to play when he came to visit. Listening to music was the only time when Epstein was really at peace, friends said. 'I have been listening to Bach's B minor Mass. In the section, Crucifixus, I have a feeling of tremendous quiet of awe. The music comes from a great distance and in this mood I conceive my *Consummatum Est*.'

Epstein exhibited *Rock Drill*, his 'great adventure' in plaster in 1915 and later dismantled it. The experimental sculpture was reconstructed some sixty years later for the Haywood Gallery.

Epstein treats the theme of pregnancy
in a subtle and naturalistic manner in
The Visitation. *The Risen Christ*,
Epstein's first specifically religious
work roused a storm of criticism.

At first the Leicester Galleries, Epstein's dealers, refused to exhibit
Adam. Now the thrusting figure stands in contrast to the elegant
interior of Harewood House.

Epstein's masterpiece, *Jacob and the Angel* carved in alabaster, towers in the front hall of Tate Britain.

In 1942 when this photograph was taken, holiday crowds in Blackpool queued in their thousands to gawp at Epstein's *Jacob and the Angel*, displayed in a Tussaud's freak show!

Epstein, almost seventy-eight, was too ill to attend the unveiling of his majestic *TUC War Memorial*.

The seventh and final portrait of Kathleen Garman. Four years before
Epstein died, the couple married and Kathleen became Lady Epstein.

Epstein's studio in Hyde Park Gate was always crowded with work in progress. Dominating the room is *Behold the Man*, a carving Epstein prized highly, without a buyer in his lifetime. Today the sculpture is installed in the ruins of Coventry Cathedral.

Epstein writes as if the inspiration were direct: 'I see the figure complete, as a whole. I see immediately the upturned hands with the wounds in the feet, stark, crude with the stigmata. I even imagine the setting for the finished figure, a dim crypt with a subdued light on the semi-transparent alabaster.' In *Consummatum Est* the figure is horizontal although the head is slightly raised. Epstein apparently drew directly on the stone, without relying on preliminary studies. He marked out the position for the head, at the end of the stone where the colour was light, and worked downwards until the whole figure was roughly drawn, 'concentrating on the hands and giving them definite shape and expression'. He was not concerned with imitating nature: 'Imitation is no aim of sculpture proper and a true piece of sculpture will always be the material worked into a shape. The shape is the important thing, not whether the eye is fooled by representation as at Madame Tussaud's waxworks.' All the time he was working on the figure Epstein wondered whether he was getting the emotion he intended from the stone. He had great respect for his material and often warned against 'doing violence to the stone'. The work absorbed him, night and day, and he gave an explicit account of his creative process:

> The sculptor with his vision, planning, working, laying loving hands upon the willing and love-returning stone, the creation of a work, the form embodying the idea, strange copulation of spirit and matter, the intellect dominating hammer and chisel – the conception that at last becomes a piece of sculpture. This seems to me fit work for a man.

On the last day of his exhibition Epstein went into the Leicester Galleries to look at *Consummatum Est* in silence. A stranger came up and spoke to him of the work, as if he sensed that he was talking to the artist. He spoke eloquently, and, when Epstein questioned him about himself, the stranger said that he was a German, a Jew, an engineer. 'What impressed me was his evident desire for anonymity. A Jew out of Germany. A man of culture and of understanding who did not wish me to make anything of him personally. We parted and that is my last impression at the end of the exhibition of *Consummatum Est*.'

In 1936, when Epstein was working on *Consummatum Est*, a chance meeting with a publisher in Paris led to a commission that excited him greatly. As a student in Paris he had come to admire the poetry of Baudelaire and had kept a treasured French edition of the poet's work since 1904.[22] Thirty years later, while enjoying a quiet drink in the Café des Deux Magots in the Boulevard Saint-Germain, Epstein was introduced to George Macy, founder of the Limited Edition Club of New York. Macy knew Epstein's flower paintings and invited him to choose a book to illustrate. In the atmosphere of Montparnasse, Epstein was prompted to suggest illustrating Baudelaire's *Les Fleurs du mal*.

Publisher and artist were delighted with the idea, and Epstein agreed to produce fifteen to twenty illustrations for the poems by July 1937 for a fee of £300: £150 on signature and £150 on delivery. The deadline proved unrealistic, for the artist was taken up with *Consummatum Est* that year and also with the débâcle of the Strand statues. He worked for a year on the drawings, and during the family's Easter visit to Paris in 1938 he made preliminary sketches. Finally, in June 1938, Epstein's carefully worked drawings were ready. Only he had made sixty, three times the amount specified in the contract, somewhat to the publisher's consternation.

Epstein considered the drawings among his best work and showed them 'solely to satisfy a craving of my own', as he wrote in the catalogue of an exhibition of thirty-seven of the drawings held at Tooth's Gallery in New Bond Street in December. 'This Bible of modern man had long called to me and brooding upon the powerful and subtle images evoked by long reading, a world comes forth filled with splendid and maleficent entities.'[23] The macabre had always fascinated and haunted Epstein, and in these magnificent drawings his nightmare world seems to come to life.

Guilty men and wild-eyed harlots couple joylessly; a skeleton strides a skeletal horse in a whirling ride; a middle-aged man creeps downstairs leaving a naked woman desolate on the landing. In *Litany to Satan* a fierce angel swoops down on the crowned king of the underworld, who has the cherubic face, thick lips and bulbous eyes of the ageing Jacob Epstein. The drawings have a depth and sense of volume, and the artist pays careful and consistent attention to detail. He has made no concession to the erotic and sensuous in his harsh 'adventure of the soul'.

The press did not forget to remind its readers that *Les Fleurs du mal* had once been a banned book. Even the *New Statesman* indulged in rhetoric: 'Not only are [the drawings] impertinent, they must be classed as among the emptiest works that he has ever exhibited . . . compared with Picasso's *Guernica* drawings, these are hardly more significant than graffiti. One does not need to be a Blimp in order to feel that ugliness is not enough.' 'Upstairs', the critic concludes, 'there is a roomful of Paul Nash paintings, most of them not new, but a nice enough sight for one's sore eyes.' That was the crux of the matter. Little, if any, of Epstein's work can be described as 'nice'. *The Times* dismissed the drawings in a moderately approving paragraph: 'As exercises in the macabre they show imagination and in form and movement they reveal the plastic powers of the artist.'[24]

Only L. B. Powell, writing in the *Birmingham Mail*, entered imaginatively into the spirit of Epstein's drawings. He saw the work as resembling examples of Gothic fantasy: 'And there is a curious reflection for you: the Gothic gargoyle was an adventure of the soul – a phrase which Epstein uses in description of his work. Adventures of the soul are not, unfortunately, popular nowadays.' Epstein had, in fact, sketched the gargoyles of the Pont Neuf in Paris in preliminary drawings. The critic concludes, 'The directness of inspiration from the text is evident in most examples and is matched, in a unique degree, by ease and grace of accomplishment. *Les Fleurs du mal* is a theme felt acutely enough and of the artist's joy in creation there is no doubt.' A far cry from the *Daily Mail*'s view that 'horror and near-obscenity with no aesthetic value . . . stamp Epstein's new drawings'.[25]

He was, to be sure, no retiring soul, but this time the criticism really wounded him. He had sold fifteen out of the thirty-seven drawings when two weeks after the exhibition opened he withdrew them from the gallery. The show of work that he had considered among his best was 'My greatest failure . . . from the point of view of any intelligent appreciation.' He found the gallery directors out of sympathy with his drawings and 'really rather ashamed of them'. Apart from an exhibition of drawings and paintings of children in 1939 – and this time he had his son Jackie as a favourite model – Epstein exhibited no more graphic work in his lifetime.

Despite his enthusiastic forays into new ventures, Epstein's reputation and livelihood in the 1920s and 1930s rested on his portraits in bronze. He was forced to accept commissions. 'I cannot afford to refuse commissions and do not believe in people who are supposed to,' he told Arnold Haskell in 1930.[26] Two-thirds of the ninety portrait bronzes he modelled in the 1930s were commissioned. His ability to capture a likeness and his psychological insight made him popular with the public and critics alike. Obviously when his sympathy and imagination were engaged the work sparkled. But he was incapable of producing hack work, and to see a group of Epstein portraits together is to experience a meeting with vivid characters.

By the 1930s, as his fame increased, the male sitters who posed on his wooden box in the Hyde Park Gate studio were almost all elderly and distinguished, or at least very wealthy. They included an emperor in exile, a president-to-be and a Prime Minister (Ramsay MacDonald), as well as film producers, oil magnates and academics. The women, by contrast, were usually young and beautiful, oozing sexuality. He portrayed black jazz singers and dancers of the period and yet could, when challenged, create a dignified and complex portrait of a woman academic, fair minded and determined, as his *Professor Lucy Martin Donnelly* demonstrates.[27] The range and quality of his sitters were in themselves impressive.

In 1936 Epstein was asked by Oliver Locker-Lampson to make

a study of Haile Selassie of Abyssinia, who was in exile, to help raise funds for Abyssinia's hopeless struggle against Fascist Italy. Epstein went to the Abyssinian delegation in Kensington to model the Emperor. He was deeply impressed by the calm dignity displayed by Haile Selassie and produced an impressionistic portrait of a doomed emperor, saddened and yet undefeated. The fragile head of the troubled ruler sits uneasily on his neck, and although Epstein created a work of compassion and integrity the unfinished bust 'had no popularity and was only a matter of great expense to myself'.

His bust of Chaim Weizmann, the first President of Israel – revealing the Zionist politician as a man of vision, with hooded, scooped-out eyes, parted lips and flared nostrils – was, by contrast, of great interest to Jewish groups and sold well. With the level of commissions that he accepted, it was not surprising that not all of Epstein's patrons were satisfied with his work.

Since the sculptor had first come to England in 1905, George Bernard Shaw had been a generous supporter of his work, providing him with letters of introduction and vigorously supporting campaigns against his detractors. When Epstein came to sculpt his benevolent friend, Shaw, who was seventy-four, was 'distinctly nervous'. Generous as ever, the writer had insisted that Epstein be commissioned to do the work. A. R. Orage, former editor of the *New Age*, had arranged a commission from an American patron, a Mrs Blanche Grant. The sittings were not a success. 'Shaw sat to me with exemplary patience and even eagerness,' Epstein said.

> He walked to my studio every day and was punctual and conscientious. He wise-cracked, of course. In matters of Art he aired definite opinions, mostly wrong, and I often had to believe that he wished to say smart, clever things to amuse me . . . Shaw was puzzled by the bust of himself and often looked at it and tried to make it out. He believed that I had made a kind of primitive barbarian of him. Something altogether uncivilised and really a projection of myself.

Epstein was convinced that Shaw, who was so generous to young talent, was not really interested in the plastic arts; he felt that he had made a bust with 'elements so subtle that it would be difficult to explain'. The tensions between sitter and artist made it difficult for Epstein to work with the spontaneity and directness that produced his best work. When the bust was cast in bronze, Epstein offered Shaw a copy of it, but was told that Shaw would not have it in the house. Epstein told his sister privately that the first time Shaw came to sit for him he stripped. The artist was appalled. 'He had such an ugly body. I couldn't stand it.'[28] Perhaps that affected the outcome.

Margaret Epstein wrote to GBS in December 1937. She had heard from Orage that Shaw did not like the bust, that it was 'offensive to his household and that he was unlikely to buy a cast of it'. Shaw replied on 29 December:

Dear Mrs Epstein

Only Orage the irresponsible could have . . . supposed that I would throw an Epstein bust back in the sculptor's face as a thing of no value. Of course I never thought of doing anything of the kind. I could at least have sold it and given Jacob the price.

What happened was this. Jacob, as you know, is a savage, always seeking to discover and expose the savage in his sitters . . . when he said to me 'I will show you what you really are', I knew quite well that he would do his best to represent me as an Australian bushman. The result was a very remarkable bust but as I am neither an Australian nor a bushman my wife . . . absolutely refused to . . . have it in her house on any terms. And she expressed her feelings very emphatically to Orage . . .

What interests me at an exhibition of Jacob's work is always the work in which the truth breaks through the biological theory, which began as a phallic obsession and held him back for years. It does sometimes. It did in the Weizmann bust. He is always picking out the women models on whom he can lavish exquisite modelling in detail but on the whole makes them lizards, not women. Why do you let him do it?

. . . One Chaim Weizmann as such is worth a dozen bushmen labelled Bernard Shaw.

If all this makes you angry just think how you would feel if you ordered a statue of Jacob to remember him by, and you received instead a statue of Ishmael!
Faithfully[29]

At this time, when his family life was at its most entangled, Epstein sculpted almost a family album. He produced the first portrait of Jackie, a robust baby boy, with arms outstretched; his fifteenth (and last) study of Peggy Jean, on the verge of womanhood; and an elegant and delicate portrait of Kathleen, surely an act of contrition as well as love after his adventure with Isabel. In this portrait, Kathleen is wearing a high-necked dress, her long-fingered hands resting on her breast. Epstein described the process in his autobiography in a lengthy passage entitled 'Bust of a Lady'.

The sculptor is to model a bust and the beautiful sitter has arrived . . . To the exclusion of all else his vision is concentrated on the model . . . His searching and loving eye roams over the soft contours of the face and is caught by the edges of the brow enclosing the eyes, and so to the cheek-bones, and then downwards past the eyes, mouth and nose. The mask is lightly fixed and the salient points established . . . the expression of the eyes and the shape and droop of the upper eyelid, the exact curve of the under-lid is drawn . . . The nostrils are defined and for this a surgeon's sharp eye and exactitude of observation and handling, are necessary; a trembling sensitiveness, for the nostrils breathe; and from thence to the contours of the lips and the partition of the lips. Then the contours of the cheeks, the faintest indication of cheekbones and the oval of the head, never exactly symmetrical must be shown, and when so much is achieved − a halt. A sonnet of Shakespeare or Faust's invocation to Helen comes to mind.

Perhaps it was with a feeling of relief that Epstein sculpted a new member of his family in 1937. A young communist, Norman Hornstein, the American son of Russian-Jewish immigrants, had noticed Peggy Jean at Montparnasse, drinking coffee. Hornstein invited Peggy Jean to a concert of Hungarian music but the family were leaving for London the next day and the young Hornstein, who was studying medicine at Edinburgh University, followed them. After a brief, rapturous romance the couple were married in the autumn of 1937 at a register office. They all celebrated the occasion at a family lunch at the Ivy restaurant. Hornstein's left-wing politics endeared him to both Margaret and Epstein, who had been anxious about the nineteen-year-old Peggy Jean's future. They had even considered sending her to a finishing school in Brussels or to a domestic science college, but Peggy Jean was not interested. Epstein sculpted his new son-in-law, a curly-headed young man, serene and serious, with a noble countenance. He was the only one of Peggy Jean's admirers that he really liked. Margaret was delighted. She felt that her 'daughter' would have a chance of happiness with Norman Hornstein. 'At first I was afraid he was too beautiful, but Communism has been his religion, and that has kept him good I think.'[30]

Epstein's portraits in 1937 included one of a talented and wealthy American sculptor, Sally Fortune Ryan, who was greatly influenced by his work and became his only pupil. Sally Ryan, who was twenty-one when Epstein sculpted her, persuaded her lover, Ellen Ballon, to sit for him in 1938 and was to purchase several of Epstein's important works. After his death, together with Kathleen, she helped to perpetuate his memory by setting up the Garman–Ryan Collection, now in the New Art Gallery, Walsall.

Some of Epstein's portraits in the pre-war period reflected his political leanings. Victor Gollancz, publisher of the Left-Wing Book Club, brought the Soviet ambassador and his wife to the studio one afternoon. Mrs Maisky was particularly impressed by Epstein's still unsold *Madonna and Child*. Although the title was completely at odds with communist ideology, she thought that the Soviet authorities would be interested in purchasing the majestic group, and Epstein supplied her with photographs. No commission resulted, but he did make a bronze of the round-headed diplomat with the inscrutable expression. That year too he was commissioned to sculpt Rabbi Stephen Wise, a liberal visionary American.

Throughout the decade Epstein had been preoccupied by religious themes – from Genesis to the two figures of Christ. By 1938 his visual imagination was focused on images from the Old Testament. He often made rapid sketches for large works and he modelled two small maquettes of scenes from Adam's life. In one, Adam is protecting the crouching Eve with his body, his head upturned, saying to God, 'I heard Thy voice in the garden and I was afraid; I hid myself.' In the second, Adam is carrying the dead body of Abel, while Eve crouches behind him in deep grief. The two sketches were cast in bronze but never realised as large monuments.

His financial position, always precarious, was becoming desperate in 1938. Although Peggy Jean was now married and living with her new husband, Kathleen's three children – Theo, aged fourteen, Kitty aged twelve and Esther aged nine – were growing up, their needs more demanding. He had received no major commissions since 1929 and his prospects were not encouraging. When he did have smaller commissions he was never able to create a bust for the money alone. He always spent more time and produced more studies than a commission demanded.

In 1938, in a gesture of reckless defiance, he began to sculpt his giant figure of *Adam*, a seven-foot-high, three-ton figure worked in a block of alabaster. Like all his religious figures, Adam seen through Epstein's eyes is elemental man, powerful and forbidding. He stands squarely, his enormous head reaching backward and upward to the sky, defiant yet supplicating too, perhaps. This time the genitals are shown in generous proportion, certain to excite comment.

12

The Lean Years

THE YEAR 1939 began badly for Epstein. He could no longer ignore his looming financial problems: a large tax bill was due, and Philip Sayers, the Irish dealer who had lent him money to obtain a mortgage on the house, was threatening to call in the loan. And other creditors were pressing. He knew that most of the family's money problems were due to his obsessive and reckless buying of African figures in the 1930s, yet he did not even contemplate selling any of this superb collection. Instead, he was reluctantly forced to sell twenty-eight of his paintings by Matthew Smith, works that he had been collecting for over twenty years. The Leicester Galleries had advanced him money on the Smith paintings and would pay him no further sums for his work until he could refund their advance. Matthew Smith's vivid oils of nudes and still lifes had decorated his large living room in Hyde Park Gate for years and were like living presences to him. He was to keep only one, *Woman with a Fan*, which he could not bear to part with.

Matthew Smith came home from France at Christmas 1938 to arrange the exhibition. He had been given a room in the British section of the Venice Biennale that year, and now that his own reputation was more established he was gentler and more at ease with Epstein, although he had some misgivings about flooding the market with such a large release of his work. In January 1939 Epstein visited him every day at Oddenino's Hotel; as the date of the sale approached, the sculptor was in 'a great state of nerves'.[1] Despite Matthew Smith's heavy cold, the two men hung the collection together and, to Epstein's immense relief, half of the exhibits were sold before the doors were even opened. The exhibition was a great success, a sell-out, and Epstein was overwhelmed with gratitude. He began to bombard Smith with gifts in appreciation: an array of medicines, a book on El Greco and a weekend visit to the cottage at Loughton.

Commissions were sparse but he did have one great happiness. Peggy Jean gave birth to her first child, Leda, on 23 August, just before war was declared, making Epstein a grandfather. He sculpted Leda at two months, at four months and at seven months. He also used his little granddaughter as a model for the baby in *African Mother and Child*. His young family served as wonderful models; a head of five-year-old Jackie he called *Ragamuffin*:

> It is the life, free, careless and apprehensive at the same time
> – of the little boy with his lively intelligence and quick ways,
> especially his eyes and also his expressive hands in their
> infinite and unconscious gestures that I wish to capture. I find
> that I must have great patience as there is no such thing as
> posing and I have to watch for the return of a gesture and the
> movement of a head.

His delight in studying, drawing and sculpting children, and his versatility as a craftsman, were disconcerting to his dealers. With apparent ease, Epstein could scale down the forceful dynamism of his carving of an Adam to model an infant's head with great delicacy and yet without sentimentality.

His 'long-promised' exhibition at the Leicester Galleries was due to open in June. The galleries titled the show 'New Sculpture and Drawings of Children by Jacob Epstein'. No doubt they hoped that this time there would be no 'monster' to deflect attention from smaller and more saleable objects. But early in 1939 Epstein found himself with some free time and worked at *Adam* relentlessly, day and night, in order to finish the monument in time for the exhibition. He was extremely circumspect in describing his new work to the Leicester Galleries, saying merely that he was sculpting a statue of Adam. The three gallery directors turned up at his studio in the spring to look at the finished piece. They were obviously stunned at the size and explicitness of the *Adam*: a naked giant, head thrown back defiantly, it was bold even for Epstein. *Adam* is the only carving he endowed with oversized genitals, almost as though he were saying to the public, 'Well, you asked for it!' The gallery directors looked, walked round the free-standing carving and left without speaking a word. The next day Epstein received a letter stating that the directors regretted that they could not see their way to showing *Adam* in their galleries.

Epstein found their worries laughable. He had, he said, seen at the Leicester Galleries coloured engravings from France which were far more explicit. He was anxious to have his work shown but told the directors that if they refused to exhibit *Adam* he would withdraw the rest of his work. Loath to relinquish the exhibition at this late hour, the three directors came again to visit the studio. This time Epstein left them alone for hours to make up their minds. They agreed, with great misgivings, to allow him to exhibit his *Adam*, a work that was, in its earthy energy, its tremendous power and its upward momentum, intensely personal to Epstein. 'Into no other work had I merged myself so much,' he wrote. 'I feel that generations spoke through me and the inner urge that took shape here was the universal one.' That Epstein was inspired by a Whitmanesque desire –

> Singing the phallus,
> Singing the song of procreation
> Singing the need of superb children and therein superb
>   grown people[2]

– seems undeniable. Yet to imagine that he was unaware of the effect that the prodigious phallus that he had sculpted would have upon the English public in the 1930s appears disingenuous.

The exhibition, which opened in June 1939, three months before the Second World War broke out, was of course dominated by *Adam*. Apart from the usual diatribes and headline disapproval, there were interesting reactions. In August, *Lilliput*, a popular illustrated magazine, showed a photograph of Mussolini, stripped to the waist and ranting, with the caption 'Modern Caesar', and on the opposite page a photograph of Epstein's arrogant sculpture captioned 'Modern Adam'. In the reproduction, the figure of *Adam* was discreetly turned to the wall.

Not long after the exhibition had opened, Epstein discovered an unwelcome reminder of *Adam*'s fame on his doorstep. 'This morning on my gate a copy of *Action*, the paper of Mosley's Fascists, was hung up. At last the Fascists have got at my house. I opened it and found an incitement to break up the *Adam*. I must warn my gallery to keep a look out.'[3]

To the surprise of the Leicester Galleries and to Epstein's initial satisfaction, *Adam* was sold that summer to Charles Stafford, a smooth-talking entrepreneur and the director of a gold mine, who bought the statue for a reported £7,000. In fact the figure was really £750, but even at that price, as Epstein pointed out, a quarter of the sum received went to the gallery and another quarter to the Inland Revenue. Nevertheless, any sale was welcome – that is, until Epstein realised what the fate of his *Adam* would be.

By the 1930s, shrewd showmen had begun to realise the commercial potential of Epstein's large controversial monuments, hawking them round the country humiliatingly as a freak show at country fairs. In 1931, after the 'scandal' of the exhibition at the Leicester Galleries, Alfred Bossom, MP, had bought *Genesis* and initially raised a large amount of money for charity by sending the statue on a provincial tour. Later he sold the work at a handsome profit.

As to *Adam*, Stafford sold the exhibition rights to another entrepreneur, a Mr Lawrence Wright; after travelling round the country, the statue eventually turned up in a sideshow at Louis Tussaud's waxworks in Blackpool, with huge crowds queuing to pay their shilling to be shocked. In the spring of 1940, the giant statue was shipped across the Atlantic and exhibited at the Famous Gallery, New York, where, advertized as 'Mr Epstein's masterpiece', *Adam* was a bait to sensation-seekers in America. The *New York Daily Mirror* reproduced a photograph of the carving with polka-dot underpants painted over the notorious genitals.[4]

In the summer of 1939, however, the sensation of *Adam* was soon overshadowed by the threat of war. At 11.15 a.m. on the morning of 3 September, the Prime Minister Neville Chamberlain announced that Britain was at war with Germany. The streetlights had gone out in London two days before and the blackout plunged the city into gloom. The grim news from Europe, with the voices of Hitler and Mussolini booming over the radio, the issue of gas masks and the fear of imminent air raids, affected every family in the capital. The Epsteins remained in London and Jacob grumpily refused to go down into the basement when the sirens sounded, but they were worried about the children. Jackie and a governess were sent to stay at Deerhurst in Epping Forest for the duration; Margaret and Jacob travelled to Loughton by taxi every Sunday to see him. Norman Hornstein had qualified as a doctor and went to work at a hospital in Aylesbury, and Peggy Jean and her baby lived in a village near by, close enough to London to visit Hyde Park Gate regularly.

Mrs Garman, Kathleen's mother, had moved from Herefordshire to the Sussex village of South Harting in the 1930s; Kitty had lived for most of her life with her grandmother, and Esther and Theo were evacuees, going to school near by. Kitty attended a secondary school at Petersfield in Hampshire, but when the girls discovered that she was illegitimate they teased her cruelly and her grandmother took her away and found a governess to address her education. At weekends Kathleen came to South Harting, sleeping in a hut. She brought several of Epstein's bronzes and paintings to store in safety because of the bombing that began in 1940. During the week she stayed in Chelsea to be near him. All Epstein's children were scattered, and family life, such as it was, was seriously disrupted.

Peggy Jean remembers one Christmas when Margaret was dressing the tree and the festive table was laid with a set of Bavarian glasses. Epstein ran downstairs in a hurry, on his way out to see Kathleen. Margaret enjoyed visiting auctions and picking up bric-à-brac and jewellery for the models, and he had asked her to buy a jade necklace – for Kathleen. When he pressed her for it that evening, Margaret told him that she had not been able to purchase the necklace, the asking price was too high. Epstein, enraged, overturned the table and stalked out to the sound of smashing glass, his overweening arrogance reminiscent of the stance of his *Adam*. Margaret always forgave him. She saw in his son Jackie a mirror of Jacob's temperament: 'a terrible mixture of goodness and bad moods, highly strung, a temper like a volcano one moment, and sweet and good-hearted the next'.[5] When he came back from visiting Kathleen overnight Margaret would warn the children that they must be 'especially nice to Daddy'.[6] Ever since Kathleen's arrival Margaret had been afraid of losing him; and perhaps her unfortunate tendency to self-sacrifice reinforced Epstein's egotism.

Epstein's restless temperament made idleness a torment. All through 1939 he worked on his autobiography, *Let There Be Sculpture*, helped by both Margaret and Kathleen. In fact Kathleen more or less wrote the chapter 'I Listen to Music'; Epstein loved music himself, but had little theoretical knowledge.[7] He would be sixty in 1940 and had practised his art in Britain for thirty-five years. In his autobiography he was extremely discreet about his personal life: there was no mention at all of Kathleen, who only features as a model in an illustration; the details of his marriage to Margaret were also glossed over and her first marriage and divorce ignored. He tactfully included photographs of two portraits of Margaret. It was when he came to dealing with the press and with his critics that Epstein lashed out. He detailed the scandals of his public commissions, the Strand statues, the Oscar Wilde tomb, *Rima* and the Underground figures *Night* and *Day*. Then he quoted at length the critics and correspondents who had slated or praised him. In a chapter on journalists he observed,

Art Critics, of course, never want to know what an Artist thinks. They know what they want to think. As they're today, very often, practising artists themselves, or well-to-do amateurs, there is the element of rivalry and jealousy to reckon with . . . I have all my life suffered from these gentry.

One fondly imagines they will die off . . . [but] I have found new spawn rising up from the same muddy depths the old ones were bred in, with the same horrid characteristics, jealous, carping, biting and snarling, and always the hatred that attempts to belittle works whose superiority makes their own failures seem worse.

Though he was insufferably arrogant at times, Epstein's attitude could embrace a magnificent defiance. He was writing in 1939, aware of the impending horror of Hitler, who had already invaded his parents' homeland of Poland, and of the particular threat to the Jews. In his book he proclaimed, 'Artists are of all races and climes, and to band together in racial groups is ridiculous. I am most often annoyed, rather than flattered, to be told that I am the best or foremost Jewish artist. Surely to be an artist is enough . . . This pernicious racialism in art should be forever banished.' Not even a Hitler could shift him from his ideals.

Epstein did not, in any way, deny his Jewish identity. His name proclaimed it and the majority of his patrons and friends were Jews, as the At Home book at Hyde Park Gate in the 1930s reveals.[8] He still kept in touch with the Educational Alliance in New York, the Jewish cultural organization that had helped him so much as a youth. When they held an exhibition in the autumn of 1940 he sent two bronzes, both of family members: *Leda*, a portrait of his granddaughter, and the sombre *Ishmael*, a portrait of his son-in-law, Norman Hornstein.[9]

In 1943 he visited an exhibition of paintings by Josef Herman, a refugee from Poland, and, as Josef remembered, 'Epstein had a wonderful eye.'[10] He recognised Herman's talent and the two men became friends, and later exhibited together. On one memorable Friday evening during the war, Jankel Adler, the influential Polish painter, and Jacob Epstein, the son of Polish parents, were the guests of Josef Herman in his Hampstead studio. Epstein brought his tallis (prayer shawl) as a tablecloth and beer bottles held the candles as the three Jewish artists celebrated the eve of the Sabbath in their own highly unorthodox fashion.

In the early years of the war, galleries were reluctant to hold exhibitions and buyers were reluctant to spend money on art. The Epsteins were forced to canvass friendly collectors to buy sculptures or even paintings at reduced prices.

A Mr Samuels of Liverpool proved a sympathetic friend. In June 1941 Margaret Epstein wrote him a desperate and rambling letter setting out their debts in detail and sending information from the 'Epstein frontline'. Epstein, she reported, was 'working hard, slogging at an Alabaster group all day, every day except Sunday and Monday'. They spent delightful weekends among the flowers in Epping Forest with Matthew Smith. But at Hyde Park Gate there were final demands to meet. 'Don't let this give you worry,' Margaret added blithely; 'there might be some Jewish common acquaintance who would advance Epstein on his future £500. Trusting for his art and honour and goodwill to pay back when he comes into his own again.' At the last crisis, she said, the bank had advanced them money. 'It is well worth trying to put quickly some bright heads together to secure that Epstein should go on hammering and chiselling. That hammer and that chisel will make marks that will live longer than Hitler and have an infinitely higher place in history than Hitler's nightmares of mass murders and tortures.'[11] Margaret, now sixty-eight, overweight and with a weak heart, continued to struggle heroically to protect Epstein and his work. The house was large and expensive to maintain, and although they sometimes had 'staff', beautiful young girls who were more useful as models than in the kitchen, in wartime with money tight there was little comfort for either of them.

The alabaster group that Margaret mentioned in her letter was to become *Jacob and the Angel*, Epstein's most mysterious and powerful interpretation of the giants of the Bible. Ever since he had discovered an old Bible in the cottage at Loughton, Epstein had been deeply immersed in the stories of the Old Testament. He had carved them first in *Genesis*, then in *Adam*. This time he did not attempt to explain or elaborate on the work.

In the Bible story, Jacob, about to make his peace with his brother Esau whom he has wronged, sends his wives, sons and servants ahead of him on the journey, over the brook. 'And Jacob was left alone,' the story continues, 'and there wrestled a man with him until the breaking of the day.'[12] The stranger cannot defeat Jacob but dislocates his thigh, and the patriarch, still clinging to him, demands a blessing from the stranger, whom he takes to be God.

In a radical departure from the original story, Epstein's sculpture, in glowing alabaster streaked with veins of pink and brown recently cleaned by the Tate, depicts two muscular figures locked in a deeply sensual embrace. The angel dominates, his arms tightly clasping a youthful Jacob in an almost maternal embrace, while the boy looks upward in mystical surrender. The sculpture suggests a meeting of spiritual strength and carnal awareness. From the back, the slab of the flat angel's wings seems almost to frame the figures, a part of the great block of stone that Epstein had wrestled with. His skilful carving has effectively given the sculpture 'colour', with the angel's face translucent, while Jacob is seen partly in deep shadow. The biblical story of the mysterious encounter between his namesake and the metaphysical stranger evidently prompted Epstein to draw parallels with his own strivings: his endless struggle to create life from inanimate matter; the fusion of carnal and spiritual love or the ultimate struggle with himself, with his own soul, at a time of war and personal hardship. However, he used the biblical story as a springboard: in his interpretation the struggle is over and the youth has found peace.

In February 1942 *Jacob and the Angel* was exhibited at the Leicester Galleries to a press eager for sensation. By now his large work was so difficult to sell that its main commercial value lay in its freak-show appeal. For almost twenty years Epstein's majestic carving suffered the indignity of cheap exposure, turning up first at a sideshow in Blackpool, then at a seedy Oxford Street dive. The work changed hands more than once; the owner in the early 1950s, Tony Crisp, sent it to Durban, South Africa, before it eventually found a 'home' at Tussaud's in Blackpool.

There was some comment in the press. The *Daily Mirror* remarked in a leader, 'A lot of people are perturbed that Epstein's

4-ton masterpiece *Jacob and the Angel* should have finished up at a 3-penny peepshow in a Blackpool amusement park,' and added rhetorically, 'Is it really inspiring for famous sculptors to have their work exploited in this manner?'[13] But that kind of high-minded hypocrisy served only to draw attention to Epstein's humiliation, although he never revealed publicly how mortified he felt at the slighting of his carvings. It remains an enigma that he did not choose to sell one of his precious African heads to protect his reputation. In his thirty-five years in England his work had attracted more insults and brutal attacks than that of any other artist. 'I would have liked *Adam* to have been shown at the Tate Gallery,' he said, and that is where he felt all his large carvings should have been shown, 'but', he continued, 'you know it would have been rejected – the trustees of the Tate are lacking both in imagination and initiative.'[14] In fact, the Tate took fifty-four years to amend its judgement.

In May 1942 Epstein was offered £750 for *Consummatum Est* by the showman Charles Stafford, who knew the commercial value of a monumental Epstein. 'I hate to have the work dragged through the mud of a cheap show,' wrote Epstein to his patron, Mr Samuels.[15] Samuels tried, unsuccessfully, to raise a subscription to buy *Consummatum Est* for Liverpool Cathedral. In the end, Stafford won.

From 1954 to 1961 *Adam, Jacob and the Angel* and *Consummatum Est* all became part of a spectacularly successful sideshow at Louis Tussaud's, pulling crowds for years. In 1958 the waxworks bought up *Genesis* to complete their Epsteins, which were displayed in 'the anatomical department' at Blackpool. On the seafront 'a loudspeaker blaring swing tunes and a dozen mari-onettes dancing on strings' advertized the attractions of the base-ment department. Holidaymakers were invited in to see 'the strangest thing you have ever seen'. Epstein's carvings were 'surrounded by human heads shrunk to the size of apples by Indian head-hunters, moving marionettes and the embalmed bodies of Siamese twins'.[16] Commercially the Epsteins were a great draw, attracting up to 17,000 visitors a day in the 1950s. But the exploitation of Epstein's works of art smeared his reputation and made it more difficult for him to gain credence with art lovers for years.

Epstein's standing as a portrait artist, however, ensured that he still received some commissions and, although he was never an official war artist, the Ministry of Information began to order bronzes from him. They paid only a nominal fee, but the formal recognition conferred was important. In 1942 he made busts of Major-General Alan Cunningham and of Air Marshal Viscount Portal. He also made a head of Helen Patton, the daughter of the reviled American general. D. N. Pritt, the communist MP for Hammersmith, and his wife asked Epstein to sculpt their portraits, and his known left-wing sympathies may explain why the Establishment were loath to employ him on their staff. It was not until well after the war that Epstein resumed carving his great monuments.

As a release from the studio, Epstein sometimes met up with Matthew Smith, who was still friendly with Augustus John. Although John and Epstein remained wary of each other, with Smith to hold the peace the three men, all in their sixties, shared a wealth of memories of Bohemia. They met at the Café Royal, the scene of so many battles and triumphs, and at the newly decorated Queen's restaurant in Sloane Square. As a joke, the trio suggested to the proprietor that they should decorate one wall with a mural. The owner was horrified at the idea of his ageing clients ruining his new wall.[17]

Matthew Smith – Matt, as Epstein called him – helped Epstein discreetly with money whenever he could, as this letter sent in the autumn of 1940 reveals:

Dear Matt
Thanks for the cheque for £5, although I ought not to accept it but as you surmise things are none too good and were you here I couldn't even blow it with you . . .
Money is getting frightfully difficult to come by. I've fished for portraits but nothing doing yet, perhaps a bite soon, the fisherman needs patience. I am afraid my Micawberlike

nature will give way if things get more serious. At present I'm suffering from an awful boil in the groin brought on by sleeping in the wine cellar (the wines are all gone) where there is hard ground. [The blitz on London in 1940 had made even Epstein take shelter in the air raids.] If I'm to be any good as a sculptor I must get rid of this damned boil.

Went to see John's drawings, difficult to know what I think of them. There is of course consummate ease and ability, but they strike me as cold. I never thought that once. Perhaps you must be young to think John is 'romantic', which is, of course what he'd like to be thought.

Hope to see you soon here,

Ever Yours

Jacob[18]

The close friendship with Smith remained a boon to Epstein. The painter would often spend a night at Loughton as a relief from the bombing, or come to Hyde Park Gate, where he felt at home in the large front living room with his oil *The Woman with a Fan* hanging beside the grand piano. As well as knowing Margaret and Peggy Jean and her family, he was also a close friend of Kathleen and her children. To Theo, in his early attempts to become a painter, Matthew was unfailingly encouraging, and wrote a foreword to the young artist's first show.

For the first time in 1942, the two friends exhibited together at Temple Newsam House, a Tudor and Jacobean mansion set in acres of parkland four miles outside Leeds. A former stately home, Temple Newsam was owned by Leeds Corporation (now Leeds City Council) and gave public access to both permanent collections and temporary exhibitions of art. Epstein showed eighty-six works in all, sculpture, watercolours and drawings. Matthew Smith proved himself a true friend. 'I was enormously impressed by the Epsteins,' he wrote to Philip Hendy, the director (later director of the National Gallery). 'I do not think they could ever look better than at Temple Newsam. It is an honour to have a few canvases hanging around them.'[19]

Both Matthew Smith and Epstein believed that the sculptor had gained a great deal of his interest and skill in painting flowers from his loving observation of Smith's paintings. Epstein did not realise that Smith secretly resented his friend's 'borrowing' his energy. Once when they were walking round a show of Epstein's at Tooth's Gallery together, Epstein said innocently, 'There's a lot of Matthew Smith here,' and Matthew managed to swallow hard and agree.[20]

In drab wartime London, the Christmas exhibition at the Leicester Galleries was a cheerful event in the social calendar. Epstein's exuberant watercolours of flowers were enormously popular. When he had exhibited his paintings in the winter of 1940–1 a bomb had dropped on Leicester Square, and although the blast had shattered the galleries' windows no damage had been done to Epstein's paintings. In 1942, the Christmas show passed without enemy interference and his thirty paintings sold out quickly. Two years later the Christmas show comprised seventy of Epstein's flower paintings and scenes of Epping Forest, each priced around twenty-five guineas. 'Yesterday I went quite berserk,' wrote Virginia Graham to Joyce Grenfell in November 1944. 'I happened to go to a Private View at the Leicester Galleries of Epstein's paintings. There were about 10 people there and they were frantically buying up everything . . . I thought, God, I must be quick, they're taking all the best . . . So I bought two.'[21] Flower painting had become a vital part of his income in wartime. At the cottage in Epping Forest, the Irish gardener/handyman was given firm instructions never to sweep the fallen petals from the grass. Painting 'a frenzy of flowers' was a wonderful and colourful experience for Epstein, and for once he knew that his work was almost guaranteed to sell.

Despite his failure to win approval for his large works, and the necessities of making a living, Epstein could not function without the promptings of a dream. As a youth of sixteen he had found inspiration in poetry, and as a man in his sixties he was still a romantic delving into great literary works. Since the late 1930s his imagination had been besieged by the idea of the fall of man from grace and the struggle between the forces of good and evil. Milton's *Paradise Lost* enthralled him, and in 1943 he began a series of preliminary illustrations to Book I of the epic poem. In his drawing of Lucifer, he shows the prince of angels, his great wings unfurled and his hand placed despairingly on his head; in a second drawing he depicts three of the rebellious angels marooned in the Lake of Hell. The central and largest angel in the trio bears a marked resemblance to the artist. Jacob had also introduced a fallen angel with his own features in his illustration to Baudelaire's poem 'Litany to Satan' in *Les Fleurs du mal*.

It is too simplistic to conclude that Epstein sought to expiate his sins by illustrating his own fall from grace, but his dramatic depiction of sin, and of himself as sinner – the angel turned devil – is striking. In 1944 he modelled a small group of three figures, Satan, Beelzebub and Belial, and a relief panel, *The Fall of Lucifer*: 'a complex of slashing diagonal strokes unleashing the fury of Lucifer's downfall'.[22] This unfinished panel recalls Epstein's early interest in Rodin, and in Rodin's *Gates of Hell* specifically, although he did not particularly admire that work. It was not until after the war that the large single figure of Lucifer appeared.

When times were lean Epstein set out to improve his technique. From 1939 onwards he made a series of studies: small, realistic nude figures, these were not the smooth, seductive, saleable nudes for the drawing room that his dealers would have liked; rather they were his self-taught anatomy lessons with a nude shown swimming against the waves, arms extended, or clutching her breasts, poses that helped Epstein to explore the tensions and energy of the body. Betty Peters, the principal model for the study, was spotted by Epstein one evening in the street at the beginning of the war as he and Kathleen left the Ivy restaurant. They stopped to talk to the small, sinewy African woman with her hair piled high on her head. Epstein invited her to pose for him and she was glad to supplement the small income she earned from running a hostel for black seamen.

To Epstein, Kathleen was still a girl, although by 1943, when Epstein modelled her as *The Girl with Gardenias*, she was a woman in her forties who had borne three children. His admiration for Kathleen's trim body, her long legs and firm breasts is evident. In one hand she carries a gardenia; other flowers float down her legs and one blossom rests on the ground. He is able only to show one shoulder fully; the other still carried the scar of Margaret's bullet. Epstein's figures with a forward movement often seem somewhat precariously balanced. Kathleen, wearing a flimsy garment, seems poised to take off. The large, free-standing bronze has a theatrical air about it which may not be inappropriate.

By 1944 Epstein's complex family life was recovering from wartime strains. Jackie was again living at Hyde Park Gate and Kathleen's three children, Kitty, Theo and Esther, were living at 272 King's Road. He had seen Jackie every weekend at the cottage at Loughton during the war. He was growing up to be a mischievous boy and, to Epstein's bafflement, was interested in machinery and had a passion for motor cars. (Jackie Epstein was later to become a world-class racing driver.) Epstein tried to coax his young son into a love of art, paying him a shilling every time he produced a painting when he was at Loughton, but nothing could wean him away from cars.

The Garman children, by contrast, were quite unworldly. According to one witness, they 'read poetry and played Debussy' and lived in a house stuffed with works of art. Epstein sculpted his Chelsea family in 1944. His two girls, Kitty and Esther, had been fostered in the 1930s, and by sculpting them Epstein had an opportunity to come closer. He created a beautiful bust of Esther with her long plaits and swanlike neck; aged fifteen, Epstein's youngest daughter was growing into a graceful and gentle girl. His first bronze of Kitty, her elder sister, revealed a wistful young woman of eighteen with a luxuriant head of hair and a hint of frailty. Kitty was overawed at first and sat stock still until her father said, 'Kitty, can't you move about, talk to me. I'll get someone to make you a cup of tea.' 'After that,' she recalls, 'we became friends and I dared to call him "Daddy".' [23] He said afterwards of *Kitty with Curls*, 'The portrait has a kind of perfection.'

Theo, who had been drawn by Epstein as a child and as a five-year-old had served as a model for the boy in his father's *Day*, was never subsequently sculpted by him. Now aged twenty, the young man was distant and tense with his father and increasingly jealous; the mental illness that was to cloud his life had already afflicted him. Epstein offered to take him as a pupil in his studio, believing that sculpture would cure all ills. Sadly the rapprochement never happened.

Epstein was passed over by the pundits of modern art during the 1940s. The trustees of the Tate, including Henry Moore, politely excluded him. However, when Picasso came to London in 1945 for his major exhibition at the Victoria and Albert Museum, the great man made a point of acknowledging Epstein at a party held at Felix Topolski's studio in Little Venice. Invited for 8 p.m., Picasso, the guest of honour, arrived at ten. When he caught sight of Epstein among the guests he rushed up and kissed him.[24]

At the end of the war Epstein's portraits for the Ministry of Information were so popular that he was invited to create more busts of wartime leaders. Among others he sculpted Field Marshal Sir Archibald Wavell, who had just published his anthology of poetry, *Other Men's Flowers*. He was a sympathetic sitter and the two men talked about literature during the sessions. Epstein's head of the wartime Home Secretary, Ernest Bevin, square and brutal, reminded Evelyn Silber irresistibly of a Sumerian head in his own collection.[25] To this writer, although there is no obvious similarity, it recalls Karl Marx in Highgate Cemetery.

Of the new and welcome commissions, the most notable was Winston Churchill, now a neighbour. After losing the general election of 1945, Churchill had moved from 10 Downing Street to 28 Hyde Park Gate, opposite the Epsteins. Although he was no longer Prime Minister, policemen patrolled, photographers hovered and large official cars arrived, introducing a worldly air to the quiet cul-de-sac. Churchill came to Epstein's studio with his secretary and a plainclothes detective, who stood at the door. Epstein noted, 'I offered this gentleman a chair, whereupon Churchill abruptly dismissed him. Lighting his cigar, with his secretary seated behind me for dictation, we were all set for a fair

start. After an hour this secretary was dismissed and a second
appeared for further dictation to the accompaniment of a second
cigar.'

Churchill then decided to go to his country home at Chartwell
and he gave Epstein three more sittings there. But the light was
poor and Epstein felt that he had made only a study. The head
shows Churchill firm and thoughtful, the chin pugnacious but the
eyes saddened and a worried furrow in his brow. Although Epstein
felt misgivings about the work, he sold many casts and it remained
one of his most popular pieces.* The two old warriors became
friendly and a rivalry existed between them, as Wynne Godley,
who was to become Epstein's son-in-law in the 1950s, remembered: 'Epstein was a very merry man, very jovial. One day
Churchill came into the studio, looked at Epstein's luscious collection of busts and remarked, "You wouldn't want to go to bed with
any of his women, would you?' When Wynne repeated the remark
to Epstein, he retorted: 'Well, you wouldn't want to go to bed with
any of Churchill's women, would you?"'[26]

The commission that gave Epstein the most pleasure during this
period was of the pianist Myra Hess. She was not, of course,
directly connected to the war effort, but her wartime lunch-hour
concerts at the National Gallery had helped greatly to raise morale
in the dark days and the commission was paid for by public
subscription. When Kenneth Clark put the proposition to Epstein,
he replied, 'I am delighted at the idea of doing a bust of Dame
Myra Hess. I have always been a great admirer of her pianoforte
playing.'[27] The grand piano from the living room was brought into
the studio and Epstein enjoyed the luxury of listening to a performance by a world-class musician while he worked.

As he created portrait heads, the unfinished torsos of his larger
pieces stood about the studio as if in reproach, but he was able to
devote almost a year to the endlessly fascinating subject of Lucifer
as the war drew to a close. He studied the darkly beautiful angel

---

*In March 2001 the magisterial Churchill head was loaned to the White House by
Prime Minister Tony Blair as a gesture of goodwill to the new President, George W.
Bush.

from biblical as well as literary sources and decided to sculpt
Milton's angel as he first alights in hell:

> He above the rest
> In shape and gesture proudly eminent
> Stood like a tower, his form had not yet lost
> All her original brightness, nor appeared
> Less than archangel ruined and the excess
> Of glory obscured.[28]

His *Lucifer*, an immensely tall, bronze figure with a golden
patina, is a strange romantic creation, tentative and thoughtful
and obviously androgynous, despite his male genitals.
Mysteriously Epstein decided to give Lucifer the face of his
former Indian model Sunita, who had appeared as a Madonna
and later as *Israfel*. Sunita, whom he had first met in 1924, had at
one time lived in the house in Guilford Street, and had also
modelled for Matthew Smith. The fallen angel has Sunita's broad
brow, long wavy hair and enigmatic gaze. Two enormous wings
frame him as he lands in hell, his right foot pointed daintily as if
in dance. Epstein said that the key to the figure was the phrase
'son of the morning'. (In Isaiah 14:12 the defeat of the King of
Babylon – that is, Lucifer – is poetically celebrated: 'How art
thou fallen from heaven, O Lucifer, son of the morning! How
art thou cut down to the ground, which didst weaken the
nations.')

   In the autumn of 1945, shortly after the war ended, *Lucifer* was
transported to the Leicester Galleries for an exhibition in October
and November. The bronze was so huge that the front of the
galleries had to be dismantled to ease the shrouded statue inside.
Epstein showed only one bronze with the great work, a head of
Yehudi Menuhin, in an exhibition which included drawings by
Mervyn Peake. He was to sell several casts of the Menuhin bust,
but *Lucifer*, which had been enormously expensive to cast and had
caused him to 'probe inside himself', remained unsold. Ironically
the criticism this time was very positive. 'Epstein was seen at his

best,' said T. W. Earp in the *Daily Telegraph*. 'The actual modelling was superb.'[29]

Then, in 1946, Epstein received wonderful news. Professor A. W. Lawrence, brother of the late T. E. Lawrence, had arranged for the Seven Pillars of Wisdom Trust to purchase *Lucifer* for £4,000. Despite exaggerated newspaper reports, this was the highest price Epstein had ever received for his work. There was a 'family' connection, which must have helped. Sylvia Garman, Kathleen's elder sister, had been a close friend of the reclusive writer and also knew Professor Lawrence well. Both of the Lawrence brothers admired Epstein's work, and in the 1920s T. E. Lawrence had tried, unsuccessfully, to have Epstein appointed to create a memorial to Thomas Hardy.

A. W. Lawrence, a professor of archaeology at Cambridge, was delighted with his acquisition and offered it as a gift to the Fitzwilliam Museum. To his disappointment they turned it down. Epstein then suggested that he offer the work to the Victoria and Albert Museum, but the offer was again rejected, this time on the grounds that the museum did not exhibit works by living artists. The gift of *Lucifer* was next offered to the Tate. Epstein wrote to the director, John Rothenstein, on Professor Lawrence's behalf. The director was away and Epstein invited the Tate trustees to visit; once again the gift was turned down. The rejection was unanimous. Epstein knew that some of the trustees had not even seen the statue; his name alone seemed enough to frighten them off. This time he fought back. In an interview with the *Manchester Guardian*, he described the Tate Gallery trustees' refusal as 'a discouraging performance'. Other newspapers took up the story, and as a result the city art galleries of Liverpool, Manchester and Birmingham all requested the work. 'I was visited by the Lord Mayor of Birmingham and Director of the Art Gallery, Mr Trenchard Cox, who asked that Birmingham should be honoured with the gift,' Epstein wrote.

The struggle was dispiriting at a time when Epstein had grave personal worries. The winter months were bitterly cold in 1946–7 and fuel shortages made heating the large house difficult and

expensive. 'Peggy has been very unwell with bronchitis,' he wrote
to Matthew Smith on 8 January 1947. 'Jackie also developed a bad
cough during Christmas so there is trouble all round. I am keeping
well but the lack of work gets me very impatient.' He was arranging a show of flower paintings in Glasgow at Connell's Gallery
and 'hoping for the best'. The letter ends, 'When will we see you
again? Ever yours, Jacob.'[30]

The 'trouble' was soon to become much more serious. At the
beginning of March, Epstein, Margaret and Jackie travelled by taxi
to Loughton for the day, taking with them John Finch, a young
man who had been engaged the previous year to help take care of
Jackie. As usual, when the taxi brought them home it was Margaret
who stayed behind to pay off the driver. Walking up the cold stone
steps she missed her footing and fell. Wrapped in a black fur coat,
with the large bunch of keys that she always carried round her
waist, she fell heavily to the bottom of the steps and gave a cry.
Epstein, appalled, carried his wife indoors, helped by Finch and
the cook. She was unconscious and was rushed by ambulance to St
Mary Abbot's Hospital near by, where she died later the same day.
At the inquest the coroner recorded a verdict of accidental death.
The shock from a fractured skull, bruised brain and internal haem-
orrhage had killed her. On her death certificate her age was given
as sixty. That was the charade she had played out in order to
pretend to be the mother of Epstein's son Jackie. Her real age was
seventy-four.

For over forty years she had loved and protected Epstein and his
art with ferocious devotion and raised his children as her own. She
had willingly given her life to him as his closest confidante, champion and guardian. Struggling against ill health that marred her
appearance, she maintained an inner strength and dignity that
impressed all who met her. Cecil Gray, a friend of the couple for
thirty years, wrote of Margaret and Epstein,

> No man can ever have had a more loyal and devoted life-
> partner. I can well believe that towards enemies, real or
> imaginary, she could behave ruthlessly, but . . . I can honestly

say that I never had from her anything but kindness and courtesy.

She had a soft spot in her heart for me [a fellow Scot] on account of her deeply ingrained sense of racial loyalty, which she managed somehow to reconcile with her international Communistic leanings. She was a Red of the Reds, but she was also a Scot among Scots, carved like a monumental statue, as if by the master's hand, out of Aberdeen granite. Whenever I met Peggy Epstein I always felt very acutely that man is the weaker vessel.[31]

Among the many letters of condolence that Epstein received was one from his new neighbour, Winston Churchill, written from 28 Hyde Park Gate, three days after Margaret's death.

My dear Mr Epstein
I am deeply grieved to learn of your wife's death. I know what a terrible blow this will be to you. I beg you to accept my keenest sympathy in your sorrow. Mrs Churchill is abroad but I know she joins herself with me in this.
Believe me,
Yours sincerely
Winston S. Churchill[32]

A sad aftermath to Margaret's death was the discovery in the locked room where she stored her trunks of a secret horde of junk: sacks stuffed with broken trinkets and a mouldering fur coat, covered with cat's fur and dust and everywhere an overpowering smell. In her later years Margaret Epstein had taken to visiting auction sales and buying compulsively, a consolation perhaps, for her impossible home life. Epstein, who had not realized the extent of his wife's addiction, could not bear the sight and had the room cleared out completely before the funeral, with the loss of valuable letters.

Peggy Jean, who had just gone off to America to join her husband, came home for the funeral. Margaret had bought two plots for herself and Epstein in Highgate Cemetery, where she lies buried.

13

Into the Light

EPSTEIN'S WORLD WAS in shreds in the spring of 1947. Margaret was dead and he had sent twelve-year-old Jackie back to New York with Peggy Jean. The big old house was empty; there were no servants living in any longer, and Epstein was desperately lonely. He had expected Kathleen to marry him after a decent interval but she made it clear that this was not going to happen. 'You're not going to bloody well make an honest woman of me after living with me for twenty-five years,' she told him.[1]

As a girl Kathleen had been a free, brave spirit, and she retained her fire and her independence. In the years when she was forced to make her own life, she often had members of the Garman family staying in her house in Chelsea. A young Canadian musician, Beth Lipkin, whom Kathleen had met before the war, had attached herself to the household. She adored Kathleen and acted as her amanuensis, making herself indispensable. In her forties, with long dark hair, she was attractive to both men and women. 'She wore flowing, pre-Raphaelite clothes, with sandals,' recalled another friend of the family. Niall Lawlor was a young Irish journalist whom Theo Garman had met in 1946 in a Chelsea pub. Theo asked to draw the young man and the following year Lawlor visited the family, remembering Kathleen's house as 'sparsely furnished in impeccable taste'. He was also invited to Hyde Park Gate, where Epstein was unveiling a bust of Gabriel Pascal, the film producer. Pascal was rash enough to criticize the sculpture and tell him that he had made the jowls too heavy. 'Epstein picked up his sculptor's hammer in a flash of temper. "You dirty bourgeois," he said, "you know nothing about art." [2] Lawlor concluded that the sculptor had no capacity for self-criticism.

Epstein and Kathleen still dined out once or twice a week. They often visited the newly opened Caprice restaurant, where the proprietor collected Epstein's work and where the film fraternity often dined, so that there was the possibility of gaining commissions. He made only six portraits in that turbulent year, but he did begin work on a major carving of a biblical figure, *Lazarus*. This time Epstein chose to temper the drama inherent in the story of the man miraculously raised from his death (John 11:1–44) with a quiet compassion and a restraint rarely seen in his work. He carved the figure from a block of pale cream Hopton Wood stone in his studio, the eight-foot-tall body still swathed tightly for burial and only the head turned wearily towards the light, with eyes still closed, in this, Epstein's most spiritual work. He worked on it in the large empty house where he himself was gradually emerging from a nightmare at a time when the nation was gradually counting the cost of victory. He did not finish until 1948, or exhibit until 1950.

In March 1950 *Lazarus* was the central feature of an exhibition of Epstein's new work. Almost without exception the critics praised it. Wyndham Lewis, writing in the *Listener*, considered this latest work 'perhaps the most impressive of his giant carvings'. T. W. Earp of the *Daily Telegraph* thought that it 'ranks among the sculptor's major achievements', while Denys Sutton, assessing Epstein's importance two years later, found *Lazarus* 'one of the most moving works of our time'. [3]

Unfortunately no buyer came forward to purchase *Lazarus*. There were no anatomical features to tempt the proprietors of seaside peep-shows, and Epstein felt dejected, as this letter to Meum reveals. There is no date, but it was almost certainly written in the summer of 1950, after the exhibition at the Leicester Galleries and a profile in the *Observer* of June 1950. Meum was in hospital suffering from cancer at the time.

My own dear little Meum,

Poor you lying in hospital. The bright – the happy Meum how sorry I am to hear this sadness. Never mind the wretched 'profile'. It is all about a shabby old man in a shabby old house. A 'shabby' profile altogether. The chap who wrote that sensed a feeling of depression and disappointment. This must have forced itself strongly on him. Since Peggy's death there has been a great deal to disappoint me, much that does not bear thinking or brooding on. It is a long and very complicated tale. I do not want honors, you know that. I am too old to be honored. I hope you saw the Lazarus: that I think is beautiful but it is disregarded as you know. I will try to get it to America. Do not write of your youth. You are the ever beautiful, the ever lovely, the ever youthful Meum. Get well – get well. If wishes could help you would get well right away.

[Two sentences are scratched out here.]

I never thought I would be as lonely as I am.[4]

Although Kathleen was now partly living at Hyde Park Gate, she was elusive and often away. 'In a big, somewhat shabby, house not far from the Albert Hall, with worn oilcloth in the hallway, stands a vivid bust of the composer Vaughan Williams, left like a visitor's hat on a wooden chest near the front door,' the *Observer* profile began.

Epstein himself answers the door, in a cricket shirt, shapeless trousers with braces and blue plimsolls . . . It seems a pleasant but rather empty encounter, until one gets into the studio. Here there are blocks of stone in shapes that at once convey vitality. One becomes aware of an energy in this house . . . Nothing about him startles you until you shake his hand and become conscious of its astonishing bulk. The sense of being in touch with a man of unusual force grows as the impressions of an amiable teaparty at a trestle table recede.[5]

Epstein's aching disappointment over the fate of *Lazarus* was

eventually to be assuaged. In 1951 A. H. Smith, the distinguished
historian and Warden of New College, Oxford, sat for his portrait,
commissioned by the college, in Epstein's studio. The Warden, an
art lover, noticed the *Lazarus* standing majestically in a corner and
told Epstein that his work would look magnificent in the cloisters
of his college. Within a year the carving was bought. Epstein was
so delighted that his work would be housed in a suitable setting
that he agreed to let the college have the figure for the modest sum
of £700. After a visit to the site Epstein and the Warden decided
that the carving would be better protected inside the New College
Chapel, where it now stands. The installation of *Lazarus* at New
College was a great event. Epstein wrote to Peggy Jean, 'We all
travelled down with Matt Smith' – the party also included
Kathleen, Kitty and Esther – 'and the presentation of the statue in
the Chapel was most impressive. I got very little from this statue,
but I think the placing was worthwhile.' For Epstein, who had seen
so much of his work rejected and debased, the outcome was 'one
of the happiest of my working life'.[6]

Since he had begun work on *Lazarus* in the spring of 1947
Epstein had gradually reassembled his life. Kathleen and Esther
came to Hyde Park Gate in the summer of 1948, although at first
'it went against the grain very much living here at all', Kathleen
wrote to Peggy Jean.[7] She kept her own house in Chelsea for Theo
and went over there frequently to look after him. Epstein's home
was badly in need of repair and Kathleen had the kitchen roof
mended and most of the house painted. More vitally she tried to
rationalize Epstein's finances, bringing in an accountant, who
reduced his tax bill from £1,300 to £600. It was an expensive
establishment to run: there was the interest to pay on the house
loan, and Epstein's bill from the bronze moulders was never less
than £100 a month. Kathleen thought the Kensington house
'ridiculously big . . . but it does give [Epstein] the feeling of
security and isolation that he needs for his work'.[8] More worldly
than Margaret had been, and also very much younger, Kathleen
insisted on cutting down on household expenses. Despite Epstein's
protests, no living-in servant was employed in the house; there was

only a cleaner who came in during the week. On Saturdays Kathleen kept up the tradition of Margaret's 'At Homes', entertaining as many as fifteen guests, because, she said practically, 'usually in one way or another it leads to sales'.

A newspaper article appeared in the summer of 1948 incorrectly reporting that the couple had married, and Epstein asked Kathleen to write to Peggy Jean to tell her that it was not true. 'Some day we might,' she said, 'but things seem to me best as they are.' She told Peggy Jean that her father was well and rather touchingly seemed to seek her approval. 'I make your father laugh quite a bit and we have a lot of fun in between times. Wouldn't it be hateful to be a stepmother?' Kathleen asked her lover's daughter. 'Isn't it nicer as it is?'[9] Epstein wrote to Peggy Jean very freely, almost as if he were writing a diary, and she obviously knew that her father would have preferred to be married. But with Theo's mental health a constant worry, with her own friends and her years of pleasing herself, Kathleen was reluctant to commit herself.

In 1948 their daughter Kitty, now aged twenty-two, married the up-and-coming painter Lucian Freud, who was twenty-five. The German-born grandson of Sigmund Freud, he had moved to London with his family in 1931 after the rise of the Nazis and became a naturalised British subject in 1939. Four years earlier Freud had had his first one-man show at the Lefevre Gallery. Kitty went to live in the flat he rented in Delamere Terrace in Paddington. Sadly, their marriage was to last only four years.

As an artist Epstein still felt ostracized. 'The highbrows disregard my work,' he said, referring specifically to the Rothensteins, Kenneth Clark and Philip Hendy. He was also permanently worried about money, never able to keep up with income-tax demands. 'My main anxiety is that I do not feel secure in any way, although I am constantly selling things and working on portraits.' An invitation to exhibit at a 'Sculpture in the Open Air' show at Battersea Park in May 1948 cheered him. The exhibition was an imaginative initiative by the London County Council to bring art to the people, and when Epstein visited the site he was delighted. For the first time the public would be able to see the large carvings he valued, *Behold the Man* and *Lazarus*, open to the sky and not dwarfed by the confines of a gallery. They looked at their best among the trees, as did the bronze of Kathleen, *Girl with a Gardenia*. When he attended the opening with Kathleen he was pointedly ignored. Moore's *Three Standing Figures* was the only sculpture shown on the posters. 'The Battersea show was a scream,' he told Peggy Jean.

> Moore was made hero of the opening, leading the members of the Cabinet, Cripps and Bevan, straight to his work and ignoring everything else. Bevan avoided me and so did Moore, they rushed around very self-important and posing for the photographers. Nevertheless the photographers were busy photographing Kathleen and myself.

He enclosed photographs to amuse his daughter. 'The show, in spite of the monstrosities there, bodes well. There are Rodins and Maillols and my things look, I think, in harmony with the trees and outdoors.' The sculptor Maurice Lambert, he wrote, had 'sent me a friendly and sympathetic letter, protesting against the domination of the intellectuals'.[10] Epstein was referring to Kenneth Clark and 'that miserable little Rothenstein'.

During the summer he kept busy with portraits, still working, when he had spare time, on *Behold the Man*. In the autumn he was cheered by an offer from the Aberdeen City Art Gallery to buy *Girl with a Gardenia*. 'After all the Battersea exhibition did me a good turn although the organisers never wanted me to have a look-in.' But his confidence in official taste was so dented by this time that he half expected the statue to come back. 'I seem banned in London,' he complained to Peggy Jean. He did send a few of his works for exhibition to the second Edinburgh International Festival but could not afford the expense of a full show.

In the autumn he was working on a bust of Jawaharlal Nehru, the Prime Minister of India. He had modelled a head of the Indian leader in December 1946, when Pandit Nehru, who was attending a Commonwealth conference, came to visit his studio. After the meeting and three sittings Nehru wrote appreciatively from the Dorchester Hotel,

My dear Epstein

Before I leave London I want to send these few lines to express my deep pleasure at having met you at last, and my gratitude for all the trouble you have taken.

I hope we shall meet again in a less hurried atmosphere.[11]

In 1948, however, when Nehru sat for Epstein again, the assassination of Mahatma Gandhi and his political difficulties at home had darkened Nehru's mood. Epstein wrote to Peggy Jean,

I have finished the Nehru, or rather Nehru has returned to India . . . his last sittings were very unsatisfactory. He seemed easily fatigued and practically slept during two sittings and I could not get on with it . . . it all left me wondering about him . . . Nehru is now a silent and I think embittered man, and gives me the impression of disillusionment and all this is in my bust.[12]

Despite Epstein's hopes, the bust of Nehru did not sell to any wealthy Indian. Epstein put this down to Lady Mountbatten's influence. '[She] doesn't like it because it's too serious and not half handsome enough for her.'[13] Her husband, Lord Louis Mountbatten, had been the last Viceroy of India and it was widely known that Lady Mountbatten was having an affair with Nehru.

Epstein was in a bitter mood all that year. In January he wrote to Peggy Jean about the 'gratitude' of Henry Moore. Moore had asked Epstein to lend some of his collection for an exhibition of 'Sculpture through the Ages', while neglecting to invite Epstein to lend any of his own work. 'You can imagine the answer they got from me.'[14]

*   *   *

By 1949 Jackie had been away in America for nearly two years. Epstein missed him and more than once asked Peggy Jean to remind the boy of his father. He was naturally paternal, although his way of living and his volatile temperament meant that his children grew up in an atmosphere of high art and emotional and financial insecurity. Esther, now aged twenty, left Hyde Park Gate to move in with Mark Joffe, a publisher whose wife had disappeared a few months after the birth of their son Roland. Esther, a gentle, loving girl, looked after the six-year-old boy. Theo's recurrent mental illness was a constant worry; he rarely came to Hyde Park Gate. To compound the family misfortune, Kathleen's sister Helen, who was now married to an elderly Italian lawyer, was discovered to be suffering from a brain tumour. Esther went out to Italy to help take care of Helen's one-year-old baby. In August 1949 Kathleen travelled to Italy to be with her sister when she had surgery. Epstein decided to visit Peggy Jean and Jackie and Norman Hornstein in Cape Hatterns, a small island off the coast of North Carolina where they had recently moved. He loved the sea and enjoyed swimming and walking along the beach. It was the first real rest he'd had for years, away from the complex world of celebrities and critics and dealers. He could not resist drawing Peggy Jean's oldest child, Leda, and her little brother Ian.

Now that Kathleen had moved in, Epstein felt able to bring his son Jackie home with him. On the way back he visited New York and made some business calls to gallery owners. There was good news waiting for him on his return. He was invited by the Arts Council to contribute to an exciting new enterprise, the Festival of Britain, designed to reinvigorate Britain after the postwar austerity. Since the final victory in 1945 the country had endured a drab period of food and petrol shortages and rationing. By employing Britain's most talented architects, artists and designers to work together to transform twenty-seven acres of the Thames Embankment into a dazzling miniature city representing the history and achievements of Britain, the Labour government hoped to transform the nation's mood. The injection of colour and light in illuminated fountains which rose along the waterfront, the hundreds of trees in bloom and thousands of flowering bulbs, the fun and fizz of the exhibits did, amazingly, act as a tonic to the nation.

For Epstein, invited for the first time in twenty years to make a monument for a public building, the commission marked a turning point in his career. 'My commission for the 1951 Festival of Britain was announced on the wireless and aroused a lot of attention,' he told Peggy Jean in January 1950.[15] He had also received an invitation from the Philadelphia Museum of Art, who wanted him to sculpt a statue – and he would soon be invited to create a large monument for an important church building in central London. Approaching seventy, he was about to embark on the busiest period of his career. 'When I had the strength I didn't have the work,' he used to joke. 'Now I have the work, I don't have the strength.'

Epstein's modest *Youth Advancing*, the curiously conservative bronze figure he modelled for the Festival, lacks the passion he usually brought to his work. His realistic portrait of a young male nude, head up, arms thrust forward with clenched fists, one foot lunging forward, was placed on a circular plinth between two pavilions. The face, with wide staring eyes and long hair, based on the head of a Chinese boy, is not noticeably oriental. Epstein, it seems, was playing safe, and his figure attracted no flak.

By contrast, the younger sculptors at the Festival were making strange linear constructions, exploring new materials: Reg Butler welded metal to create the spikiest exhibit in *Bird Cage*; Eduardo Paolozzi created a quirky wall fountain of steel and concrete by arranging cups and basins on scaffolding; but the sculpture which most captivated the massive audience that visited the Festival was Richard Huws's forty-three-foot bucketing *Water Sculpture*. The public were beginning to expect art to be a 'happening'. Henry Moore, with a large *Reclining Figure* opposite the entrance to the exhibition, was still in the ascendancy, but his monumental style was being challenged and so, of course, was Epstein's.

After the public humiliation of *Rima* and the London Underground sculptures, the importance to Epstein of having his work included prominently at the Festival was immense. In the postwar world, perceptions of his work had changed: his *Lazarus* was greatly admired and his presence at the Festival of Britain gave him a certain standing. The climate of opinion in the country had changed too: in the light of the recently revealed Nazi atrocities, public expressions of anti-Semitism were now insupportable and this too made acceptance of Epstein's work easier.

Cathedrals and churches had suffered severe damage in the bombing and in the postwar world the ecclesiastical authorities were beginning to reconstruct their shattered buildings. Four Palladian houses occupied by the nuns of the Convent of the Holy Child on the north side of Cavendish Square in central London had been partly destroyed in the war. In 1947 the order employed Louis Osman, a young architect with an imaginative approach to the artist's contribution to architecture, to restore their houses. As well as rebuilding many of the inner rooms in the convent, Osman built a connecting bridge with a plain supporting wall above it to link and buttress the two central blocks. An integral part of the design of the bridge was to be a 'large magnificent group of sculpture'. Without it, he said, his plan for the bridge would be 'quite ridiculous and meaningless'.[16] The nuns had already told their architect in conversation that they intended to employ a Catholic sculptor to create a Madonna and Child for their convent when they could raise the funds. But Osman was determined to have his sculpture and convinced that Epstein was the only artist who could produce a work of the scale and grandeur required. Without telling the convent, he approached Epstein and explained the position frankly. He had no guarantee of payment or acceptance but badly wanted the sculptor to accept the challenge. Epstein, as rash as Osman, was thrilled by the prospect and replied that he 'would like to go right ahead and do it'.[17] He produced a wonderful maquette within a week. 'I got so interested in the Mother and Child that I neglected everything else and in the Madonna and Child there is no money, so I have had to keep myself going by doing portraits of extraordinarily dull people,' he told Peggy Jean later.[18]

Epstein's name first appears in the convent's minute book of

5 April 1951, when the nuns, taken unawares, were confronted by the model and unanimously (and one suspects rather thankfully) agreed that they could not afford it and that 'this decision must be *firmly made* to Mr Osman'.[19] Osman was not a man to be deterred easily and appealed again and again for Epstein's work. Despite the community's fears of the expense of the work, of the possible scandal, of the non-Catholic artist and his style of work, he persisted. The nuns demurred; Osman threatened to resign. The nuns were faced with an impasse: 'One does not lightly turn down the work of so great an artist, nor break with a good architect midway in building operations.' In the meantime Louis Osman appealed to the Arts Council for backing and, while the community was still hesitating, 'Kenneth Clark blew in, pronounced it beautiful and saying "Take it, take it," blew out again.'[20] The Arts Council made a small grant towards Epstein's work. At the end of June the convent capitulated. The Reverend Mother made it clear that the order could not bear any of the cost and Epstein agreed to co-operate with any suggestions made by the community. 'The nuns are favourable to my going ahead with the Madonna on condition that they have a say in "advising me",' he wrote to Kenneth Clark. 'I don't know whether theologically or aesthetically. Short of baptism I don't mind listening to them.'[21]

Epstein was away for the summer, but in the autumn several nuns came to his studio to gaze at the emerging figures. Accounts of the meeting between the sculptor and the sisters give us a glimpse of this encounter: it seems clear that the two parties were engaged in a decorous flirtation. 'Epstein examined our habits closely and would walk round us looking for a model. He said, "It's the boney [sic] structure that interests me."' He modelled the figure's garments on the nuns' habits and, after listening to their reservations, agreed to alter the Madonna's expression: the face of the Virgin in the maquette was based on Kathleen, but the nuns disliked her 'upward agonized gaze', so he substituted another model. Marcella Bazetti, a gifted Italian pianist, was a friend of Kathleen's, a young woman with an introspective, inward expression, and he sculpted her face as the Madonna, looking down in

peaceful offering of her child. 'He was ready to accept our suggestions and criticisms with the humility of a really great man,' the
convent's report concludes.[22] In the light of the many accounts of
Epstein's arrogance, this simple tribute from the sisters of the Holy
Child is particularly telling.

He refused 'all but negligible personal remuneration', a letter
from the convent to other communities appealing for funds for the
project revealed. The community had become completely transformed and were now devoted to Epstein's statue, which portrayed
the Madonna 'poised between heaven and earth . . . The finished
work, to be cast in lead into which some silver has been melted,
should be completely satisfying to the mind and we hope to the
hearts of all who see it . . . it may be that God has chosen a great
artist, almost in spite of us, to create something that is worthy to
live into the future.'[23] The group at Cavendish Square gave
Epstein enormous satisfaction and, after the scandals of the 1920s
and the horrors of cheap sideshows, restored him to an honoured
place in the artistic community.

Apart from this absorbing project Epstein was juggling with
other commitments. The invitation from the Philadelphia Museum
to create a symbolic sculpture for Fairmount Park, which
surrounded the museum, with the rather nebulous title of *Social
Consciousness*, was accepted. The Americans offered Epstein over
£4,000, with casting and expenses paid by the donors. This was the
most generous offer he had ever received, and in August 1951
Epstein sailed to the United States to view the site and make his
arrangements. He spent a few days in New York with his helpful
brother Irving, seeing old friends, and relaxing with Peggy Jean
and her family off the North Carolina coast.

He returned to England at the beginning of October. He was still
deeply in love with Kathleen and wrote her love letters when he
was away, always beginning 'Sweetheart'. The couple tried to time
their separate visits abroad together. Kathleen had been visiting
her sister Helen with Theo and Beth Lipkin, who had returned to
England to become inseparable from Kathleen, a situation which
Epstein just tolerated. The family had acquired a pet, a Welsh

sheepdog puppy, Frisky. Originally it was for Jackie, but, now a teenager mad about cars, he had just acquired a motorcycle and had no time to look after a dog. Frisky became Epstein's devoted friend, and the artist was to sculpt him. 'He has made friends with everyone in the street, especially the policemen who guard Mr Churchill's house,' he told Peggy Jean.

The year 1952 was when Epstein was finally acknowledged by the Establishment as the senior sculptor in Britain. In January *Lazarus* was installed at New College Chapel; photographs of Epstein's thirteen-foot-high *Madonna and Child* and reports on its progress were often in the press. To crown it all, the Tate was to hold a retrospective exhibition of his works, a mark of recognition that he had long craved. Having looked to the Tate for support for years, now aged seventy-two he thought the overdue recognition was because 'they had exhausted the interest in Moore & Co and everyone . . . is fed up with the Abstractionists'.[24]

In May, before the exhibition, he was edgy. He had a woman with a child living in to do the cooking, but Kathleen was away in Italy, where her sister was undergoing a second operation on her brain. 'All this isn't good for me who also needs looking after,' he complained to Peggy Jean. 'The hundred and one things of practical life I am as little prepared to trouble with as anybody else. Kathleen's boy Theo' – Epstein could hardly be blamed for labelling him 'Kathleen's boy' since he had seen so little of his elder son – 'gets worse and worse, all treatments have been tried with no results.'[25]

The retrospective opened on 25 September 1952 with three rooms showing fifty-nine of his sculptures and twenty of his drawings. The magnificent bronze portrait heads dominated the exhibition: rulers, artists, intellectuals, politicians, beautiful women from the stage and studio, and children from newborn infants to young men and women. The retrospective gave the impression that Epstein was principally a modeller, although the introduction to the catalogue noted that an important part of his work was of a monumental nature. Since a number of his large carvings were unavailable because they were either in an architectural setting or

in a sideshow, illustrations of them were published in the catalogue. The five-foot-four-inch marble *Genesis* was the only monumental carving; the other two marbles included were *The Doves*
and a *Study of Two Arms*, described by Epstein as 'the hand of a
woman resting tenderly in the hand of a man'.[26] This had been
carved in 1923, in the early years of his lifelong love affair with
Kathleen Garman.

The loyal Matthew Smith hosted a party at the Caprice after the
show's opening and Epstein admitted to Peggy Jean that his
exhibition was 'having a great success', but still he felt an outsider.
He sensed that John Rothenstein, the director of the Tate, although
outwardly friendly, was 'hostile', and that the Arts Council were
equally unfriendly. Whether he had simply grown accustomed to
years of disdain from the art establishment and could not believe
in his success and acceptance it is hard to know.

The exhibition was 'a triumphant vindication of [Epstein's]
courage in the face of unjustifiable hostility and stupid prejudice',
wrote Philip James in the catalogue, quoting the only words that
Epstein had allowed in the preface to his first exhibition in 1917 at
the Leicester Galleries: 'I rest silent in my work.' Those words
remained, he said, 'an expression of the innate simplicity and
modesty of a great artist'.[27] Epstein was natural, unaffected and
direct. Whether he was either simple or modest is another question. He had grumbled to Peggy Jean about the 'excessively dull'
people he was commissioned to portray, yet in his later years he
sculpted some of the most outstanding personalities of the century
– Churchill and Nehru, of course, as well as Bertrand Russell – and
in 1949 he had made a memorable portrait of the composer Ralph
Vaughan Williams, his face ravaged by time, yet both thoughtful
and forthright. Epstein felt an innate sympathy towards sitters
connected with the arts, and Vaughan Williams, a courteous man,
invited the sculptor to hear him conduct his annual performance of
Bach's St Matthew Passion.

Neither could he complain of boredom when sculpting the head
of the poet T. S. Eliot in 1951; in fact the two became friends. In
1958 Epstein, one of a small number of guests at the poet's seven-

tieth birthday party, lit the candles on Eliot's cake. The writer
W. Somerset Maugham also sat for him in 1951 and addressed him
assiduously as 'Maestro'. He portrayed Maugham as an imperious
Roman emperor with narrowed eyes, hawk-like nose and mouth
turned down, the whole face criss-crossed with fine lines. Epstein
seems to have made his own sliding scale of fees for sitters; to
people in the arts he charged too little for his work, as T. S. Eliot
pointed out in a letter.

The film world could afford to pay well, although he was not so
interested in the stars. He made portraits of Anna Neagle, of Gina
Lollobrigida, the Italian sex symbol, and of Portland Mason, James
Mason's baby daughter, in 1952. The actor Michael Wilding wanted
Epstein to sculpt Elizabeth Taylor as a wedding present from him,
but Epstein was doubtful about the commission. She was unwell at
the time and he was preoccupied with his large commissions, the
Madonna and Child and *Social Consciousness*. Although she was
very beautiful, he thought she was too spoiled to take her sittings
seriously. For whatever reason, he did not make a bust of Elizabeth
Taylor. 'I suppose only film stars will be able to afford works of art
in the future,' he reflected gloomily to his daughter.

As he aged he became busier than ever, taking on large
symbolic and religious works and still greatly in demand as a
portrait sculptor, sculpting ten or twelve portraits in 1952. He
began to employ artists to mould the plaster in his studio. Noreen
Smith and her husband Jan worked for him and remember the
experience vividly.

The studio was crammed with pieces of casts, arms, legs,
tools, piles of cloth to keep the clay work damp. There were
shelves of heads, mostly well known. Everywhere you looked
you would catch the eye, of Menuhin, Emlyn Williams,
Conrad, Robeson and many lovely children's heads. Of
course, there were the huge stone figures and always work in
progress. We frequently worked practically over the heads of
sitters or listened to somebody reading a story to a child while
we mixed plaster.

He was unusual in that he would never let anyone do the actual modelling or carving. He did it all himself. When he had modelled in clay and asked me to cast it in plaster he was aware of every line and wrinkle, every curl and eyelash, the exact depth of the eye, and wanted this perfectly reproduced in plaster . . . He would sometimes watch me chipping out and working on a face with small tools. He loved to see it emerge again. He appreciated the job well done and would say so. He never wanted me to do his work but he wanted me to make it easier for him to do his own.[28]

Both Jan Smith and Noreen loved their work and admired Epstein, their employer. They would all have lunch together, and at teatime on a sunny summer's day they would sit on the steps. Epstein would say, 'Can you pour a cup of tea for the postman?' He was a regular visitor who hung his hat on the gate and chatted with them.

Hyde Park Gate being a very select address, some of the neighbours must have been dismayed by Epstein's democratic habits. 'He adhered to no convention,' Noreen Smith remembers. 'He didn't kow-tow to any of the bigotries.' He occasionally invited the Smiths out to dinner at the Caprice. Frisky, his adored dog, accompanied them, and was welcomed royally with a plate of his favourite chocolates placed discreetly on the floor. That year, 1953, Epstein made an affectionate sculpture of Frisky jumping up.

Dining out with friends or colleagues who understood his work was one of Epstein's rare relaxations. He was struggling to finish his work *Social Consciousness*, today sited on the West Terrace of the Philadelphia Museum of Art just outside the entrance. The difficulties he had were inherent in the over-ambitious nature of the commission. Originally, *Social Consciousness* was planned as part of a vast and grandiloquent plan to span the history of America in a series of sculptures set on the bank of the Schuylkill river, Philadelphia. The work was begun in 1914, and Epstein was one of six sculptors invited to complete the series after the First World War. By 1951 Epstein had signed the contract, but he found it difficult to interpret his vague and lofty theme. For inspiration he turned, as he had when he was a youth, to the vigorous sweep of Walt Whitman's verse. Whitman, after all, had represented his country as the mother in his poem 'America'. The core of Epstein's monument is an eleven-foot-high seated mother, the strongest figure in the group. These lines of Whitman were in his mind; and after his death they were engraved on the monument:

> A grand, sane, towering, seated Mother
> Chair'd in the Adamant of time.[29]

He made a maquette of the mother with the strong, dignified features of Sunita, arms wide in welcome, symbolizing America the free, welcoming in her immigrant children. The concept was extraordinarily dense and encouraged Epstein's histrionic tendency. He first made a maquette of a warrior with a sword and a mourner on either side of the central figure, then radically altered the flanking figures halfway through his work, again turning to Whitman's poetry. Two towering figures stand beside the mother. The one on her left is an elongated, Christ-like figure raising up a fallen man, the symbolism easy to read. The one on her right, a tall, swathed woman supporting a dying boy, represents the figure of death. Today the three sets of figures seem difficult to interpret and lacking in unity. But when Henri Marceau, director of the Philadelphia Museum and co-chairman of the project, came to visit Epstein in October 1953 he was delighted and wrote enthusiastically to his colleague in Philadelphia,

> *Social Consciousness* is magnificent – really great and impressive, deeply moving work . . . I was completely over-whelmed by its impressive scale, its dignity and power and by a quiet tenderness I had not expected to find. To my mind it completely tells the story of a rather difficult abstract theme.[30]

By September 1953 Epstein was able to send all three huge plasters to the foundry to be cast. The scale had been so large that he had needed more height than his studio could provide; the Royal College of Art near by loaned him a huge studio to work in. He only had to slip out of the back of his house to be there in five minutes. He was touched by the warmth and interest of the students, who often watched him at work.

Epstein was learning to reconcile himself to recognition and even appreciation that year. On Ascension Day, 14 May, the sun shone for the unveiling of his *Madonna and Child* in Cavendish Square. A large crowd gathered, and the street was cordoned off for the opening ceremony, performed by R. A. Butler, the Chancellor of the Exchequer of the Tory government. The memory of the unveiling of *Rima*, when Prime Minister Baldwin had pulled the cord and released a storm of protest, faded at last, as Butler described Epstein's statue as 'a synthesis of beauty'. 'No work of mine has brought so many tributes from so many diverse quarters,' Epstein said, and the newspapers were full of photographs of Epstein and Kathleen. The critics, the religious press and the public joined in the chorus of praise. This was one of his creations which gave him great joy for the rest of his life. He often used to sit on the steps of the fountain opposite looking up in wonder at his work. Sister Helen Forshaw, a student at the convent in 1958, remembers 'seeing Epstein sitting in Cavendish Square looking at his *Madonna*'. One spontaneous tribute which particularly touched him came from a bus driver, who slowed down his bus as he passed the statue and, spotting Epstein, called out, 'You've done it this time, Guv'nor.'[31]

On Christmas Eve the *Madonna* was floodlit and the Epstein family gathered outside to hear children singing carols. A note in the convent records reveals that Kathleen paid for the illumination for years until Marylebone County Council offered to take on the cost, since the statue was so popular with the public.

That same year, 1953, Epstein was awarded the honorary degree of Doctor of Law at Oxford University but he was still something of an old rebel. The Royal Society of Sculptors had wanted to give him a gold medal for his services to sculpture. Forty years earlier they had refused his application for membership. Their award came too late.

Like the Cavendish Square convent, Llandaff Cathedral had been badly damaged in wartime. George Pace, a Yorkshireman, was appointed as the architect and in his plans for reconstructing the building he had designed a giant reinforced-concrete arch to support the cylindrical organ loft. Pace had written to Epstein the previous year, asking him whether he would be interested in sculpting 'a great figure of Christ Reigning from the Cross'. 'Epstein spoke of the Llandaff Christ, I remember,' said Jan Smith. 'He was very excited and enthusiastic about the project. He went in the train with the painter Stanley Spencer' – who had been asked to create a mosaic of the Last Judgement for the underside of the arch, but the work was never carried out. 'Spencer talked all the time on the journey and Epstein finally told him to shut up.'[32]

Epstein found the prospect enormously challenging and could not resist it, although, as he told Peggy Jean, Llandaff had no money and he was working for his 'church charity'. The sculpture, it was decided, should be cast in gilt plaster. The undertaking was so large that Epstein modelled it in sections, mainly in the huge studio in the Royal College. First he modelled the head and neck, then the chest and shoulders, with the top of the arms and the drapery. Next he modelled the hips and lower arms and then the legs and gown. He modelled the halo, the hands and feet in his own studio. Jan Smith cast them and took them over to the Royal College, where they were fixed to the whole figure. 'They looked right, *very right*,' he said.[33]

By the end of October, the work was formally commissioned and in the same month the newspapers reported that his great alabaster figures, *Jacob and the Angel*, *Consummatum Est* and *Adam*, the sensational shockers at sideshows, were up for sale, but Epstein's value as a religious sculptor was now assured. The impressive statue he created for Llandaff, a gaunt, compassionate draped figure, enormously elongated and on tiptoe, was not unveiled for four years. 'Epstein', said Jan Smith, 'was pleased with the figure but felt that plaster was vulnerable and was prepared to use his own money to have it cast in durable metal.' Finally the cathedral authorities relented. 'Epstein has charged little enough, we ought to be prepared to sanction £1,500 to preserve his work,' Dean Simon wrote to his architect.[34]

Official recognition came too from the Office of Works, which commissioned a full-length figure of the former Prime Minister of South Africa, Field Marshal Jan Christian Smuts, for Parliament Square. The figure involved Epstein in endless correspondence, visits from politicians and art experts, and the deliberations of committees that he disliked so much. The figure was to be ten feet high and in field marshal's uniform, 'with all the tabs and buttons correct. Everyone who knew Smuts wants to tell me how to do it.' Smuts's statue, striding forward with hands clasped behind his back, was nicknamed 'The Skater'. Epstein disliked official monuments, and his over-life-sized figure of the South African statesman reveals that the sculptor was ill at ease with the commission.

Then in 1953 came the irrefutable evidence that Epstein had arrived. One morning in November he went to open the front door to his friend Arnold Haskell, when he saw an official-looking envelope on the floor and went to put it aside. 'Must be a tax demand.' Haskell persuaded him to open it, and he discovered to his amusement and delight that Her Majesty's Government were offering him a knighthood. Epstein enjoyed all the flurry and attention in spite of himself, and, of course, he welcomed the long-delayed recognition of his achievement that the honour brought when the New Year Honours of 1954 were announced. 'Dear Peggy Jean,' he wrote on 20 January,

> The excitement over my knighthood has been terrific. The house was besieged by newspapermen and photographers. I never knew I was so popular. Her Majesty the Queen is away so the Queen Mother will deliver the accolade . . . A dark lounge suit is correct. Thank Goodness no top hat and rubbish of that sort . . . Knight Commander of the British Empire. That sounds fine. I think the whole thing came from Churchill. I don't know anyone else who would be interested and the recommendation is from the Prime Minister.[35]

All his life Epstein had been carefully careless of his clothes. In his seventies he wore loose trousers, always with braces, and dressed for comfort and ease of movement. Even that morning in February when he was about to go to Buckingham Palace for the investiture in his dark lounge suit, he escaped into the studio, and the daubs of plaster had to be hastily rubbed off his clothes.

The ennoblement of Epstein was a grand occasion – even the press now treated him with respectful affection – but the year was marred by personal tragedy. His relationships were complex and always dominated by his own needs. He colonized his women and loved his children but on his own terms, commandeering them when he needed them. His second family in particular suffered from their parents' irregular union and the inevitable distance from their father. When the Garman children were growing up the passionate nature of the love affair between Kathleen and Epstein left the three children feeling excluded. Theo, Kathleen's eldest child and only son, was extremely close to his mother and resentful of his father. Subject to fits of depression for years – even attempting to take his own life – he was highly disturbed, and Kathleen spent most of her time looking after him. Despite a well-received exhibition of his paintings at the Redfern Gallery in 1950, Theo Garman had stopped painting altogether. Then, one terrible night in February 1954, complaints about Theo's behaviour were made to the police in Chelsea. Kathleen, alerted, had sent an ambulance to the King's Road to take her son to hospital to prevent his arrest. Epstein was never quite certain how it happened but, in struggling against restraint from the ambulancemen, Theo suffered a heart attack and died instantly. He was twenty-nine years old. The family were distraught. Epstein at least could retreat into his work and his studio, but for Kathleen and for Theo's sisters Kitty and Esther the loss was devastating.

Two years earlier Kitty had divorced Lucian Freud, and she and her two young daughters, Anna and Annabel, were staying at Hyde Park Gate at this time. Epstein was delighted: he found consolation in young children; he loved the girls and drew and sculpted them. There was also a small boy staying in the Epstein household that year. Esther Garman's love affair with Mark Joffe was over and she brought his son Roland to stay with Kathleen and Epstein. Esther was a tender-hearted girl and very beautiful. A young student who fell in love with her committed suicide when she refused to marry him and Esther became severely depressed. She received treatment for the depression, took a room by herself and in November 1954 was about to start working in a bookshop with a woman friend and begin an independent life. On her first night in her new room she gassed herself. Within the space of ten months, two out of three of Kathleen and Epstein's children had died in tragic circumstances. Brother and sister were buried in the village of South Harting in Sussex, the village where they had lived during the war with their grandmother as a constant support.

Epstein fortunately was overwhelmed with work all the following year. He had the great Llandaff figure to complete and was often at the college all day, eating lunch in the canteen with the students, and the demands for him to make portrait heads still came in. 'The day of beautiful women is over and I am only engaged by elderly businessmen – tycoons I suppose,' he complained to Peggy Jean.[36] One of these tycoons, Lord Woolton, the owner of Lewis's large department store in the centre of Liverpool, visited Epstein to ask whether he would create a gigantic sculpture on the façade of the store's tall, porticoed entrance. During the Blitz the centre of Liverpool and the docks had been bombed heavily, and Lewis's store had been flattened by a landmine in 1941. The sculpture was intended to symbolize the city of Liverpool rising from the flames of war. No doubt the commission paid handsomely, and Epstein could use the money to shore up finances depleted by the 'church charity', the Llandaff statue that he was working on at the time.

Beside *Christ in Majesty*, at the Royal College Epstein's plaster cast for the Liverpool store's *Resurgent*, a giant, naked youth standing on a ship's prow, arms flung out triumphantly, must have looked a brash figure. He had experimented with a group of figures on the prow of a ship but decided that the store needed a more prominent image.

Christmas was bleak for them all. Epstein worked at the college all through the holiday on his two large projects, alone in the building except for a caretaker.

In his seventy-fifth year Epstein was busier than ever, in demand as a sculptor of religious subjects. In January 1955 the executor to the late Bishop Woods of Lichfield asked for Epstein's advice; he wanted a talented young sculptor whose fees would not be immoderate to create a memorial to the bishop. Kathleen was keen for Epstein to take on the commission himself: she loved the cathedral and knew the area; as a girl she used to ride over to visit the deanery with her father. Kathleen was of course still grieving deeply over the deaths of her two children and Epstein was anxious to lift her mood. Together they travelled to Lichfield and met the clergymen 'from the Middle Ages'. Epstein admired the cathedral and he agreed to make a bust of the late cleric.

He and Kathleen had been lovers for thirty-four years, and in old age he wanted no more scandal. On 28 June 1955 he and Kathleen were married quietly at Fulham Register Office with the omnipresent Beth Lipkin as one of the witnesses. Epstein's affairs were always news, but the couple managed to dodge the photographers and journalists. Epstein himself was evidently relieved to be able to regularize their union. 'Our odd position has been a source of embarrassment for a long time and now I hope things will be better.'[37]

14

'Very little of a gadabout'

O N 7 JULY 1955, nine days after his wedding, Epstein was on board the SS *Liberté* sailing for New York – alone. In his seventies he was still achingly and touchingly in love with Kathleen. He had a long-standing engagement to go to Philadelphia to unveil *Social Consciousness*, but Kathleen, still shaken after the deaths of Theo and Esther, wanted to avoid the publicity. She usually visited her sister Helen in Italy in the summer, so she travelled to Italy as usual with Beth Lipkin but planned to meet Epstein in Paris on his return journey. Fifty years before, he had travelled to New York steerage class; this time he was given VIP treatment, including an outside cabin with a port-hole and a table to himself in the dining room. He was, however, besieged by reporters and photographers: 'an ignorant lot I can tell you', he wrote to his sweetheart. 'They avoided all reference to sculpture but wanted to know why I had travelled without you.'[1]

Epstein spent a few days with his brother, who had moved to Long Island: 'A singular place, once obviously wooded with beautiful trees, it is being fast converted into a suburban slum.' Then he travelled to Philadelphia to see *Social Consciousness* unveiled. He was fêted by local dignitaries, taken on a traditional cruise down the Schuylkill river and, from all the publicity, gained a commission to make a medal to commemorate the 250th anniversary of Benjamin Franklin.

No sooner was *Social Consciousness* unveiled than Epstein heard that another gigantic task awaited him. In December 1954 the Trades Union Congress had invited him to compete to carve a war memorial for the central courtyard of the new TUC building in Great Russell Street. Epstein disliked competitions and committees and had declined the invitation. It had come too soon after Theo's death, and when he was overburdened with work. The following March the TUC decided to ask him directly to create a maquette for their intended sculpture. This time Epstein accepted and produced the model before he left for America. 'Darling Girl,' he wrote to Kathleen on 24 August. 'Today I received a cable from the Trades Union Council's [*sic*] Sir Vincent Tewson. He let me know that [they] were delighted to have my proposal for the monument carried out!'[2] Epstein cabled that he would be back towards the end of September. 'I didn't want to lose that good time with you in France.'[3]

Kathleen and Epstein spent ten golden days in Paris, a much-delayed honeymoon. One afternoon they visited Père Lachaise cemetery and gazed at the tomb of Oscar Wilde. The sculptor thought it looked 'pretty good' among the forest of tombs.

Back in London, Epstein had begun to enjoy making sculpture on a smaller scale. In 1953, Louis Osman, the architect of the Cavendish Square convent, had commissioned him to adorn four oval door handles he had designed with four baby angels. Epstein based them on his portraits of children, including his grandchildren Annabel and Ian. Also, now that his giant statue for Lewis's in Liverpool was almost finished, he modelled three bas-reliefs, at his own suggestion and without taking any extra fee, to be placed below his statue and just above the entrance to the store. There were lively scenes of *Children Fighting* and *Children Playing* on either side of Annabel, Epstein's granddaughter, and Frisky, his dog.

Kathleen went every week to visit her children's graves in Sussex, but life at Hyde Park Gate was getting back to normal; musicians often came to play the piano at weekends. They had a Spanish woman to cook and clean whom Epstein called 'a character out of Don Quixote'. He was walking regularly in the park, needing to keep fit for the strenuous job ahead of carving the TUC monument. 'I think the work will do me good, perhaps keep my weight down,' he said optimistically.[4]

Early in January 1956 he was preparing a silver medal, commissioned by the city of Philadelphia for International Understanding, as a gift to Winston Churchill. On one side Epstein had engraved the profile of Benjamin Franklin; on the other the head of Prometheus, who had stolen fire from the heavens, looking through the sun's rays. The Mayor of Philadelphia presented the eighty-one-year-old Churchill with the medal; the old man, though shaky, made a gallant effort to receive it appropriately and was pleased to see his neighbour there.

By February the ten-ton block of buff-coloured Roman stone was delivered to the TUC building and Epstein realized the enormity of the task that lay ahead. 'I have let myself in for some devilish hard work as this particular block is as hard as granite and tools just break on it,' he told Peggy Jean. For the first time he allowed stonemasons to prepare the great stone for him. He had a hut built on the site to keep out snoopers and worked on a narrow plank on the wall face. Every morning he took a cab to the TUC building in Bloomsbury, too impatient to get there to wait for a bus. Then he worked until he found himself tired out and went home to lunch at Hyde Park Gate at 1.30. After a rest, he returned to the site until about 5.30. When he had finished work, covered with plaster, he looked like a workman, and sometimes taxis refused to take him. At the end of April he told Peggy Jean that he was making good progress, disturbed only by the terrific noise of drilling and clatter all around him.

The monument, devastating in its simplicity, depicts the strong figure of a mother standing, erect and implacable in her grief, clutching her dead son's body to her own, while his limbs hang down, lifeless. Mounted on a high plinth and set in a pyramid wall of green marble, Epstein's memorial emerges from the stone block and moulds itself to its shape. It is, implicitly, an anti-war statement, an article of his faith, with no concession to patriotism or popular sentiment. Epstein completed the carving by Christmas 1956, long before the building was ready, and his monument was not unveiled until the spring of 1958.

His portraits were in great demand, but now Epstein had little

time to devote to them; the commissions came from the aristocracy, from academia and from the world of the arts, and, of course,
he still made portraits of his own family. His daughter Kitty had
remarried in 1957, and her new husband was the Honourable
Wynne Godley, an economist with a profound interest in the arts.
Wynne found his father-in-law genial and vivacious, and Epstein
was taken with Wynne's noble, ascetic looks. He made a fine head
of his son-in-law, and also used it as the model for the head of St
Michael in his latest commission. He had been invited to make a
huge bronze sculpture of *St Michael and the Devil*, to be sited on
the red sandstone wall of the brand-new Coventry Cathedral.

The building of a new cathedral in Coventry beside the ruins of
the old one, almost totally destroyed by bombing in 1940, was a
symbol of hope and reconciliation in the postwar world. The architect Basil Spence designed the new cathedral in the modern spirit,
with bold simplicity, and employed the finest British artistic talent
in the country. Apart from Epstein, he invited Graham Sutherland
to create a great tapestry, John Piper to design a stained-glass
window, and the young sculptor Elizabeth Frink to model a bronze
eagle for the lectern. The architect worked patiently to persuade
his committee to accept Epstein. In the autumn of 1954 he took
Bishop Gorton of Coventry to see the Cavendish Square *Madonna
and Child*. The bishop, bareheaded and oblivious to the traffic,
stood looking up at this masterpiece and said simply, 'Epstein is
the man for us.' Later, when Basil Spence brought up Epstein's
name in the reconstruction committee, 'There was a shocked
silence, at length broken by the remark, "But he is a Jew," to which
I replied quietly, "So was Jesus Christ." '[5]

During 1955, when Epstein was working in a studio loaned to
him at the Royal College of Art, Spence visited him. 'When I
asked him if he would accept the commission to do the great figure
of St Michael, he answered, "All my life I have wanted to do
Michael. This is a great task." ' When Spence asked him what his
fee would be, pointing out that funds were low, he quoted a ridiculously small figure, adding, 'If the committee can't pay that I shall
reduce it.' His first figure was agreed.

Even then Spence's negotiations with the cathedral authorities were not over. They decided, since 'Epstein was such a controversial figure, that they must have the backing of the Cathedral Council for his appointment. I presented the case and the meeting was a stormy one . . . At last, by a majority decision it was decided that he should do a maquette, about eighteen inches.' Later Spence brought the provost of the cathedral to lunch with the Epsteins. When he was questioned directly about his religious beliefs, the artist replied, 'My beliefs can be seen clearly through my "woik".' In a radio broadcast in 1952, Epstein revealed, 'My tendency has always been religious – it may not be known, but that is a fact . . . most great sculpture is occasioned by faith. Even the African sculpture, which we don't understand, is full of their faith.'[6] Epstein's visual imagination was fired by the Christian story, but it seems clear that for him the divine spark might take many forms.

He had been invited to make the maquette for Coventry in November 1955, but his large work for the TUC prevented him from starting until the end of the following year. By November 1956 Epstein was seventy-six, feeling fatigued after a hectic year and 'full of commissions' – he had been invited by the Blake Society to make a monument to William Blake for Poets' Corner in Westminster Abbey. The St Michael project excited him greatly; he was an old man in a hurry. He made the small maquette and then, without waiting to show it to the committee and gain their approval, began modelling the head and wings of the huge figure. The first that Basil Spence knew of Epstein's initiative was when he read a report in a newspaper quoting Epstein saying that his St Michael for Coventry would be his 'masterpiece'. Spence hurried round to Hyde Park Gate to see for himself what was happening. Epstein, unabashed, showed, in addition to the small maquette, the head and shoulders of the statue of St Michael, which was to be over thirty feet high. The architect was both impressed and embarrassed. When he remonstrated, Epstein said that if the committee didn't want his work he would do it for himself. Perhaps he had decided to brave his way through the endless deliberations of the committees. At any rate his tactic worked. The bishop and provost were hurriedly summoned to view the sculpture and were delighted with what they saw. Photographs were taken and both the reconstruction committee and the cathedral council approved.

Although he was so taken up with work, Epstein did shelter and care for his family as best he could. When Peggy Jean wrote to say that she was divorcing Norman Hornstein, he was very upset and tried to intervene with his son-in-law on her behalf. Jackie was totally obsessed with racing cars and Epstein worried about his future; sometimes the sight and sound of him tinkering offended the well-to-do neighbours in their little cul-de-sac. But, as he said, he was too busy to play the heavy father. On 11 April 1957 Epstein and Kathleen spent two days in Wales, when his magnificent *Christ in Majesty* was unveiled at Llandaff Cathedral with the Archbishop of Wales presiding. He never lost his sense of wonder that he was now so honoured by ecclesiastical officials – and it was strange that a Jewish boy from the New York slums should have his work so dignified. 'It is odd that most of my work is for religious establishments – that is because of the *Madonna and Child* in London, no doubt. I have survived the bad periods when only Moore & Co. were thought to be worth looking at. I was ignored and neglected.'[7]

His studio that spring was filled with sculpture for Coventry Cathedral which reached from floor to ceiling. The finished bronze work was to comprise two figures: the winged archangel Michael, arms outstretched and a spear in his right hand, standing triumphantly over the horned and naked Devil, half lying at his feet. *St Michael and the Devil* was completed in 1958 (the new cathedral was finally consecrated in 1962). Also in Epstein's studio at this time was his fine head of Bishop Woods for Lichfield Cathedral, which was to become a half-figure; 'the funds for this are contributed by all the Bishops of England headed by the Queen'. He now had the satisfaction of knowing that his work would remain and 'not be at the mercy of selling people'.

The previous year had been occupied by his work for the TUC and he had not had a proper break since his visit to America in 1955, yet he felt uneasy about leaving home with his big work for

Coventry Cathedral unfinished. As a young man he had wanted to 'carve mountains'. In old age he had realised his ambition but at a cost. 'I feel often worn out and tired and I must stop soon or I might be stopping for ever,' he wrote in July 1957, uncharacteristically pessimistic. He and Kathleen had talked about a holiday in Italy or perhaps the Highlands of Scotland. They visited Epping Forest on Sundays but Epstein avoided their 'old house on the hill as the memory of that's too sad'. He and Kathleen dined out twice a week in Soho, 'which has been transformed by the Maltese into one big brothel'.[8]

Kathleen insisted that Epstein should have a holiday and, with Roland Joffe, the boy they were still looking after, they travelled to the Gleneagles Hotel in the Scottish Highlands. Epstein, who had been dreaming of mountains and lakes, was horrified with the worldliness of the golfing hotel, and the party soon moved to pleasant bed-and-breakfast accommodation. There they hired a car that took them into the woods, and Epstein was content to paint for several days; idleness was impossible for him.

He was still very fatigued at the end of the year and, although he had been a good walker all his life, found even walking tiring. In Westminster Abbey on 24 November 1957 his portrait of William Blake was dedicated. 'It means a lot to get accepted in the Abbey although there was not much money in it, the prestige of doing it is great,' he explained to Peggy Jean. He asked Matthew Smith to come to the dedication to 'support myself and Kathleen, as there will be present, to my knowledge, sundry evil spirits, in the shape of I won't mention who, and it would be nice to know that friends are there. A poem by the Poet Laureate will be read, which I hope will be short. The sculpture is of course by your friend, the old firm "Jake".'[9]

Matthew Smith, elderly and frail himself, loyally turned up. Apparently Epstein's enemies did not appear – and that affronted him too. He told Peggy Jean that of the large and distinguished Blake committee, only Lord Samuel attended. 'The absentees, rogues like Kenneth Clark, Herbert Read, Henry Moore, John Piper and many others . . . did not approve of my doing the work so they did not come.'[10] Two months later, in January 1958, he revealed that he had had only expenses paid. 'I'm afraid I will have to whistle for anything else. I am turned into a philanthropist who gives public sculpture away. Well, Blake got very little for his work. I manage to get nothing . . .Yours as ever, Daddy.'

Epstein still hankered for the prestige that he felt eluded him. Big commissions continued to come in and he could not bear to turn them down. The directors of Bowaters, the paper manufacturers, asked him to design a group sculpture to stand beside their new building at the Edinburgh Gate entrance to Hyde Park. In January he was already making sketches for the large new project. But ordinary work in the studio was interrupted in February by the appearance of royalty. North Staffordshire University had commissioned a bust of HRH Princess Margaret, their Vice-Chancellor, and the Palace arranged sittings. Epstein found the experience of sculpting a member of the royal family something of an ordeal. The princess always arrived accompanied by a small entourage, her lady-in-waiting and her detective both stood by during the two-hour sittings, and a crowd of press and curious members of the public watched the house. Behaving towards a royal personage was a strain:

> Royalty lives in an altogether different world than we commoners do and it is impossible to understand their mentality. As they are never contradicted and treated like gods any criticism or answering back is out of the question; as you know I am no courtier. I listened to H.R.H. but of course never agreed to any alterations which I thought unreasonable . . . I myself am pleased with what I have made and I think it is a dignified and true presentation of the Princess. As I didn't know her intimately, I couldn't show that side of her . . . The princess is quite pretty, petite and somewhat [writing illegible] gay and taut in her conversation or rather responses, as conversation in the ordinary way is impossible . . . I do not look forward to any further commissions connected with Royalty with any eagerness or pleasure

. . . I feel I have overdone the work . . . and I feel often terribly fatigued.[11]

A plaster cast of Princess Margaret's bust was being made when Epstein's ill health interrupted him. Early in March 1958 he was rushed to the London Hospital, suffering from pleurisy and a thrombosis. He stayed there for almost a month, too ill to attend the opening of Congress House and the unveiling of his war memorial. Public reaction to it, as to all Epstein's work, was mixed. While Labour MPs were deeply impressed – Aneurin Bevan described the monument as 'the best thing he's ever done' and Hugh Gaitskell found it 'superb' – the majority of the TUC leaders loathed it. 'Sooner it joins *Genesis* in Blackpool the better,' said one, and Sir Will Lawther, the ex-miners' leader, remarked, 'I'd rather see Manchester United win the cup.'[12] On a more serious note, the *Daily Telegraph*'s Terence Mulally wrote, 'As a work of art, Epstein's group appears to be almost painfully moving . . . a tragic monument on a grand scale.'[13]

'My large work for the TUC was unveiled to trumpets and quite a do but I was not there. I lay in bed and read about it. There has been a good deal of discussion and wireless comments but the architect of this building is pleased and so am I,' he told Peggy Jean. He also sent her cuttings about a sale of *Genesis*. Unfortunately the destination was Blackpool, and that too caused comment. Epstein told Peggy Jean that he was being pressed to make tomb figures for the Chapel Royal at Windsor but was resisting the opportunity. '[I] do not want to spend the rest of my life at such idiocy,' he said at the age of seventy-seven. 'The old days were best when I had no large commissions, no one bought anything and I was free to do what I wanted to do,' he grumbled, choosing to forget the hard times. 'I was happier that way and didn't ruin my health.'[14] Epstein had an enlarged heart (probably the result of long-term high blood pressure); for years he had overtaxed himself, no sooner finishing one large work than starting on another. But he was strong willed and a fighter. 'A man of great physical strength whose broad shoulders and powerful limbs regained signs of vigour to the end of his life . . . I have seen him carry heavy pieces of stone and large bronze busts in a way that not only astonished a small man like myself, but surprised our staff at the galleries who were used to heavy burdens,' wrote Oliver Brown, his dealer at the Leicester Galleries.[15] Lifting was now forbidden, of course, but he hated to think of himself as an invalid. His doctors thought he had made an 'astonishing recovery'.

After a few days at home Epstein was well enough to take a recuperative holiday, and in mid-April made his first trip to Venice, a long-cherished dream. He travelled with Kathleen and Beth Lipkin, a permanent companion for Kathleen when Epstein was sketching or spending hours gazing at sculpture. He was thrilled by Verrocchio's powerful equestrian statue of Colleoni and went to see it four times. Then the party took a boat to Padua, where the sculptor admired another equestrian statue, *Gattemelata* by Donatello, an artist who had influenced his work. On the way home the trio stopped in Paris to visit a Modigliani exhibition and were back in England after a month of sightseeing. He was always eager to get home, back to the studio. In the mornings before breakfast, he looked in to make sure that the clay was still wet for the day's work, and he often returned to the studio last thing at night. Kathleen, twenty years younger than Epstein, was out more than he was, often on business for him. He was lost without her; his son-in-law Wynne Godley remembers him standing in the middle of the road in Hyde Park Gate, his watch in his hand, waiting for his wife to come home.

He was still inundated with work. He had several commissions for portraits. Sir Russell Brain, President of the Royal College of Physicians, and Sir William Haley, formerly Director-General of the BBC and subsequently editor of *The Times*, both sat for him that summer. Through his portrait sculpture Epstein was in touch with some of the most cultivated minds in the country. Russell Brain wrote down a detailed account of his conversations with him on subjects ranging from Shakespeare and Michelangelo to Cleopatra's nose! Many of his distinguished sitters enjoyed their time with him and a few became personal friends.

All his working life Epstein took risks, and when the architect of the new Church of the Ascension at Crownhill, Plymouth, invited him to make designs for twelve hexagonal stained-glass windows, as well as an Ascension of Christ, he was excited by the idea and went to Plymouth in September to visit the church. Ironically, Epstein had spent perhaps the most unhappy months of his life in Crownhill as a private in the First World War. Perhaps he saw the commission in the church as a way of coming to terms with the past.

With a plan of studying stained glass in mind, Epstein agreed to take a holiday.[16] He, Kathleen and Beth, driven by their doctor friends John and Valerie Cowie, made a marathon cathedral tour. They travelled through France and Italy via Amiens, Beauvais, Chartres and Bourges, visiting a cathedral a day in what sounds like a punishing trip for a man who had recently recovered from a serious illness. The party visited Nîmes, Arles and Aix, picnicking and bathing in the sea whenever they could, but moving on every day as they travelled through Italy from Portofino to Milan and Como. Kathleen, who knew the country much better than Epstein from her annual visits to her sister, wanted him to see the Antelami reliefs in Parma. In the church of S. Antonio in Parma, Epstein suffered a sudden blackout, his vision temporarily affected. But he soon recovered and the journey went on. They travelled back via Switzerland to see a Holbein exhibition, then visited Grünewald's altarpiece at Colmar, a masterpiece which Epstein had long waited to see. On the way home they visited the cathedral of Laon and Reims. As a young man he had not been able to afford to visit the great art treasures of Europe and he was making up for lost time. He told Peggy Jean that he had had a 'great trip' through France and Italy, 'making a special study of stained glass'.

As always, he was excited by the new, big work for what he called the 'Hyde Park Group'. He had been given no brief for the sculpture, and he never titled it. Given that the monument was to stand at the south entrance to Hyde Park, he chose the theme of escaping from the city: as a boy he had found refuge from the ghetto in Central Park. He illustrated his theme with a half-realistic, half-mythical family: father, mother, child and dog escaping from the thraldom of town life, surging towards open spaces in the park, spurred by the large, horned figure of Pan; the mother, with extremely exaggerated, long arms, propelling the family forward. He set out his plans in a detailed working drawing. Sadly, although the group possesses extraordinary energy and brio, it lacks the conviction and the certainty of his best work. 'Epstein's articulation of figures in forward movement is rarely entirely successful,' Evelyn Silber remarks,[17] and in his last large bronze, known as the *Bowater House Group*, this failing is all too apparent.

He was seventy-eight in November, still working too hard, taking on too much, sometimes longing for a simpler life. 'I hope you are well in your primitive house in the woods,' he wrote to Peggy Jean in North Carolina. 'I sometimes think I would like to get away to something like that myself and . . . stop doing this laborious task of pleasing sitters and others who commission me to work for them. With love from Daddy.'[18]

But he was as busy as ever and commissions for portraits continued to come in, commissions that Epstein could not afford to turn down, from academics, churchmen, businessmen and aristocrats and their children; the Office of Works commissioned a life-sized portrait of Lloyd George for the House of Commons. Despite his fame, his fees for his prestigious public works were modest, and his insistence on developing his work as he saw fit, even if he was not paid to do so, costly. At the end of the year he sculpted a fine head of Charles McInnes, Professor of Imperial History at Bristol University. McInnes was blind, a genial man with wide interests. Epstein found him a sympathetic sitter and portrayed him as a man with a vivid inner life, a tinge of humour in his gaze. He sometimes despaired of duller subjects; they exhausted him.

'I'm very little of a gadabout these days,' he wrote to Peggy Jean in February 1959 in a letter which suggested that his grand-daughter Leda should come over during the holidays and bring a friend. 'I get very tired and I must reserve my energy for the large works I have in hand.'[19] He had been offered a doctorate at York

University but had to refuse, as he would have had to attend in person to accept the honour.

In April he went to Paris with Kathleen and Beth to meet his brother Irving and his wife. After a week of intensive sightseeing, mainly in the Louvre, he saw his brother and sister-in-law off to New York and went on to Venice, which he had so much enjoyed the year before. Epstein went back to look at Verrocchio's statue, and they visited the little church on the island of Torcello to see the mosaics. On his way home Epstein stopped in Paris to buy two additions to his extraordinary collection of 'primitive' art, one of them an African 'parrot head'. Although his house was still mortgaged and his expenses limitless, for his collection, his passion, he did not count the cost. Back home he was eagerly at work again – that was his real joy.

The summer of 1959 was one of the hottest for years but Epstein made no concession to his health, finishing off portraits and working on his statue of Lloyd George. He had almost completed his large *Bowater House Group*, and was fatigued from the exertion. On the evening of 18 August Matthew Smith, himself ailing, rang up and asked the Epsteins to come round, promising that he had a bottle of something nice. Kathleen suggested that the next day would be better: Jacob was looking tired and the following day they were going out to dinner and could call round to the artist's home in Chelsea Cloisters beforehand. But Jacob insisted that they should visit their friend that night. In the lift going up to see him, Jacob had a dizzy spell and had to take emergency tablets for his heart, but still insisted on the visit. He was stout and looked robust, while Matthew Smith looked frail and ill – he couldn't even lift the bottle of champagne he had sent for to greet his friends. The Epsteins had loaned him a little Renoir landscape to hang beside his bed. Despite their ailments the two old friends talked with almost frenetic animation of their memories of the old days.

After working all the next day in the studio, Epstein took Kathleen, Beth and his beloved dog Frisky out to dinner at a favourite restaurant, Ciccio's in Campden Hill. After dinner, he wanted to walk home across Kensington Gardens, but Kathleen forbade it. When he came home he took a chair out on the porch to watch the stars come out; he was in a happy mood, singing Schubert songs. He fell into a deep sleep and woke feeling refreshed. Before he went up to bed, Epstein insisted on going into the studio to cover up the clay, despite Kathleen's protests; he went upstairs, calling out that the group was finished. Sensing that something was wrong, Kathleen told Beth to phone for the doctor and rushed upstairs after him. When she went into the room she found him lying on the floor beside the bed, his eyes still open. He had suffered a massive heart attack. In a few seconds he was dead.

At his death the sense of shock not only in the family but in the nation was palpable. In the course of all the battles that had raged round him Epstein himself had become something of a public monument. *The Times* devoted a column and a half to the obituary of 'perhaps the most outstanding sculptor of his generation and certainly the most controversial'.[20] In the *Sunday Times*, Henry Moore, who had so often disappointed his old colleague, made an apologia:

> I first met Jacob Epstein in the mid-1920s, a time when I was unknown and he was the most famous sculptor in Britain, and I have two reasons to be grateful to him . . . He bought works of mine before I had had an exhibition and he showed an excitement in my work, as he did in everything else that he liked or loved, which was characteristic of the man . . . He took the brickbats, he took the insults, he faced the howls of derision with which artists since Rembrandt have learned to become familiar. And as far as sculpture in this century is concerned he took them first . . . We have lost a great sculptor and a great man.[21]

The scholarly *Burlington Magazine* devoted an editorial to censuring Epstein's critics. But perhaps the most pertinent comment came in the 1960 Catalogue of the London Group. 'The greatness of Epstein has been fully acknowledged in the obituary notices of the world's press and there is little left to be added.' After outlining Epstein's role in the London Group, and touching on the savage attacks on his work, the writer concludes, 'Like Rembrandt, an intense individualism combined in him a power of perception and connoisseurship in all the arts . . . More than anyone else, his pioneering hand and heart have helped to remove this country from the stigma of parochialism.'[22]

Epstein was buried at Putney Vale cemetery on 24 August 1959, with a copy of the Whitman poems that had meant so much to him. Dr Hewlett Johnson, the Red Dean of Canterbury, took the service, Peggy Jean came over from America, and Epstein's children from different mothers met for the first time and mourned together.

He had kept his tallis (prayer shawl) and menorah, and his religious feelings had remained intensely personal. A memorial service was held in St Paul's Cathedral on 10 November; it would have been Epstein's seventy-ninth birthday. His friend Canon Mortlock gave the address, with a plaster cast of the Llandaff Christ hanging in the north transept for the occasion. 'If we ask how it was that a boy born and bred in the Jewish faith and never embracing any other, should become the interpreter of the sublime mysteries of our religion there can be no clear answer. Such things belong to the inscrutable wisdom of God.'[23]

The tributes that came in from those who knew him reveal what an impact he had made on them. 'We must never forget what a great man he was,' Matthew Smith, who was to die six weeks later, wrote to Kathleen.[24] T. S. Eliot's note, written two days after his death, is fresh with shock: 'A few minutes ago on my way home I saw the evening newspapers. I write in haste for both of us to say how deeply we grieve. It is as if some of my world has crumbled away. You have our warmest sympathy. We loved him. Affectionately, Tom Eliot.'[25]

Otto Klemperer, the conductor whose musicianship Epstein much admired, had been sculpted by him two years earlier in 1957. 'I shall never forget the hours I was permitted to spend with the great man.'[26]

When he died, his monumental work, the carvings and large bronzes which contained so much of Epstein's passion, remained in an anomalous position. On the one hand there was *Lazarus* in Oxford, the *Madonna and Child* in London, the *Christ in Majesty* outside Cardiff, and the *St Michael and the Devil* in Coventry, works which were universally admired. On the other, four of his carvings were still drawing motley crowds in a Blackpool sideshow. Before he died he had twice tried to give away *Behold the Man* to the Church without success. The statue was stored in a shed in Battersea Park until, happily, the monument was presented to Coventry Cathedral in 1969, where it broods, mysteriously, among the ruins.

His earlier *Madonna and Child*, with Sunita as model, was purchased by Sally Ryan, Epstein's pupil, for the United States, and presented to the Church of Riverside, New York.

His reputation was partly restored in the 1960s when his four 'freak-show' carvings, *Adam, Consummatum Est, Jacob and the Angel* and *Genesis*, were rescued, bought by Lord Harewood and Sir Jack Lyons, in time to loan them to a large memorial exhibition of 170 sculptures held at the Edinburgh Festival in 1961. Since then the four outlawed carvings have found respectable homes. *Adam* stands in the entrance hall of Lord Harewood's home, Harewood House; *Consummatum Est* is at the Scottish National Gallery of Modern Art; *Genesis* at the Whitworth Gallery, Manchester; and *Jacob and the Angel* at Tate Britain. In recent years Epstein's stock has risen and younger sculptors ranging from Elizabeth Frink to Anthony Gormley have paid tribute to his work.

In keeping with his complex life, Epstein left a complex heritage. In 1960, the year before the Edinburgh exhibition, the Arts Council held a show of 'The Epstein Collection of Tribal and Exotic Sculpture', 347 of the 'greatest, most famous and widely illustrated works of African and Pacific sculpture ever to reach Europe'.[27] That was about a third of Epstein's huge collection, and after the exhibition his whole collection was dispersed by auction and private sale. A magnificent retrospective of his work was held at Leeds City Art Gallery and at the Whitechapel Art Gallery in 1987.

Kathleen Epstein donated two hundred of her husband's plaster casts to the Israel Museum in Jerusalem and to kibbutz Ain Herod in Galilee. But her most significant gift to this country came in 1974, fifteen years after Epstein's death, when she donated the Garman–Ryan Collection, now at the New Art Gallery, Walsall, to the Walsall Borough Council. The collection, with works by Epstein, his family and friends as its nucleus, contains drawings, paintings and sculptures and artefacts accumulated by Kathleen and her friend, the sculptor Sally Ryan. Heiress to a considerable fortune, Sally Ryan was suffering from cancer and was preparing for the future. In the 1960s the two women began acquiring works for their collection and had decided on the name. Ryan died in 1968, Kathleen in 1979, but their legacy, the acclaimed New Art Gallery in Walsall, charts Epstein's career and reflects his influence.

Of the five children that Epstein fathered, three are still living: Peggy Jean Lewis lives in North Carolina with her daughter Leda; Kitty Godley divides the year between the USA, where her husband lectures, and Suffolk; and Jackie Epstein and his wife live in London.

Jacob Epstein's impact on the cultural development of the country of his adoption was greater than has ever been acknowledged. He was, from the beginning, an outsider, an alien figure in England before the First World War. He was classless in a class-ridden society, international in an insular society and revolutionary in a conservative society. His overt sexuality offended even the bohemians, and he did not attempt to conform to the manners or to adapt to the rules of behaviour of his adopted country – or even to modify his accent to placate those around him.

In art he was regarded as 'unEnglish' in spirit, tackling Christian themes as a Jew, drawing inspiration from African, Asian, South American and Oceanic cultures to express them, finding a raw vitality and variety in forms which were at that time dismissed as 'barbaric'.

His life, like his art, was the stuff of myth, and because of the anti-Semitism of the era and Epstein's polemical personality, it became almost impossible to separate the man from his widely varied creations.

In the 1930s, when he no longer received large architectural commissions, he began to produce too much. By the end of his life his output included over 450 portrait bronzes and some 50 large carvings.

His expansive bohemian style, which required him to support two families as well as a priceless art collection, entailed a high cost. Occasionally he would skimp the portraits he found less interesting. In his large works he is at his strongest when he shaped the struggle of human life – sexual love, pregnancy, maternal love, death – and at his least convincing when he portrayed man in triumphant mode.

An intensely human and kind man, he could be utterly ruthless and self-indulgent. Since boyhood he had rebelled against authority and family tradition; this was his only route to artistic expression. Yet all his life he remained drawn to religious themes. 'I saw a great deal of Jewish orthodox life, traditional and narrow. As my thoughts were elsewhere, this did not influence me, but I imagine that the feel I have for expressing a human point of view . . . comes from those early formation years,' he wrote as a man of sixty.[28] Epstein's burning ambition was to make works of art that would serve mankind; to attain this he was ready to sacrifice himself and anybody who stood in his way. In an increasingly secular society he dealt in heroic themes from the great faiths; and at a time in England when other artists turned to decorative or abstract work, he remained faithful to the human figure.

In the end he mellowed and the country embraced him. He was a life force.

Notes and References

The following abbreviations are used:

ANAGW   Archives of the New Art Gallery, Walsall
HMC   Henry Moore Centre for the Study of Sculpture, Leeds City Art
          Galleries
HRRC   Harry Ransom Research Center, University of Austin, Texas
NYPL   New York Public Library
RSPB   Royal Society for the Protection of Birds
TGA   Tate Gallery Archives

The earlier chapters draw on Jacob Epstein's autobiography, *Let There Be Sculpture* (London, 1940). Except when indicated otherwise, where Epstein's own words are quoted, they are taken from *Let There Be Sculpture*. In appendices to his autobiography, Epstein drew up a ledger of admirers and opponents to reveal the controversy that arose over his large architectural sculptures; where these are quoted from, they are referred to as 'Epstein, Appendix One', etc.

Preface
1   JE to John Quinn, 29 November 1911, NYPL.
2   In interview with author, 1998.
3   JE to John Quinn, 1 May 1914.
4   An anonymous verse quoted in *Art Beyond the Gallery in Early Twentieth-Century England*, Richard Cork (London, 1985).

1   The Ghetto
1   Harry P. Kraus, *The Settlement House Movement in New York City, 1886–1914* (New York, 1980).
2   Jacob A. Riis cited in *The Jewish Encyclopedia*, vol. IX, section on New York (New York, 1905).
3   Kraus, op. cit.
4   JE to Helen Moore, 12 July (no year), ANAGW.
5   JE to Mrs Fish, undated, ANAGW.

6   JE to Helen Moore, undated.
7   Jane Babson, *The Epsteins: A Family Album* (London, 1984).
8   Peggy Jean Hornstein met her grandfather when she visited New York in 1936. Interview with the author.
9   Hutchins Hapgood, *The Spirit of the Ghetto* (New York, 1902).
10   Ibid.
11   Babson, op. cit.
12   Hapgood, op. cit.
13   Thomas Eakins to Helen Moore, 4 December 1900, ANAGW.
14   JE to Helen Moore, undated, ANAGW.
15   Ibid., undated.
16   Ibid., 20 January 1901.
17   Ibid., 3 March 1901.
18   Ibid., 10 March 1901.
19   Ibid., 18 May 1901.
20   Ibid., 24 February 1901.

2   Expanding

1   Jacob Epstein's 'Notes for an Autobiography', ANAGW.
2   Walt Whitman, 'We Two Boys Together Clinging' from *Complete Poetry & Selected Prose and Letters of Walt Whitman*, ed. Emory Holloway (London, 1938).
3   JE to Edward Warren Ordway, 12 April 1903, NYPL.
4   Ruth Butler, *Western Sculpture Definitions of Man* (New York, 1975).
5   JE to Edward Warren Ordway, 16 April 1903, NYPL.
6   Auguste Rodin to 'Jacob Epstein and Madame', 24 December 1904, HMC.
7   JE to Edward Warren Ordway, 16 April 1903, NYPL.
8   Ibid., 5 July 1903.
9   Arthur Ransome, *The Autobiography of Arthur Ransome* (London, 1976).
10   JE to Edward Warren Ordway, 4 September 1903, NYPL.
11   Ibid., 19 October 1903.
12   Ibid., 17 January 1904.
13   Ibid., March 1904.
14   Ibid., undated.
15   Ibid., 16 November 1904.
16   Ibid.
17   Auguste Rodin to 'Jacob Epstein and Madame', 24 December 1904, HMC.

3   Taking Off

1   M. Ross (ed.), *Robert Ross, Friend of Friends* (London, 1952).
2   JE to Edward Warren Ordway, 4 February 1904, NYPL.
3   Elizabeth Barker, 'Epstein's Early Career', *Burlington Magazine*, December 1988.
4   Ezra Pound cited in Frances Spalding, *British Art Since 1900* (London, 1986).

5 William Rothenstein, *Men and Memories*, vol. 2 (London, 1974).
6 Ibid.
7 Wyndham Lewis, *Rude Assignment* (London, 1950).
8 Augustus John to Alick Schepeler, summer 1906 in Michael Holroyd, *The Years of Innocence: A Biography of Augustus John*, Vol. 1 (London, 1974).
9 Ibid.
10 Arthur Ransome, *Bohemia in London* (London, 1907).
11 Rothenstein, op. cit.
12 Richard Cork, *Art Beyond the Gallery in Early Twentieth-Century England* (London, 1985).
13 Augustus John to Dorelia McNeill in Holroyd, op. cit.
14 Ibid.
15 Alan Crawford, *C. R. Ashbee: Architect, Designer and Romantic Socialist* (Yale University, 1986).
16 Epstein, Appendix One.
17 Ibid.
18 Epstein, *Let There Be Sculpture* (London, 1940).
19 Augustus John to Arthur Symons in Holroyd, op. cit.
20 Epstein, Appendix One.
21 Rothenstein, op. cit.

4 The Liberty of Art

1 Augustus John to Lady Ottoline Morrell, September 1908, in Michael Holroyd, *The Years of Innocence: A Biography of Augustus John*, vol. 1 (London, 1974).
2 Ibid.
3 JE to Lady Ottoline Morrell, 22 October 1908, HRRC.
4 Hugh Lane, *Lady Gregory* (London, 1973).
5 Michael Pennington, *An Angel for a Martyr: Jacob Epstein's Tomb for Oscar Wilde* (London, 1987). The donor was Mrs Helen Carew, a wealthy widow.
6 Eric Gill to *British Medical Journal*, May 1908, in Walter Shewring (ed.), The Letters of Eric Gill (London, 1947).
7 Eric Gill to William Rothenstein, 25 September 1910, in Shewring, op. cit.
8 Ibid.
9 Fiona MacCarthy, *Eric Gill* (London, 1989).
10 Eric Gill to Augustus John, 5 December 1910, in Shewring, op. cit.
11 MacCarthy, op. cit.
12 Robert Ross cited in Frances Spalding, *British Art Since 1900* (London, 1986).
13 Wilfried Scawen Blunt, *My Diaries*, part 2 (New York, 1921).
14 Judith Collins, 'Early Carving' in *Jacob Epstein: Sculpture and Drawings*, HMC (Leeds, 1989).
15 Eric Gill to W. Rothenstein, 25 September 1910, in Shewring, op. cit.
16 Oscar Wilde, 'The Ballad of Reading Gaol', 13 February 1898.

17 Evelyn Silber, *The Sculpture of Epstein* (Oxford, 1986).
18 JE to Eric Gill, 31 March 1911, L.A. Williams, Andrew Clark Library.
19 JE to John Quinn, 12 November 1911, NYPL.
20 JE to William Rothenstein, 20 June 1911, in Holroyd, op. cit.
21 JE to John Quinn, 29 November 1911, NYPL.
22 JE to John Quinn in B. L. Reid, *The Man from New York: John Quinn and His Friends* (New York, 1968).
23 Ibid.
24 Humphrey Carpenter, *A Serious Character, A Life of Ezra Pound* (London, 1988).
25 Epstein, Appendix Two.
26 Ibid.
27 Ezra Pound, *A Memoir of Gaudier-Brzeska* (London, 1970).
28 Ibid.
29 Article by Gaudier-Brzeska on the Allied Artists' Association Exhibition 1914, cited in Pound, op. cit.

5   Gathering Force

1   Lytton Strachey cited in Michael Pennington, *An Angel for a Martyr: Jacob Epstein's Tomb for Oscar Wilde* (Reading, 1987).
2   Epstein, Appendix Two.
3   Humphrey Carpenter, *A Serious Character, The Life of Ezra Pound* (New York, 1988).
4   *New Age*, London, December, 1908.
5   Jacob Epstein's 'Notes for an Autobiography', ANAGW.
6   Modigliani, *Caryatid*, ANAGW.
7   Richard Cork, *Art Beyond the Gallery in Early Twentieth-Century England* (London, 1985).
8   Ezio Bassani and Malcolm McLeod 'The Passionate Collector' in *Jacob Epstein: Sculpture and Drawings*, HMC (Leeds, 1989).
9   Arnold L. Haskell, *The Sculptor Speaks* (London, 1931).
10 Gertrude Stein, *The Autobiography of Alice B. Toklas* (London, 1933).
11 JE to John Quinn, 23 November 1912, NYPL.
12 Ibid.
13 Ibid., 11 January 1913.
14 Ibid., 17 March 1913.
15 Ibid.
16 Evelyn Silber, *The Sculpture of Epstein* (Oxford, 1986).
17 JE to John Quinn, 17 March 1913, NYPL.
18 Ibid., 21 October 1913.
19 Ezra Pound to Isobel W. Pound, November 1913, in D. D. Paige (ed.), *Ezra Pound: Selected Letters 1907–1941* (New York, 1971).
20 Carpenter, op. cit.
21 Fiona MacCarthy, *Eric Gill* (London, 1989).
22 Jacob Epstein, *Let There Be Sculpture* (London, 1940).
23 Draft of T. E. Hulme's article for the *New Age* by courtesy of Evelyn Silber of the Leeds City Art Galleries.

24 Quoted in Nina Hamnett, *Queen of Bohemia* (London, 1986).
25 Wyndham Lewis, *Blasting and Bombadiering* (London, 1937).
26 Ibid.
27 Ibid.
28 Carpenter, op. cit.
29 JE to Quinn, August 1914, NYPL.

6 Surviving

1 Mark Gertler to Dora Carrington, July 1914, *Letters to Carrington*, introduction by David Garnett (London, 1970).
2 Ibid.
3 Jane Babson, *The Epsteins: A Family Album* (London, 1984).
4 JE to John Quinn, 19 August 1914, NYPL.
5 Ibid., 4 September 1914.
6 *New Age*, 21 January 1915.
7 Ezra Pound to John Quinn, 8 March 1915, in D. D. Paige (ed.), *Ezra Pound: Selected Letters 1907–1941* (New York, 1971).
8 JE to John Quinn, 28 April 1915, NYPL.
9 Evelyn Silber, *The Sculpture of Epstein* (Oxford, 1986).
10 Ibid.
11 JE to John Quinn, 2 April 1915, NYPL.
12 B. L. Reid, *The Man from New York*: *John Quinn and His Friends* (New York, 1968).
13 *Observer*, 14 March 1913.
14 JE to John Quinn, 17 March 1916, NYPL.
15 Evelyn Silber, *The Sculpture of Epstein* (Oxford, 1986).
16 JE to John Quinn, 22 May 1916, NYPL.
17 Arnold Haskell, *The Sculptor Speaks* (London, 1931).
18 JE to John Quinn, 17 March 1916, NYPL.
19 Michael Pennington, *An Angel for a Martyr* (Reading, 1987).
20 *Weekly Dispatch*, 24 December 1916.
21 John Quinn to War Office and Exemption Tribunal, 26 June 1916. Artists' Archives, World War I, Imperial War Museum.
22 Artists' Archives, World War I, Imperial War Museum.
23 Victor Arwas, the owner of the drawing, in interview with the author.
24 Undated letter from Epstein to Meum, courtesy of Maria Hollingsworth, Meum's niece.
25 Ashley Gibson, *Postscript to Adventure* (London, 1970).
26 JE to John Quinn, 11 February 1917.
27 Lawrence Binyon, 'The Art of Jacob Epstein', *New Statesman*, 17 March 1917.
28 *New Age*, 8 March 1917.
29 JE to Bernard Van Dieren, 8 March 1917, HRRC.
30 JE to John Quinn, 11 February 1917, NYPL.
31 Hugo Vickers, *Gladys, Duchess of Marlborough* (London, 1979).
32 'Art and War – Sculptor's Exemption', *Illustrated Sunday Herald*, 10 June 1917.

33   JE to Van Dieren, 18 June 1917, HRRC.
34   JE to John Quinn, 20 July 1917, NYPL.
35   Ibid., undated.
36   Letter from Sir Martín Conway to Sir William Robertson, 13 December 1917, Artists' Archives, Imperial War Museum.
37   Letter No. 3937 from Sir George Frampton and Letter No. 4014 from Major-General Donald, both missing from Imperial War Museum's records.
38   JE to Van Dieren, undated.
39   Ibid.
40   Dorothy Lindsell-Stewart to Sir Martin Conway, 25 March 1918, Imperial War Museum.
41   JE to Van Dieren, undated.
42   JE to John Quinn, 26 July 1918.

7   Casting Off

1   *Sketch*, 24 July 1918.
2   Evelyn Silber, 'Private Concerns', *Jacob Epstein: Sculpture and Drawings*, HMC (Leeds, 1989).
3   Clare Sheridan cited in Jacob Epstein, *Let There Be Sculpture* (London, 1940).
4   Arnold L. Haskell, *The Sculptor Speaks* (London, 1931).
5   Kathleen Hale, *A Slender Reputation* (London, 1994).
6   Betty May quoted in Epstein, op. cit. (London, 1940).
7   As well as citing criticism of 'My First Christ' in Appendix Three of *Let There Be Sculpture*, Epstein includes a large extract from Father Vaughan's accusations in the body of the book.
8   Oliver Brown, *The Memoirs of Oliver Brown* (London, 1968).
9   *Nation*, 14 February 1920.
10   Bernard Van Dieren, *Epstein* (London, 1920).
11   JE to John Quinn, 27 September 1920, NYPL.
12   Ezio Bassani and Malcolm McLeod, 'The Passionate Collector' in *Jacob Epstein: Sculpture and Drawings*, HMC (Leeds, 1989).
13   Michael Wishart, *High Diver* (London, 1978).
14   JE to Kathleen Garman, undated, ANAGW.
15   Ibid., undated.
16   Margaret Epstein to Dorothy Lidsell-Stewart, 'Meum', 23 February 1922, courtesy of Maria Hollingsworth.
17   'Dolores, the Queen of the London Studios', *American Weekly Inc.*, New York, 1930.
18   The Hon. Kitty Godley in interview with the author.
19   *American Weekly*, op. cit.
20   Ibid.
21   Ibid.
22   *American Weekly*, op. cit.
23   Ibid.
24   JE to Kathleen Garman, undated, ANAGW.
25   Haskell, op. cit.

8   A Tolerant People

1   Henry Moore, *Henry Moore at the British Museum* (London, 1981).
2   Muirhead Bone to Cunningham Grahame, 13 February 1923, RSPB.
3   Sir Lionel Earle to the Hudson committee, 26 June 1923, RSPB.
4   Album of drawings, HMC.
5   *The Times* and the *Manchester Guardian*, 21 March 1924; *Country Life*, 22 March 1924.
6   *British Guardian*, 12 June 1925.
7   Jacob Epstein, *Let There Be Sculpture* (London, 1940).
8   Margaret, Maharanee of Sarawak to the Hudson committee, 22 May 1925, RSPB.
9   *Hansard*, 4 July 1925.
10   *Punch*, 3 June 1925.
11   Epstein, op. cit.
12   Epstein, Appendix Four.
13   Epstein, *Let There Be Sculpture*.
14   Arnold L. Haskell, *The Sculptor Speaks* (London, 1931).
15   *New Statesman*, 26 January 1924.
16   Epstein, *Let There Be Sculpture*.
17   Jocelyn Baines, *Joseph Conrad, A Critical Biography* (London, 1960).
18   JE to Kathleen Garman, undated, ANAGW.
19   Ibid., undated.
20   Roger Berthoud, *The Life of Henry Moore* (London, 1987).
21   JE to Kathleen Garman, undated, ANAGW.
22   Ibid., undated.
23   Peggy Jean Horstein, in interview with the author.
24   Siraj Ayesha Sayani, Sunita's great-niece, correspondence with author, spring 2001.
25   Alice Keene, *The Two Mr Smiths* (London, 1995).
26   Ibid.

9   Mr Epstein's Latest

1   Jacob Epstein, *Let There Be Sculpture* (London, 1940).
2   *Evening News*, 23 November 1925.
3   James K. Feibleman, *Philosophers Lead Sheltered Lives* (London, 1952).
4   Ibid.
5   JE to Kathleen Garman, 11 October 1927, ANAGW.
6   Ibid, mid-November 1927.
7   Ibid., undated.
8   Ibid., undated.
9   Ibid., undated.
10   Ibid., undated.
11   The *New York Evening Post* is cited in *Let There Be Sculpture* but no date is given.
12   Peggy Jean Horstein in interview with the author.
13   Paul Robeson in interview for a BBC Radio documentary, 'Sir Jacob Epstein, Sculptor and Humanist', transmitted 7 August 1960.

14 JE to Kathleen Garman, undated, ANAGW.
15 Jane Babson, *The Epsteins, A Family Album* (London, 1984).
16 JE to Kathleen Garman, 21 January 1928, ANAGW.
17 R. H. Wilenski, *The Meaning of Modern Sculpture* (London, 1932).
18 Hermione Lee, *Virginia Woolf* (London, 1986).
19 Babson, op. cit.

10 A Respectable House

1   *The Times*, 5 April 1929.
2   Charles Holden interviewed in the *Manchester Guardian*, 3 August 1929.
3   Peggy Jean Hornstein in interview with the author.
4   *Daily Mirror*, 21 March 1929; *Daily Graphic*, 21 March 1929.
5   Arnold L. Haskell, *The Sculptor Speaks* (London, 1931).
6   Terry Friedman, 'Epsteinism', in *Jacob Epstein: Sculpture and Drawings*, HMC (Leeds, 1989).
7   Haskell, op. cit.
8   Epstein, Appendix Six.
9   JE to Kathleen Garman, undated, ANAGW.
10 Cyril Connolly, *Architectural Review*, vol. LXXI, 1932.
11 William Gaunt, 'Jacob Epstein and the Old Testament', *Studio*, vol. 103, 1932.
12 Emlyn Williams, *Emlyn, an Early Autobiography, 1927–1935* (London, 1973).
13 John Gielgud to Evelyn Silber, 9 November 1983.
14 The Hon. Kitty Godley in interview with the author.
15 Haskell, op. cit.
16 BBC Radio interview: JE in conversation with Hubert Wellington, 1952.
17 *Daily Mirror*, 14 April 1931.
18 Ezra Pound to John Drummond, in D. D. Paige (ed.), *Ezra Pound: Selected Letters 1907–1941* (New York, 1971).
19 Henry Moore cited in Philip James (ed.), *Henry Moore on Sculpture* (London, 1996).
20 'Isabel Rawsthorne 1912–1992', catalogue of the Mercer Art Gallery, Harrogate, 1997.
21 Peggy Jean Hornstein in interview with the author.
22 JE to Kathleen Garman, undated, ANAGW.
23 *Lincolnshire Echo*, 1 December 1933.
24 The second appearance of Oliver Locker-Lampson, last seen in Chapter 8 when he neatly deflected an attack on *Rima* in the House of Commons. Barrister, war-hero and MP, this colourful character championed a number of pro-Jewish causes in the 1930s.
25 Peggy Jean Hornstein in interview with the author.
26 Ibid.

11 Time and Eternity

1 Photograph of Epstein and Isabel Nichols attending the first night of the film *Thunder over Mexico*, reproduced in *Jacob Epstein: Sculpture and Drawings*, HMC (Leeds, 1989).
2 Jackie Epstein in interview with the author.
3 Jacob Epstein, *Let There Be Sculpture* (London, 1940).
4 Ibid.
5 Ibid.
6 Epstein's drawing of the Hon. Kitty Godley is in the Collection of the New Art Gallery, Walsall.
7 The Hon. Kitty Godley in interview with the author.
8 Peggy Jean Hornstein in interview with the author.
9 Courtesy of Maria Hollingsworth, Meum's niece, ANAGW.
10 Peggy Jean Hornstein in interview with the author.
11 Jane Babson, *The Epsteins: A Family Album* (London, 1984).
12 Ibid.
13 Peggy Jean Hornstein in interview with the author.
14 Arthur Lett-Haines to JE, 5 December 1933, TGA.
15 *Evening Standard*, 2 December 1936.
16 Epstein, op. cit.
17 Ibid.
18 Ibid.
19 Ibid.
20 *Daily Telegraph*, 18 November 1935.
21 All newspaper references to Epstein's backcloth for *David* are cited in Terry Friedman, 'Epstein and the Theatre', *Jacob Epstein: Sculpture and Drawings*, HMC (Leeds, 1989).
22 An edition of *Les Fleurs du Mal* inscribed 'Jacob Epstein, 1904' is in the New Art Gallery, Walsall.
23 Catalogue of 'Drawings by Jacob Epstein for *Les Fleurs du mal* by Charles Baudelaire', A. Tooth & Sons, London, December 1958.
24 Epstein, op. cit.
25 Ibid.
26 Arnold L. Haskell, *The Sculptor Speaks* (London, 1931).
27 Evelyn Silber, *The Sculpture of Epstein* (Oxford, 1986).
28 Babson, op. cit.
29 George Bernard Shaw to Margaret Epstein, 29 December 1937, cited in Dan H. Laurence, *Bernard Shaw, Collected Letters, 1926–1950*, London, 1987.
30 Babson, op. cit.

12 The Lean Years

1 Alice Keene, *The Two Mr Smiths* (London, 1995).
2 Walt Whitman, 'From pent-up aching rivers' in 'The Leaves of Grass', *Complete Poetry & Selected Prose and Letters of Walt Whitman*, ed. Emory Holloway, London, 1938.
3 Jacob Epstein, 'Notes for an Autobiography', ANAGW.

4 *New York Daily Mirror*, cited in Richard Buckle, *Jacob Epstein, Sculptor* (London, 1963).
5 Jane Babson, *The Epsteins, A Family Album* (London, 1984).
6 Peggy Jean Hornstein in interview with the author.
7 The Hon. Kitty Godley in interview with the author.
8 The Epsteins' At Home book, HRRC.
9 JE to Abbo Ostrowsky, Organiser of the Alliance Exhibition, 3 September 1940, YIVO Institute, New York.
10 Josef Herman in interview with the author.
11 Margaret Epstein to Mr Samuels, 18 June 1941, TGA.
12 Genesis, 32: 24–30.
13 *Daily Mirror*, 28 April 1942.
14 Stephen Gardiner, *Artist against the Establishment* (London, 1992).
15 JE to Mr Samuels, May 1942, TGA.
16 *Evening Standard*, 8 June 1949.
17 Keene, op. cit.
18 JE to Matthew Smith, undated, but the exhibition of Augustus John's drawings he describes was held at the National Gallery in 1940.
19 Matthew Smith to Philip Hendy, 7 July 1942, HMC.
20 Keene, op. cit.
21 Virginia Graham to Joyce Grenfell, 29 November 1944, in *Joyce and Ginnie: The Letters of Joyce Grenfell and Virginia Graham* (London, 1977).
22 Edward Schinman and Barbara Ann Schinman, Eds, *Jacob Epstein* (New Jersey, 1970).
23 The Hon. Kitty Godley in interview with the author.
24 James Laver, *Museum Piece* (London, 1963).
25 Evelyn Silber, *The Sculpture of Epstein* (Oxford, 1986).
26 The Hon. Wynne Godley in interview with the author.
27 JE to Kenneth Clark, 17 January 1944, TGA.
28 John Milton, *Paradise Lost*, book I (Oxford, 1913).
29 *Daily Telegraph*, 15 November 1945.
30 JE to Matthew Smith, 8 January 1947, Guildhall Library Manuscript Section.
31 Cecil Gray, *Musical Chairs* (London, 1948).
32 Winston Churchill to JE, 6 March 1947, HMC.

13 Into the Light

1 Niall Lawlor in interview with the author.
2 Ibid.
3 *Listener*, 23 March 1950; *Daily Telegraph*, 9 March 1950; Denys Sutton, 'The Significance of Epstein', *Country Life*, vol. 1, December 1952.
4 JE to Dorothy Lindsell-Stewart, undated, courtesy of Maria Hollingsworth.
5 *Observer* profile, 11 June 1950.
6 JE to Peggy Jean Hornstein, 24 January 1952, TGA.
7 Kathleen Garman to Peggy Jean Hornstein, 24 August 1948, TGA.

8 Ibid.
9 Ibid.
10 JE to Peggy Jean Hornstein, undated, TGA. (The Battersea Park Exhibition, 'Sculpture in the Open Air', opened in May 1948.)
11 J. Nehru to JE, 7 December 1946, HMC.
12 JE to Peggy Jean Hornstein, 31 October 1948, TGA.
13 Ibid.
14 Ibid., 21 January 1950.
15 Ibid.
16 Louis Osman, *Journal of the London Society*, 20 February 1957.
17 Ibid.
18 JE to Peggy Jean Hornstein, 8 March 1952, TGA.
19 Archives of the Convent of the Holy Child Jesus, Mayfield, Sussex.
20 Ibid.
21 JE to Sir Kenneth Clark, 1 July 1951, TGA.
22 Convent of the Holy Child.
23 Ibid.
24 JE to Peggy Jean Hornstein, undated, TGA.
25 Ibid., 3 May 1952, TGA.
26 Catalogue of the Tate Gallery Epstein Exhibition, September–November 1952.
27 Philip James, ibid.
28 Noreen Smith in interview with the author.
29 Walt Whitman, 'America', *Complete Poetry & Selected Prose and Letters of Walt Whitman*, ed. Emory Holloway, London, 1938.
30 Henri Marceau, Director, Philadelphia Museum, to R. Ingersoll, Fairmount Park Association Archives.
31 Convent of the Holy Child.
32 Noreen Smith in interview with the author.
33 Ibid.
34 Dean Simon to George Pace, 31 January 1954, cited in Evelyn Silber, *The Sculpture of Epstein* (Oxford, 1986).
35 JE to Peggy Jean Hornstein, 20 January 1954, TGA.
36 Ibid., 3 September 1954.
37 Ibid., 27 June 1955.

14 'Very little of a gadabout'
1 JE to Kathleen Garman, 7 July 1955, ANAGW.
2 Ibid., 24 August 1955.
3 Ibid., undated.
4 JE to Peggy Jean Hornstein, undated, ANAGW.
5 Basil Spence, *Phoenix at Coventry* (London, 1962).
6 Interview on BBC Home Service, 1952.
7 JE to Peggy Jean Hornstein, 2 April 1957, TGA.
8 Ibid.
9 JE to Matthew Smith, 1 November 1957, Guildhall Archive.
10 JE to Peggy Jean Hornstein, 27 November 1957, TGA.

11 Ibid.
12 Stephen Gardiner, *Artist against the Establishment* (London, 1992).
13 Terence Mulally, *Daily Telegraph*, 28 March 1958.
14 JE to Peggy Jean Hornstein, 16 April 1958, TGA.
15 Oliver Brown, *Exhibition: The Memoirs of Oliver Brown* (London, 1968).
16 JE to Peggy Jean Hornstein, 27 October 1958, TGA.
17 Evelyn Silber, *The Sculpture of Epstein* (Oxford, 1986).
18 JE to Peggy Jean Hornstein, 27 October 1958, TGA.
19 Ibid., 9 February 1959, TGA.
20 *The Times*, 22 August 1959.
21 Henry Moore, *Sunday Times*, 23 August 1959.
22 Catalogue of the Annual Exhibition of the London Group, 1960.
23 Cited in Richard Buckle, *Jacob Epstein, Sculptor* (London, 1963).
24 Matthew Smith to Kathleen Garman, courtesy of Alice Kadel.
25 T. S. Eliot to Kathleen Garman, 21 August 1959, HMC.
26 Otto Klemperer to Kathleen Garman, 13 September 1959, HMC.
27 Ezio Bassani and Malcolm McLeod, 'The Passionate Collector', in *Jacob Epstein: Sculpture and Drawings*, HMC (Leeds, 1989).
28 Jacob Epstein, *Let There Be Sculpture* (London, 1940).

Select Bibliography

Babson, Jane. *The Epsteins: A Family Album*, London, 1984.

Baines, Jocelyn. *Joseph Conrad, A Critical Biography*, London, 1960.

Berthoud, Roger. *The Life of Henry Moore*, London, 1968.

Brown, Oliver. *Exhibition: The Memoirs of Oliver Brown*, London, 1968.

Buckle, Richard. *Jacob Epstein, Sculptor*, London, 1963.

Carpenter, Humphrey. *A Serious Character, The Life of Ezra Pound*, New York, 1988.

Cork, Richard. *Art Beyond the Gallery in Early Twentieth-Century England*, London, 1985.

——. *A Bitter Truth: Avant Garde and the Great War*, New Haven and London, 1994.

Ede, H. S. *Savage Messiah*, London, 1971.

Epstein, Jacob. *Let There Be Sculpture*, London, 1940.

Feibleman, James K. *Philosophers Lead Sheltered Lives*, London, 1952.

Friedman, Terry. *The Hyde Park Atrocity: Epstein's Rima: Creation and Controversy*, Leeds, 1988.

Friedman, Terry and Silber, Evelyn (eds). *Jacob Epstein, Sculpture and Drawings*, Leeds and London, 1987.

Gardiner, Stephen. *Artist Against the Establishment*, London, 1992.

Garnett, David (ed.). *Letters to Carrington*, London, 1970.

Gibson, Ashley. *Postcript to Adventure*, London, 1970.

Gray, Cecil. *Musical Chairs*, London, 1948.

Hale, Kathleen. *A Slender Reputation*, London, 1994.

Hapgood, Hutchins. *The Spirit of the Ghetto*, New York, 1902.

Haskell, Arnold L. *The Sculptor Speaks*, London, 1931.

Holroyd, Michael. *The Years of Innocence*: *A Biography of Augustus John*, Vol. 1, London, 1974.

The Jewish Encyclopedia, Vol. IX, Section on New York, New York, 1905.

Keene, Alice. *The Two Mr Smiths*, London, 1995.

Kraus, Harry P. *The Settlement House Movement in New York City, 1886–1914*, New York, 1980.

Lane, Hugh. *Lady Gregory*, London, 1973.

Laurence, Dan H. (ed.). *Bernard Shaw, Collected Letters, 1926–1950*, London, 1987.

Laver, James. *Museum Piece*, London, 1963.

Lee, Hermione. *Virginia Woolf*, London, 1986.

Lewis. Wyndham. *Blasting & Bombardiering*, London, 1967.

——. *Rude Assignment*, London, 1950.

MacCarthy, Fiona. *Eric Gill*, London, 1989.

McGregor, Sheila. *A Shared Vision*. Exhibition Catalogue, The New Art Gallery, Walsall, London, 1999.

Moore, Henry. *Henry Moore at the British Museum*, London, 1981.

Paige, D. D. (ed.). *Ezra Pound: Selected Letters 1907–1941*, New York, 1971.

Pennington, Michael. *An Angel for a Martyr: Jacob Epstein's Tomb for Oscar Wilde*, London, 1987.

Pound, Ezra. *A Memoir of Gaudier-Brzeska*, London, 1916.

Powell, L. B. *Jacob Epstein*, London, 1932.

Ransome, Arthur. *The Autobiography of Arthur Ransome*, London, 1976.

——. *Bohemia in London*, London, 1907.

Reid, B. L. *The Man from New York: John Quinn and his Friends*, New York, 1968.

Ross, M. (ed.). *Robert Ross, Friend of Friends*, London, 1952.

Rothenstein, William. *Men and Memories*, Vol. 2, London, 1974.

Scawen Blunt, Wilfred. *My Diaries*, Part 2, New York, 1921.

Shewring, Walter (ed.). *The Letters of Eric Gill*, London, 1947.

Silber, Evelyn. *The Sculpture of Epstein with a Complete Catalogue*, Oxford, 1986.

Silber, Evelyn and Finn, D. *Gaudier-Brzeska*, London, 1996.

Spalding, Frances. *British Art Since 1900*, London, 1986.

Spence, Basil. *Phoenix at Coventry*, London, 1962.

Stein, Gertrude. *The Autobiography of Alice B. Toklas*, London, 1933.

Van Dieren, Bernard. *Epstein*, London, 1920.

Whitman, Walt. *Complete Poetry & Selected Prose and Letters of Walt Whitman*, edited by Emory Holloway, London, 1938.

Wilenski, R. H. *The Meaning of Modern Sculpture*, London, 1932.

Williams, Emlyn. *Emlyn, an Early Autobiography, 1927–1935*, London, 1973.

Index